THE FINANCIAL SUCCESS PRINCIPLES

FROM VISION TO IMPACT

BECCA HEISSEL
AAS, JACK CANFIELD CERTIFIED TRAINER

CAROLINE PASSMORE
CMA, MBA, LSSBB

MATTIE MURREY
MA, CCC-SLP, NFAA

The Financial Success Principles:
From Vision to Impact

By Becca Heissel, Caroline Passmore, and Mattie Murrey

ISBN: 978-1-968960-04-9 (Paperback)
ISBN: 978-1-968960-03-2 (Ebook)
Library of Congress Control Number: 2025917536

Cover Design by Andrew Magee
Printed in the United States of America

Upword Publishing
Denver, CO
upwordpublishing.com

First Edition

Praise of
The Financial Success Principles

Start with your head and your heart before you set out to learn business tactics. That's what I love about *The Financial Success Principles*. Such an important book! So many people rush and strive to make their mark, hoping to bring in big bucks. Take it from Becca and her co-authors—financial success is worthless... unless you know why you're seeking it. And only then can you achieve it. You're going to love getting a mindset reset, and that's when the money will find you. Financial abundance is the reward, not the goal. – GEORGE WALTHER, author of *Power Talking* and Hall of Fame speaker.

This book highlights what you don't know you don't know. Being aware and prepared will change your mindset to move your business forward. This can not be done alone; that's why reaching out for support and guidance is so important for your finances! – STEVE RAMONA, The Human SEO - Energy Industry - Podcast/TV Host

This book is the foundation every entrepreneur needs. From mindset and money to taxes and strategy, The Three Wise Women created a powerful roadmap to help business owners dream big, earn more, and lead with purpose. It's time we flip the statistic that says 86% of business owners make under $100K—and this book is how we start. – SARANSH OBEROI ("Obi"), Chef, Author, TV Personality

This book is refreshing. In a world where we are often told "what" to do without the "how," this is very practical and actionable advice. This is not a book you read; it's a book you study, take notes on, and put what you're learning into practice. I love the four cups analogy, and I love the clear distinction between a budget and a forecast, and why the forecast is so much more useful. This is something every business owner should read, especially if you feel the slightest bit unclear about your accounting and finances. —SETH DAVID, Director of Education, Nerd Enterprises

I really enjoyed this book. It's easy to read and easy to understand, without ever talking down to readers who don't have an accounting background. At the same time, it's not oversimplified. As an accountant, I appreciated that. The examples are clear and relatable. Honestly, it was a fun read—yes, a fun accounting book! Highly recommended. —DEBRA KILSHEIMER, CPA, Behind the Scenes Financial Service

As someone who has run a 7-figure business, I was curious about what *The Financial Success Principles* would have for me. I was delighted to see how useful it was in laying out solid principles for understanding money, along with paradigms that are useful at multiple business levels. It helps that it's also an easy read, with some great stories and analogies to make things real. Well done! — PAMELA BRUNER, CEO, Attract Clients Online

As a bookkeeping firm owner, I've seen a lot of business owners wrestle with their finances like it's some kind of voodoo mumbo jumbo. This book changes that. It takes the confusion and overwhelm and turns it into clarity, confidence, and actual direction. Whether you're trying to make sense of your numbers or just want to stop dreading tax season, this book delivers the financial pep talk (and practical guidance) every entrepreneur needs. — GREG CULLUP, Owner of The Numbers Guy, LLC

For six years, Becca Heissel rode shotgun in my CPA firm, soaking up every insight and asking the questions most professionals overlook. I watched her transform from a curious learner into a fierce advocate for business owners. Becca didn't just listen—she researched. She saw the shame, fear, and self-doubt that many entrepreneurs feel about their finances and traced it to its root: a complete lack of financial literacy. Her discovery that only 25 states mandate financial literacy in schools and that 86% of business owners earn less than $100k ignited a passion within her that continues to this day. This book is a result of that fire. Alongside her co-authors Mattie and Caroline, they have created what I believe should be required reading for every current and aspiring business owner. It's a financial literacy manual, business survival guide, and mindset reset all in one. If you've never been taught how to manage money or never thought you could be a business owner, now is your chance. Turn the page. Start the movement. – **MADDIE BROWN**, CPA, Founder of Smashing Numbers

The Financial Success Principles: From Vision to Impact is a powerful reminder that clarity alone isn't enough; it's what you do with your vision that creates success. As Chapter 12 says, "If you have a vision without action, you'll end up with something even more painful: regret." This book is a beautiful extension of Jack Canfield's legacy, offering real, practical strategies that empower you to take inspired, imperfect action with confidence. Intention becomes transformation when paired with attention, and this book shows you how. – **DEBBI SLUYS**, Founder of Dare to Declare

The Financial Success Principles is a refreshing, relatable, and empowering guide for women stepping into entrepreneurship. From the first page, the authors create a welcoming space to redefine your relationship with money, not through fear or jargon, but with clarity, compassion, and confidence. What resonated most was the invitation to see money as a neutral tool and trusted ally instead of a source of shame or stress. That mindset shift alone can change a business's direction. The storytelling is honest and vulnerable, blending financial principles with personal experiences in a way that makes readers feel seen, supported, and capable. Readers will leave with not only a healthier money mindset but also clear tools to take inspired, measurable action toward their goals. Whether you're starting out or ready to scale with intention, this book is a must-read for building both profit and purpose. – **CATHY JUILFS**, CFP®, AIFA®, CEBS | CEO/President

I started my journey as a solo entrepreneur 10 years ago, wearing all the hats and figuring things out as I went. While reading *The Financial Success Principles: From Vision to Impact,* I had a moment of clarity: money has been my not-so-silent business partner all along. It's made me feel proud, stressed, hopeful, and confused—and if I'm honest, it's had more control over my decisions (and emotions) than I realized. This book gives you the tools to shift that dynamic. It offers a clear, doable roadmap for building a healthy, empowered relationship with money. I wish I'd had it when I was starting out—it would have given me so much more clarity. – **ANN MCKITRICK**, MS, Speaker, Educator, Consultant

The Financial Success Principles: From Vision to Impact is a book about financial success and a guide to discovering your purpose, claiming your confidence, and building a business that reflects your heart and vision. Becca and her co-authors offer the clarity and practical tools every entrepreneur needs to create a life of freedom, fulfillment, and sustainable impact. – **GLORY ST. GERMAIN**, CEO of Ultimate Music Theory, International Best-Selling Author of *The Power of WHY Musicians Book Series, and Teach Music Change Lives*

The Three Wise Women do a phenomenal job of laying out a variety of important financial topics for business owners in a simple and straightforward way. Implementing their financial clarity tools and intentional systems will go a long way to increase your profitability—helping reduce taxes, cut through confusion, and eliminate anxiety as you build your business. Becca has a huge servant's heart, and together, this team has created a practical, empowering guide that every entrepreneur should read. I encourage anyone seeking help with implementation to reach out. —**DAVID GEAKE**, Strategic Tax Consultant

I love that this book offers a true foundation for business owners—from expanding their vision to making an impact and leaving a legacy. It's not just a self-help or storytelling book. It's a practical, powerful guide that covers everything from business planning, taxes, investments, and bookkeeping to cultivating an abundance mindset. A rainbow of wisdom with nuggets of gold on every page. — **MARGUERITE MARIAMA**, Ph.D., co-author of *The Book on Love* and the upcoming book, *Artivism: A Sixties Activist/Artist's Memoir and Guide for Joyfully Healing a Crazy World.*

This book is full of stuff I wish I knew. I wish I had had it 30 years ago! It's a much-needed guide for financial success—so good, it almost makes me want to start over and, this time, do it right! —**JOHN VERRICO**, Founder, Share Your Fire

This information is presented in a clear and practical way that brings real clarity to the potential chaos of the financial world. I love the relatable analogies—they really drive the points home. This book is a valuable resource not only for new entrepreneurs but also for experienced business owners who are wondering why the finances aren't working out as they envisioned. —**LAURABETH MESSIMER**, CEO G.I. Josie Nonprofit

Running a successful business requires many elements, but the foundation begins with one essential component: structure. True structure starts with a clear plan—one built by working from the end in mind. Along the way, every business needs the right support team: a reliable bookkeeper, a skilled accountant, and most importantly, a strategic business advisor who can help guide long-term vision and growth. Success is not a solo journey. It's a collaborative effort that elevates business owners beyond just survival—and into excellence. When you implement these principles, you're not just building a business; you're building peace of mind, reclaiming energy for what truly matters, and creating space to help others rise and thrive in their own journeys. —**LAURA LEE**, Money Mindset Mentors, Podcaster & Host, #1 International Best-Selling Author & Coach

This isn't just another money book. It's a guide to reclaiming your power and building wealth on your terms. – **MIRIAM LAUNDRY**, Publisher and CEO of Miriam Laundry Publishing

The Financial Success Principles isn't just about money—it's about building a life and business with clarity, confidence, and purpose. The 3 Wise Women bring together practical tools, mindset shifts, and heart-center strategy to help entrepreneurs grow without burnout. A must-read for anyone serious about success. — **DREW BERMAN**, Licensed Financial Professional, Peak Performance Strategist

Bravo to the Three Wise Women, who get to the heart of what holds women back from realizing their full potential. This is a must-read for every woman who has ever dimmed her light or struggled with a complicated relationship with money. The authors offer not only deep insight but also practical tools to help bring dreams to life by shifting long-held beliefs and behaviors. — **BECKY ESTBY**, Owner, Next Monday

As someone who has gone from managing mental health crises behind locked doors to delivering transformation in boardrooms and beyond, I know the toll that "doing it all" takes on our brains, bodies, and businesses. Chapter 11 is a masterclass in letting go without losing power. It's the permission slip every high-achieving person didn't know they needed. It doesn't just preach delegation; it teaches it. It unpacks the emotional baggage we attach to asking for help and replaces it with razor-sharp strategy, backed with truths and real-world tools to stop burnout in its tracks. From recalibrating our money mindset to reclaiming our time, it's a mic drop moment for solopreneurs, CEOs, and anyone ready to scale sustainably. If you're still wearing overwhelm like a badge of honour, read this. And then read it again. Your nervous system, bank account, and future self will thank you. – **NICOLA NOÉL**, Multi-Award-Winning Specialist Psychiatric Nurse, Solution-Focused Hypnotherapist, and Transformational Consultant

The Financial Success Principles: From Vision to Impact is filled with memorable, to-the-point insights like 'Perfection is procrastination in disguise' that stick with you and make you think. The lessons are simple, clear, and actionable—perfect for anyone considering entrepreneurship. The part about letting go of perfectionism and overplanning really hit home for me. A powerful, practical read. – **DR. ROBIN HALL**, best-selling author, *The Other Side of Illness: Unexpected Blessings*

Reading *The Financial Success Principles* lit a fire in my soul. As a spiritual teacher and recovery coach, I know how often fear, perfectionism, and old beliefs keep us from taking that first courageous step toward our dreams. This chapter is a powerful reminder that clarity comes through action, not waiting. The "Ready, Fire, Aim" approach aligns beautifully with the Soul Recovery Process—inviting us to release control, rewrite our inner narratives, and co-create with the Divine. I found myself nodding, underlining, and even tearing up as I was reminded that we don't need to be perfect to begin—we just need to show up with faith, trust our gifts, and move forward anyway. This message is spiritual, grounded, and empowering. It's not just financial wisdom—it's soul wisdom. – REVEREND RACHEL HARRISON, Host of Recover Your Soul Podcast, author, speaker

This isn't just another financial book—it's a practical guide for building a business that reflects your values, your purpose, and your potential. *The Financial Success Principles: From Vision to Impact* is refreshingly honest, empowering, and packed with tools that actually work. If you're ready to feel in control of your money and your mission—this is the book for you. —RICKY LOCKE, TEDx Speaker, Confidence Coach & Host of the Unlocked Podcast

Money as a Tool and Energy: So many of us carry silent stress and fear about money. This chapter on finances and fear is a game-changer. What I love in this chapter is the sense of having a relationship with money. Reframing our money story and moving from fear to freedom will help readers to reset and release the emotional weight they carry around finances. It offers not only guidance but grace as you learn a new way to view money as a friend and a partner. MELODY VACHAL, Director of Aging Services and Outreach at Arise Cares, speaker, and author of *Still, I Rise: A Guide to Navigating the Caregiver Journey*

As a woman of a certain age who's built a business from scratch—and weathered more than a few storms along the way—these chapters spoke straight to my heart. They're not just insightful; they're empowering. Chapter 1 reframes money in a way I wish someone had told me decades ago. Seeing it as energy, rather than fear or failure, is liberating, especially for women who were taught to stay small or silent when it comes to finances. Chapter 4 made me nod the whole way through. I've made the mistake of building without a plan, and let me tell you, fixing it later costs more than just money. The stories and metaphors (especially about the lake house view!) brought clarity without condescension. But Chapter 12 is what lit a fire in me. "Ready, Fire, Aim" isn't just a new way of thinking—it's a permission slip. To begin, before it's perfect. To trust your gut. To fall and get back up with grace and grit. That chapter reminded me that some of my proudest wins came when I launched before I felt ready. This isn't fluff. It's a field guide for women like me—seasoned, serious, and still dreaming. If you're building a business at any age, read this. It's wise, warm, and wonderfully practical. – **ROBIN LEVINE DAAS**, Consultative Design & Product Development Expert

Becca, Caroline, and Mattie clearly show in *The Financial Success Principles* that success is an inside-out job! When the vision for your business has wealth, lifestyle, and impact working together, you are building your life around purpose, energized by clarity. A must-read for everyone who wants their life to maximize authenticity and joy through their career! – **RANDI WOODWARD LARSEN**, best-selling picture book Author, *Moonlight and Wishes*

This book is a must-read for any entrepreneur or leader who's ever felt paralyzed by perfection. You'll walk away with a new blueprint for success—one that prioritizes action over analysis and progress over perfection. It's a permission slip to start messy, keep moving, and refine as you go. – **EBONY GREEN**, CCC-SLP, Entrepreneur

If you are looking to follow a clear path to entrepreneurial success, *The Financial Success Principles* is the perfect place to start! – **DEBBI-JO HORTON** (DJ), CPA, Founder DJ Horton & Associates

I would absolutely recommend *The Financial Success Principles*! One of my biggest takeaways was the reminder that even while starting my business, I should still make at least small contributions to my retirement—not just for the financial benefit, but to keep the "muscle memory" going from the auto-pilot habits I had as a W-2 employee. The book helped me reconnect with that discipline in a way that feels empowering and doable, even as an entrepreneur. It's a smart, approachable guide for building financial success. – **JONNA DAVIS**, MPA, Founder AOE Bookkeeping LLC

The Financial Success Principles does a great job of blending mindset with practical tactics when it comes to business ownership and finances. It's packed with useful guidance on things like business structure, budgeting, and taxes—but what sets it apart is that it doesn't just acknowledge mindset, it builds everything around it. That piece is often missing in other books, and it makes a big difference. I'd highly recommend this book to anyone thinking about starting a business—or already deep in it. The tips and strategies are helpful at every stage. – **BREA WOODSON**, Owner and CEO at GRT Marketing

I absolutely love the mission behind The Three Wise Women! *The Financial Success Principles* is more than a book—it's a movement empowering business owners to grow with purpose, confidence, and clarity. As a fellow mom in business, I'm inspired by how these stories support others in building a business and a life they love. – **LEONA BURTON**- MIB International

Foreword by Jack Canfield, #1 New York Times Bestselling Author, Co-creator of *Chicken Soup for the Soul*® and Co-author of *The Success Principles*™

Success is not an accident. It's the result of a clear vision, strategic action, and the right mindset. Throughout my career, I've taught individuals from all walks of life how to apply timeless success principles to achieve extraordinary results—financially, personally, and professionally.

When Becca Heissel first came to my training, I saw someone with a deep passion for transformation. Not just for herself, but for every entrepreneur trapped by financial stress, uncertainty, and limiting money beliefs—because the real hurdle isn't just income but the fear of stepping away from the security of a traditional job. She didn't just learn The Success Principles—she lived them.

At 25 years old, she faced a financial challenge that seemed insurmountable. She wanted to start a family, but like many, she believed that $15,000 for IVF was out of reach. Instead of accepting that as truth, she applied five core principles—two of which come directly from The Success Principles—and made it happen. Not only did she turn a dream into reality, but she also built a framework that others can use to do the same.

That's what this book is about: turning financial dreams into reality. Becca, along with her brilliant co-authors, Mattie Murrey Tegels and Caroline Passmore, has created The Financial Success Principles to give you a roadmap for financial empowerment. These are not just theories or abstract concepts. They are battle-tested strategies rooted in real-life applications. Their mission is clear: to flip the statistics. Right now, only 25 out of 50 states mandate financial literacy in schools. Even more staggering, 86% of entrepreneurs make less than $100,000 a year. That's not just unfortunate—it's unacceptable.

This book challenges traditional financial advice, shifting the focus from restrictive spending to smarter and more evolved strategies for long-term financial success. It's about creating an abundant mindset, taking aligned action, and positioning yourself to earn and keep more of what you make. The principles inside this book will empower you to stop feeling stuck and start feeling in control of your financial future.

I'm proud to see Becca take these principles and make them her own. She is not just a certified Success Principles Trainer; she is a true advocate for entrepreneurs, a champion for financial literacy, and a living example of what is possible when you take 100% responsibility for your success. Alongside Mattie and Caroline, she has crafted a book that is practical, inspiring, and—most importantly—effective.

So, if you've ever felt like financial success was for other people but not for you, I invite you to turn the page. The blueprint is here. The principles work. And now, it's your turn to apply them.

To your success,

Jack Canfield

Co-Author of the *Chicken Soup for the Soul*® series and *The Success Principles*™

Dedication

This book is dedicated to those who were never taught, but showed up anyway.

To the dreamers who took the leap without a map.

To the business owners who were expected to know—but never given the tools.

This is for you.

– Becca

This book is dedicated to the brave visionaries I work with every day—the tradesmen, contractors, and nonprofit leaders who risk comfort for calling. You started a business not just to make money, but to make a difference—for your families, your teams, and your communities.

This is for the tradesmen with tool belts and dreams. This is for the founders who build futures from grit and grace. This is for anyone who ever whispered, "There has to be a better way."

You're not just running a business. You're building a legacy.
And I'm here to make sure it's a profitable one.

– Caroline

This book is dedicated to my grown children, proof that we can rewrite our stories. You are wiser, braver, and stronger—and you are my greatest hope for living lives that make a difference in the world.

To those who believed in me—and those who didn't.
Both shaped my courage; both forged my strength.

And to every woman who believes she can't overcome her money struggles, who carries the weight of shame she doesn't deserve— may this remind you that you can rise, too, and your story is far from over.

And finally, to every like-minded soul who dares to rise and make the world better—this is for you.

— Mattie

Message from a Ghostwriter: Why Three Voices, One Message

I'm writing this book with two extraordinary women—partners, colleagues, co-creators, and now dear friends in this journey. With a wink and a humble heart, we call ourselves the 3 Wise Women. We each bring a different story, a different experience, and a different way we've worked through the complex relationship so many of us have with money. Our perspectives are shaped by different seasons of life, different challenges, and different wins—but our hearts beat in unison for the same mission: to help women step into financial clarity, ownership, and power.

Rather than take turns speaking to you as three separate authors, we made a conscious decision to write this book in one voice—one clear, steady voice that we hope feels like a guide, a friend, or a mentor walking beside you. It doesn't matter which one of us is saying the words—what matters is that we're here with you.

Sometimes you'll catch a glimpse of our individual stories woven through the pages. But mostly, we're speaking to you as one. One intention. One rhythm. One shared belief that you don't have to figure this out alone.

So when you hear "I," know that it could be any one of us. When you hear "we," know that it includes you, too.

Let's begin!

The 3 Wise Women
Becca, Caroline, and Mattie
https://www.thefinancialsuccessprinciples.com/

Your 30,000 Foot View of The Financial Success Principles

Part 1: Setting Yourself Up for Success

This section lays the groundwork for entrepreneurial success by redefining your relationship with money and developing a clear financial vision of your journey, from vision to impact. You'll explore money as a neutral tool and energy source, identifying the beliefs and habits that shape your financial decisions. Through practical steps, you'll build financial awareness and create a dynamic business plan that aligns with your vision and adapts to your goals. Finally, you'll establish a solid foundation for your business, leveraging the right structures and systems for sustainable growth. This is where your entrepreneurial journey begins and where you begin to engage, moving from vision to impact.

Part 2: Stepping into Success

This section teaches you to implement financial strategies that turn your vision into reality. By embracing forecasting, you'll focus on growth and adaptability, leaving behind restrictive budgets in favor of empowering financial planning. You'll uncover how proactive tax strategies protect profits and reduce stress while mastering bookkeeping and accounting to gain the clarity and decision-making strategies needed for wise financial decisions. These tools and systems are your pathway to traction and success, helping you make choices that drive profitability and stability. This part represents the critical steps in your journey where vision transforms into action.

Part 3: Growing Success

This section focuses on scaling your business and achieving lasting impact. You'll prioritize profit with purpose, ensuring your business fuels both personal and professional goals. Through strategic investing, you'll shift from earning to building long-term wealth, and by mastering delegation, you'll create the freedom to focus on your highest-value contributions. This is the stage where vision culminates in impact—your entrepreneurial success becomes a vehicle for financial independence, growth, and meaningful change.

TABLE OF CONTENTS

Part 1:
Setting Yourself Up for Success

This section lays the groundwork for business success by redefining your relationship with money and developing a clear financial vision of your journey, from vision to impact. You'll explore money as a neutral tool and energy source, identifying the beliefs and habits that shape your financial decisions. Through practical steps, you'll build financial awareness and create a dynamic business plan that aligns with your vision and adapts to your goals. Finally, you'll establish a solid foundation for your business, leveraging the right structures and systems for sustainable growth. This is where your entrepreneurial journey begins and where you begin to engage, moving from vision to impact.

Chapter 1:
Money as a Tool and Energy

Section 1: Where the Magic (and the Math) Begins

There's something electrifying about starting your own business.

Maybe it's in the moment you decide, *I'm doing this*—whether it's a whisper in your gut or a scream from your soul—or maybe it's just a brave thought to yourself as you realize you've stepped into a world of possibility.

As an entrepreneur, there is no ceiling and there are no rules. Just you, your vision, and the wide-open road ahead. And the best part? You get to draw the map and it's **YOUR** map.

Being an entrepreneur is thrilling. You're chasing ideas, building dreams, defying odds. It's also late nights, big bets, and the kind of personal growth no one warns you about.

But let's be real for a second—while dreaming big is the secret sauce of entrepreneurship, *staying in the game* requires more than just hustle and heart. The harsh reality is that approximately 20% of small businesses fail within their first year, and nearly 50% fail within five years. Not because they weren't smart or passionate. Not because their ideas weren't solid. But because they didn't understand the **principles of financial success.**

That's the heartbreak—and the opportunity.

So many entrepreneurs fail *big* because they dream big without mastering their money. And that's not your fault. Most of us didn't learn how to approach money in a way that genuinely fosters personal growth. But we're going to change that.

This book isn't a boring finance manual. It's a field guide for fearless creators. A hype song for money confidence. A practical, playful, principle-driven look at what it takes to *actually* succeed financially while building the life and business of your dreams.

Because here's the deal: You've already done the hard part. You said yes to your dream. Now let's make sure that dream becomes a sustainable, profitable, legacy-building reality.

Let's make the numbers dance. Let's turn stress into strategy. Let's write a financial success story that feels like *you.*

But... before we dive into strategies and spreadsheets, we have to start at the root of it all: your relationship with money.

Because money isn't just about math. It's about meaning. It's tied to your sense of worth, your past experiences, and your future dreams. It shows up in the way you price your offers, the way you talk to clients, and the way you sleep (or don't) at night.

So if you're going to build a business that lasts—and a life that feels aligned—it starts with your mindset.

It starts with seeing money not as a source of stress or scarcity, but as a partner in your purpose.

Money isn't the enemy—it's an ally.

When you shift from fear to friendship, money becomes a tool for clarity, confidence, and possibility. Your relationship with it sets the tone for every decision you make in business and in life. And for many of us, that relationship didn't start off on the right foot.

I remember the exact moment money made me feel like I didn't belong.

I was sitting in a room full of successful women—brilliant, driven, magnetic—and while they were discussing investments, scaling, and legacy, I was silently praying no one would ask me about my finances. My palms were sweaty. My throat felt tight. I was just starting out in my 3rd yet-to-be-successful start-up business, and I felt like a failure. I didn't feel safe saying, "I'm still figuring this out." I felt like these women were miles ahead of me in their business savvy and financial understanding. I wasn't even sure what questions to ask and how to join the conversation.

That moment didn't break me—but it did wake me up.

Because money isn't just about spreadsheets and profit margins. It's about how safe we feel asking our questions. It's about what we believe we're allowed to want. It's about the unconscious agreements we've made with ourselves about how hard it has to be, how far we're allowed to go, and whether or not we're worthy of ease.

Because you can't build something powerful while hiding from the truth.

Most entrepreneurs start their journey with a focus on the big picture—vision, impact, and freedom—yes!! Whoo hoo! We've been there ourselves, as we are also entrepreneurs. Most of us, however, are only taught a one-dimensional approach to thinking about money, and that is how to earn it. We might be taught how to save it as well, and if you were given that gift, great! But we now understand that it's not just about how you earn money, but also about how you think about it, approach it, and become friends with it.

Now, before you say, "That's weird, why are you talking about money as a friend?" Well, think about what friends do for you!
- They support you in your goals
- They are there for you unconditionally, and
- They help you reach your dreams.

Having this healthy money mindset is an invaluable tool in your Financial Principles of Success.

This chapter is your call to adventure—the moment when you decide to confront your relationship with money, to step into a new world of financial awareness that will set the stage for everything that follows.

At its core, money is neutral. It's neither good nor bad—it simply is. A tool. It serves as a vital source of energy. It amplifies who you already are and what you prioritize. But for many, money becomes a source of stress, shame, or even fear. This mindset holds back even the most visionary entrepreneurs from stepping fully into their purpose.

It's time to reframe that.

Money is 100% energy. It's a tool of creation. A force multiplier.

You take a dollar and put it to work—it builds something. It becomes something more. When you treat money with intention and respect, it multiplies. When you channel your energy, your time, and your gifts into the world as an entrepreneur, money flows in return. But here's the truth: you don't chase money.

Chasing money leads to scarcity and burnout. Think of a dog chasing something—it just runs further away. Instead, shift the energy: *I don't need money, but I'm open to receiving it.* That openness changes everything.

Some of the biggest opportunities in my career came not because I pushed harder, but because I believed I deserved them. I declared, *I'm ready. I'm open. I'm worthy of this.* When you align your energy with that kind of clarity, money shows up.

Money is not just paper—it's potential. It's backed by your mindset, not just medals. When you stop chasing and start creating, you realize: *Money comes to those who are ready to receive it.*

— *Rodolfo Gargioni*

"

Section 2: The Road to a Healthier Money Mindset

Money isn't the most important thing in life—but it touches everything that is.

It touches your choices, your boundaries, your relationships, your freedom, and your health. It influences how you sleep at night, how you dream in the morning, how you show up in conversations, and how you take risks in your business. It touches your past, present, and future. There's no getting away from it.

Whether you consider yourself "good with money" or not, whether you're sitting on savings or cycling through overdraft fees, money is one of the most emotionally loaded, practically unavoidable forces in our daily lives. And yet, for something so constant, so deeply interwoven with our well-being and success, it's often the one thing we lie most about to others and ourselves. Yet, it is the one thing we need to be most honest about.

In entrepreneurial spaces, we talk about branding, strategy, content, leadership, and impact—but money? That conversation usually comes with lowered voices and nervous laughter. Just like politics and religion, it is a taboo topic in most circles. We avoid it or intellectualize it, but rarely do we slow down enough to ask: what is my actual relationship with money? What have I inherited? What am I repeating? What am I afraid of?

We start this book with **mindset** because mindset is the lens that shapes your every decision. When your relationship with money is reactive, unclear, or shame-based, that mindset filters into everything—from how you price your services to how you show up on sales calls, how you hire, how you rest, and how you allow yourself to dream. You can have the best strategy in the world, but if your money mindset is rooted in fear, it will sabotage your progress before you even begin.

Fear doesn't always look like panic. Sometimes it looks like procrastination, like perfectionism, like "I'm still working on it," or "I'll have it ready tomorrow." It looks like staying small because growth feels uncertain. It looks like telling yourself you'll raise your rates "next quarter," or that you'll invest in help "when things slow down," or that your dream can wait until you've earned it five more times over.

And the problem with that fear isn't just the feelings—it's the cost. Fear-based indecision will drain you. It will cost you time, money, confidence, and momentum. It keeps you busy spinning your wheels while quietly killing your progress.

That's why I want you to start this journey with one guiding truth: you are not your past decisions. You are not your credit score. You are not your revenue last year. You are not the overdraft fee you forgot to cancel. You are a complex human being learning things you haven't learned before—and this chapter, this book, is your space to learn, grow, and be..

This isn't about blaming yourself for not knowing better. This is about building something new. Together, we're going to peel back the layers of shame, overwhelm, and confusion that surround money, and in their place, we're going to plant clarity, confidence, and connection.

A Coffee Date with My Business: The IVF Story

To start, I want to take you to a very personal moment in my own life—a moment that changed the way I think about money forever.

It began with a decision I never thought I'd have to make: whether or not to pursue IVF. If you've been through fertility treatments or supported someone who has, you already know how layered and emotional this journey can be. For me, it was one of the most vulnerable crossroads of my life. The desire to become a mother was fierce. But the path forward wasn't simple. There were medical concerns. There was the emotional toll. And then, of course, there was the cost.

IVF is not cheap. And in the moment, the decision felt massive—not just because of the money itself but because of what the money represented. Hope. Risk. Investment. Uncertainty. There was no guarantee it would work. No promise of a happy ending. Just the chance. The possibility. A leap of faith.

I remember sitting at my kitchen table one morning, a steaming cup of coffee in my hands, the sun rising through the window, and my laptop open in front of me. I had spreadsheets pulled up, revenue projections, invoices, and a blank document where I had started to type out "what ifs." I stared at the screen and thought, *"What if I do this? What if I can afford this?"*

That's when I decided to have a conversation with my business.

Not metaphorically—literally. I imagined my business sitting across from me, sipping coffee, ready to listen. I said, "Hey, we've been building this thing together. You've helped me pay the bills. You've given me purpose. But now I'm asking something bigger. Can you help me create a life? Can you support this dream?"

I started running the numbers. I got honest with myself about what was coming in, what could be restructured, and where there were opportunities for growth. I looked not only at my income but also at my capacity. I thought about the clients I loved, the offers that drained me, and the things I hadn't yet said yes to because I was too afraid.

And slowly, as I looked at those numbers and possibilities, something changed. I stopped feeling like I was asking too much. I stopped seeing money as the barrier. AND I started to feel a sense of partnership with my business—a sense that this thing I had built wasn't just a machine or a brand or a job. It was a firm foundation, something that could support me in more ways than one.

That day, I made the decision to move forward with IVF. Not because I was certain of the outcome but because I was finally grounded in the belief that my business could carry me—and that I didn't need to apologize for wanting more from it.

Now, for me, this was a personal decision. I was using the money for a dream of mine. But isn't that what we build our businesses for? To allow us to step into our dreams and make them come true? No matter what goals you have in mind for your future, developing a healthy mindset with money is crucial to moving from vision to impact.

Befriending Money

After that coffee date with my business, I began to notice just how much of my thinking around money had been shaped by fear. Not just big fears, like "What if it all falls apart?" but the quiet ones that show up in the everyday decisions. The kind that makes you hesitate before you raise your rates. The kind that whispers, "You can't make good decisions with money." and "Don't be greedy." when you start to dream bigger. The kind that tells you you're not allowed to want more until you've earned it five more times over.

But what if money didn't have to be a source of anxiety or shame? What if, instead of fighting against it or trying to outwork it, we could build a relationship with it? One built on mutual respect, consistency, and trust?

That question shifted everything for me.

When I started seeing money as a relationship instead of a score-board or a stressor, I realized I'd been treating it like a distant authority figure—something I needed to impress or fear. I would panic when it felt far away, feel unworthy when it didn't show up quickly enough, and blame myself for not "doing better" with it. But a healthy relationship doesn't operate that way.

When you have a true friend, you don't have to pretend. You show up as you are—messy, honest, and in progress. You don't feel the need to hide your flaws or sugarcoat the hard days. You talk things through. You check in. You build trust over time, with space for mistakes, repair, and growth. And that's when it finally clicked for me: this is how I wanted to relate to money. Not with fear, or false confidence, or forced positivity. I didn't want to perform for it or run from it—I just wanted to be real with it. To build something steady, honest, and supportive.

I wanted to build a relationship with my money, not a power struggle.

Consider the story of Cathy and Penny, two entrepreneurs who each started their businesses with the same amount of capital. Cautious Cathy sees money as scarce and hoards it, afraid to invest in growth, while Penny wisely views money as an energy flow—investing smartly, taking calculated risks, and ultimately growing her vision to her intended impact.

What's the difference between these two entrepreneurs? Believe it or not, the difference is in mindset. There are other factors, of course, such as financial skills and solid decision-making, but no single factor is more important in determining their long-term success than their financial mindset. Why? Because the way you think about money directly impacts your behavior around money.

Do you see money as a foe or a friend? As a gift, or a threat? If you see money as scarce and scary, you'll act from a place of fear—avoiding investments, underpricing your services, or overworking to compensate. If you see money as abundant and fluid, you'll make empowered decisions that align with your goals.

This mindset shift is critical. When you start to see money as a tool that works *for you*—not something you work for—you unlock a new level of freedom.

Section 3: Money is Neutral: Shifting Your Mindset

A lot of us grew up experiencing big emotions surrounding money. When our families had money, things felt good, easy, and relaxed. When money ran low, life was stressful or unpredictable.

When we have big emotions about money, those emotions ultimately drive behavior in ways that aren't always advantageous to our long-term success. For example, we all likely know someone who is a "money avoider." Money avoiders tend to think that money is the root of all evil. They are afraid to have "too much" of it, feel greedy when they make it, and can subconsciously judge others who seem to have a lot of it. Typically, money avoiders are operating from a place of shame, fearing that they themselves are "not enough" or are incapable of being financially successful and secure.

On the other side of the spectrum are the "money worshipers"— those people who believe money will solve all of their problems. Money worshipers often prioritize the acquisition of money over other crucial aspects of life, like maintaining health, hobbies, and relationships. At their core, money worshipers are often operating from a scarcity mindset, worried that there will never be enough, and over-glorifying the role of money in their lives and the lives of others.

And yet, part of truly being able to use money as a tool (rather than clutching to it desperately out of fear of losing it) is learning to view money as *neutral*. In other words, understanding that having possession of money at any given moment is neither inherently good nor bad. It means detaching money from emotion. This mindset allows you to see that it's not always about how much is in your bank account right now; it's about how you use money in the big picture as a tool to fuel your goals.

Seeing money as neutral also supports you in making balanced and pragmatic financial decisions about your business. It allows you to more comfortably tolerate some calculated risk that is likely to pay off in the long-term, even if it means "having less" money in the short-term. It allows you to make deliberate choices that are rooted in the value they will add to your life, rather than the emotions and attachment you have to each dollar today.

Ultimately, viewing money as neutral allows us to have a healthy emotional distance from it that supports wise decision-making and strategizing.

So, how do we develop a neutral mindset about money in a world that doesn't encourage it?

First, remember that money is simply a tool used to achieve your goals — *not a goal in and of itself.* The amount of money in your bank account isn't a value statement about your worth, your intellect, or your potential.

Second, get honest with yourself and consider if you fall in the "money avoider" or "money worshiper" categories. These limiting beliefs will inhibit your ability to see money for what it is (a tool) and create emotional baggage that will weigh you down on your financial journey.

Third, take control of your financial reality. Look it in the face, being willing to understand it for what it is—without shame or fear. This is hard to do! So often, we have strong emotional reactions to money because we don't understand it, we don't want to face it, or we are intimidated by it. And yet, by keeping our finances at an arm's length, we give it emotional power over us that prevents progress and growth.

Lastly, practice gratitude. Take time to focus on what you *do* have, reflecting on the many ways in which your money has been your friend and your supporter in the past. Doing so will allow you to trust your money to serve you well moving forward and help reduce the scarcity mindset that fuels fear-based decisions.

By learning to view money as neutral, you'll have taken a major step toward achieving the financial mindset necessary for long-term business success, while also allowing yourself to relax and more fully enjoy your journey. It's a win-win.

Section 4: Your Money Story is Not Your Fault

One of the most healing truths you can embrace about money is this: your current mindset didn't appear out of thin air. It was shaped, influenced, and layered into you long before you had any say in the matter.

Most of us were handed our money stories before we even understood what money was. We inherited them from the way our parents handled bills, from the conversations we overheard, from the panic we felt when something broke and we were told to "be careful" because money was tight. Some of us saw success paired with exhaustion—money came, but it cost everything. Others saw money used as control. Or maybe you just never saw it discussed at all, and now the idea of being financially fluent feels foreign, maybe even taboo.

These stories? They're not your fault. But they are your responsibility now.

You didn't choose them. But you're the one who gets to rewrite them. And that's not a burden. That's a beautiful, powerful invitation.

Rewriting the Relationship

So, how do you begin to rewrite your money story?

You don't start with a spreadsheet. You start with a conversation. A real, honest conversation—with yourself, with your business, with the version of you that's brave enough to want more and scared enough to almost shut it down.

It might look like journaling. Or therapy. Or simply whispering a truth you've never said out loud: "I don't trust money to stick around." Or, "I've always been afraid that success will make me selfish." Or, "I don't know how to stop working so hard for so little." These small admissions? They crack the door open. And once there's a crack, the light gets in.

From there, you get to start building a new relationship—one where you check in instead of check out. One where you let money show up for you, even when it's imperfect. One where you trust that your financial life can be a place of safety, not stress. A place of possibility, not punishment.

When your relationship with money shifts, your entire business changes. You stop panicking when someone asks your rate. You stop shrinking your offers to fit someone else's budget. You stop clinging to clients who drain you. You stop making decisions from desperation and start leading with clarity.

Moving with Clarity

Entrepreneurs want to grow, invest, and build something meaningful—but they're scared to move, scared to look, scared to decide. So they stay stuck. And that indecision? It can be just as damaging as a wrong turn.

That's why we're starting here—with mindset. Because until you rethink your relationship with money, you'll keep darting in and out of decisions, never getting where you want to go.

> *"Money is only a tool. It will take you wherever you wish, but it will not replace you as the driver."*
> *—Ayn Rand*

There's a certain kind of restlessness that comes when you're always bracing for the next financial surprise. It keeps you stuck in a constant loop of fear, small decisions, and second-guessing. Do I sign up for the workshop? Do I finally hire the assistant? Do I launch now or wait another quarter? Will I be okay if I do this?

I used to live in that loop. And I'll be honest, sometimes I still catch myself falling back into it. But what's different now is that I have tools. I have a mindset that knows how to breathe through the discomfort and ask better questions. I know how to move—not from panic, but from clarity.

There's a phrase people throw around a lot: "Leap and the net will appear." And while I love the spirit of it, I think it's incomplete. Because sometimes, especially when it comes to money, the net doesn't appear right away. And when you're responsible for a household, a team, or even just your own peace of mind, you can't afford to leap blindly. In fact, that might even be irresponsible.

What I believe in now is this: leap wisely. Build the net as you leap. Know your numbers. Know your margins. Know what you need. And then move—with only as much caution as is *truly needed*, having faith and confidence that you've made informed decisions.

"Leaping wisely" is how you build a business that supports you through the vulnerable moments while moving you toward your big goals. It's how you build a successful business that also respects your pace, your capacity, and your values.

Tell Yourself the Truth Faster

Most people avoid honest conversations about money—even with their closest partners. How often do husbands and wives sit down and openly discuss their financial goals, fears, and dreams? The silence around money leads to assumptions, misunderstandings, and missed opportunities.

One of the most powerful tools you can wield is clarity. By facing your current financial reality, telling the truth faster, and having open conversations—whether with a spouse, business partner, or coach—you unlock the ability to make conscious, empowered decisions.

But let's be real—these conversations take bravery. Talking openly about money often feels vulnerable because money is deeply personal. And more often than not, it comes wrapped in shame.

Shame whispers in the background of our money stories:
- "I should be farther along by now."
- "I make good money—why can't I save?"
- "I'm terrible with finances."

- "Everyone else seems to have it together—why don't I?"

Shame thrives in silence. It convinces us to hide our struggles, avoid difficult conversations, and keep up appearances. It isolates us and stops us from seeking help or being honest, even with ourselves.

But here's the truth: every single person has felt financial shame at some point. Whether it's debt, poor spending choices, or simply feeling behind, you're not alone. The key to moving past shame is to bring it into the light through honesty, clarity, and connection.

Our feelings about money didn't just appear overnight. They began when we were very young, shaped by what we saw, heard, and experienced during our formative years. Whether it was watching our parents argue over bills, hearing phrases like "money doesn't grow on trees," or noticing how success and wealth were praised (or criticized), these early experiences built the foundation of our current money mindset.

We now carry these beliefs into adulthood. Some of them serve us well, and others quietly sabotage us. Maybe you learned to save diligently but struggle to spend on yourself without guilt. Or perhaps you grew up around scarcity and now fear making bold financial moves, even when opportunities knock.

Here's the thing: you didn't choose these money mindsets, but you do have the power to change them.

When you begin to shift your mindset—when you start seeing money as a partner rather than a problem—a new voice rises in the background. One that sounds more like this:

- *"I'm exactly where I'm supposed to be, and I'm still growing."*
- *"I'm learning how to manage my money with confidence and clarity."*
- *"Every small step I take is moving me forward."*
- *"I don't have to be perfect—I just have to stay present."*
- *"My business can thrive, and so can I."*

This is the sound of financial resilience. This is the tone of growth. And this is the mindset that turns **profit into purpose, and vision into impact.**

In the rest of this book, we'll dive deeper into these money mindsets—helping you identify which ones empower you and which ones hold you back. But for now, I want you to focus on one simple yet profound action: being honest with yourself.

Honesty isn't just about external conversations; it starts internally. Being honest with yourself about your financial habits, fears, and goals is the first step to creating meaningful change. From there, you can begin to look outside yourself for wisdom and support as you embark on your journey.

66

You're not in this alone.

The entrepreneurial journey is full of ups and downs—and you're not the only one making mistakes or learning the hard way. Don't be afraid to ask for help. Connect with your local business community. *Mentorship and support aren't just for beginners — they're valuable at every stage. — Jay Cooper*

99

Section 5: The 5 Financial Success Principles

Now that we've built a strong foundation by developing the right mindsets about money, let's discuss our special sauce for entrepreneurs moving from vision to impact! These aren't just strategies—they are the spine of this book. Each and every chapter will have these 5 Financial Success Principles, focusing on the theme of that chapter, that will serve as a guide as you build a healthier, more empowering relationship with money as you step into your vision for impact as an entrepreneur.

Each principle builds upon the last to help you transition from financial anxiety into empowerment, moving from uncertainty to a clear vision for the future. These chapters are designed to walk with you step-by-step, helping you reshape how you think, make decisions, and behave around money in a way that aligns with your values and supports your future.

1. Know What You Want

Defining your financial goals clearly is the first step to achieving them. Are you aiming for time freedom, financial independence, or security? Vague goals lead to vague results. When you have clarity about what you want, you can create a roadmap that leads you directly to your desired destination.

When setting a dollar goal, write down what you think you want to achieve, and then add an additional 20-30% on top of that. Why? Because fear often stops us from being honest with ourselves about what we truly want and need to support our dreams. We have already committed to stop operating out of fear, so start now by being honest with your goals.

2. Know How Much It Costs

Everything has a cost—whether in money, time, or energy. Calculate what achieving your goals will require and consider the trade-offs. This step is about grounding your vision in reality. You must fully understand what your vision "costs" in terms of time, money, or energy to ensure that you are able and *willing* to make the investment required to achieve it. You may not be, and that's OK. Adjust your goal accordingly until the trade-off required is worth the cost.

With a clearer understanding of the costs, the next step is to get a firm grasp on your current financial landscape.

3. Know Your Numbers

Awareness is power. What are your current spending habits? How do they support—or sabotage—your goals? This isn't about judgment; it's about understanding.

I recommend reviewing three months of personal spending and six months of business spending to get a more accurate picture of your habits. This deeper dive can also reveal possible personal-business expense overlap, which can be addressed as a way to help you move forward more efficiently.

With clarity on your numbers, it's time to embody the mindset of the person you aspire to be.

4. Act As If

If you believed in your financial success, how would you act? This doesn't mean reckless spending—it means aligning your current behaviors, actions, and mindsets with your future self. *Act as if* you have already reached all that you have aspired to be, and step into the mindset of the entrepreneur you will then undoubtedly become.

They say that if you want to be a millionaire, you should hang around millionaires. That advice is wise. You need to begin putting into action new ways of operating, thinking, and behaving in order to create space for them to come into existence. You *must* believe to achieve. Once you actually believe it, the people, circumstances, and support you need to be successful will naturally find their way to you.

Now that you're fully aligned with your future self and operating out of that space, it's time to take meaningful, inspired, and focused action.

5. Take Inspired Action

Small, consistent, and measurable steps lead to big results. Consider weaving the following practices into your routine for increased action and movement toward your goals:

- **Write down your big goals and display them** in a place where you can see them daily. If you're a visual person, consider adding a vision board with images to help bring your vision to life in a way that inspires action.
- **Define measurable daily or weekly actions** that align with your goals, whether it's tracking expenses, saving, or investing in growth. Make sure you can actually *measure* if you completed these actions or not. Without the ability to measure action, you can't hold yourself accountable or determine which strategies are successful.
- **Start each day by reviewing your goals,** and close the day by reflecting on how your actions throughout the day supported or distanced you from your goals.
- **Create accountability** through peers, friends, or others with whom you check in regularly on your progress. Keeping your goals "out in the light" with people you trust encourages accountability while also creating a natural support system for you to push you along when you need it, or celebrate with you when you reach an important benchmark. It's all better together!
- **Assess your goals and adjust regularly.** We often think that goals are static things — we set them, and then they just stay that way forever. But the reality is that needs can change and priorities

often shift, making it critical that we circle back to our goals to ensure they are current and meaningful to us given our context.

With inspired action, you're not only envisioning success—you're actively building it one step at a time.

Section 6: CEO Thought Leadership Insights: Money Amplifies Who You Already Are

Here's a powerful truth: Money amplifies who you already are. It's not the villain or the hero—it's the mirror. If you avoid talking about it, it will reflect your avoidance in the form of disorganization, debt, or stagnation. But if you face it head-on, even imperfectly, it will amplify your courage, clarity, and confidence.

Another idea to consider: financial intimacy. Just like emotional intimacy deepens relationships, so does financial intimacy. Couples and business partners who openly discuss money (goals, fears, and even mistakes) tend to build stronger, more resilient partnerships. It's not about agreeing on everything but about having the courage to be seen and heard in one of life's most vulnerable areas.

And here's the ultimate truth: Shame can't survive empathy and honesty. The more we openly discuss money with vulnerability and without judgment, the less power shame holds over us.

So, lean into the discomfort. Be brave. Be honest. The conversations you're avoiding today are the ones that will unlock the doors to your future financial freedom tomorrow.

Section 7: Case Study: From Scarcity to Abundance

Case Study: From Scarcity to Abundance — Jennifer's MAP to Success

Meet Jennifer, a writer who set out to turn her creative passion into a sustainable business. In the beginning, Jennifer struggled with the same two challenges many new entrepreneurs face: unpredictable income and an intense fear of charging what her work was worth.

Her relationship with money was complicated—she loved the idea of financial freedom but was afraid to ask for it.

Jennifer's mindset was rooted in scarcity. Growing up, money was always tight, and she internalized the belief that making a living doing what you love was a luxury few could afford. That belief showed up in how she ran her business—underpricing her services, saying yes to projects that drained her, and working long hours without seeing the financial return she hoped for and deserved.

Everything began to shift when Jennifer was introduced to the **MAP** framework—Mindset, Action, and Profit. Here's how it helped her write a new chapter in her financial story:

Mindset: Jennifer started by unpacking her beliefs about money through journaling and reflection. She confronted thoughts like, "Writers don't make real money" and "Who am I to charge more?" With time, she reframed these beliefs to recognize that her words had real value—and that abundance and creativity were not mutually exclusive. She embraced the idea that money wasn't the enemy, but a resource that could help her amplify her message and serve more people.

Action and Accountability: With a clearer mindset, Jennifer began to take aligned action. She raised her rates. She created a client intake process that emphasized value over volume. She joined a writing community for accountability and support, and she scheduled regular financial check-ins to track progress. These steps, though sometimes uncomfortable, gave her a renewed sense of control and momentum.

Profit: As her confidence grew, so did her income. Jennifer landed clients who respected her process and paid her worth. She created packages that reflected the transformation she delivered, not just the hours worked. She also began saving for quarterly taxes, set aside a profit margin, and reinvested in professional development without guilt. For the first time, she wasn't just surviving—she was thriving.

Jennifer's breakthrough didn't come from a magical windfall. It stemmed from shifting her relationship with money, aligning her actions with her values, and establishing systems that enabled her to grow with intention.

Her secret? She stopped viewing money as something scarce and started treating it as renewable energy—something that flows toward clarity, confidence, and purpose.

Jennifer's story reminds us that financial transformation begins with the stories we tell ourselves. With a mindset rooted in abundance, the courage to take consistent action, and a plan to create and manage profit, anything is possible.

And the best part? You don't have to do it alone. This book—and your **MAP**—is here to guide the way.

66

Self-Worth is a Wealthy Mindset:

Your mind has to be in the right place before you can make—or keep—money. If you don't believe you deserve to have it, you'll blow through it. You'll never feel like you have enough. True wealth starts when you know beyond a shadow of a doubt that you're worthy of receiving and keeping abundance. — Debbi-Jo Horton, CPA

99

Section 8: The Path Forward: Becoming a Money Magnet

When you shift your mindset and see money as a neutral tool, you become a magnet for opportunities. It's not magic—it's about clarity, intention, and inspired action. As you continue through this book, you'll build on this foundation, learning how to align your vision with impactful financial decisions.

Your journey has begun. The next step? Knowing exactly what you want—and how to get there.

Take the first inspired step today and begin reshaping your financial destiny. And remember — don't be the squirrel in the road. Make the decision, take your confident leap, and move toward your financial freedom. The power lies within you. And to move from vision to impact, you just have to start. Go get that nut!

Top 5 Takeaways from Chapter 1: Money as a Tool and Energy

1. Shifting your mindset to view money as a neutral tool and ally rather than an enemy is crucial for entrepreneurial success. A healthy money mindset sets the foundation for all financial decisions.

2. Your current relationship with money was likely shaped by past experiences and inherited beliefs. Recognizing this allows you to consciously rewrite your money story.

3. Open, honest conversations about money — with yourself, your partners, and advisors — are essential for achieving financial clarity and empowerment. Avoiding money talk leads to assumptions and missed opportunities.

4. Shifting from a scarcity to an abundance mindset unlocks new levels of freedom and opportunity in your business and life. This mindset shift is a key differentiator for successful entrepreneurs.

5. Reaching your goals requires inspired action that can be measured and tracked. Without concrete ways to measure progress, you'll never know how effective your strategies are in getting you toward your goals, and you'll be less likely to stay consistent with your commitments.

Chapter 2:
Financial Awareness—Turning Numbers Into Knowledge

Section 1: The Power of Flipping the Switch—Why Awareness Matters

You wouldn't hop in your car and start driving across the country without checking the gas gauge, plotting your route on a map, or ensuring your vehicle is ready for the journey. It's common sense, right? You check your fuel, your tires, your oil—because you know that without proper preparation, the trip could end in disaster.

And yet, many entrepreneurs approach their businesses with a similar mindset. They start building, expanding, and pushing forward, hoping it'll all work out. They trust their intuition, ride the wave of momentum, and avoid the spreadsheets that hold the real story of their business.

But here's the truth: if you don't flip the switch and turn on your financial awareness, your business might be running on fumes.

"

Some clients don't even want their monthly reports.

I ask them, 'Excuse me—but how are you running your business?' What I've noticed is this: the ones who think they know something often tune out before they even listen. You might be starting with a concept they believe they've already mastered—so they're not really hearing you. But someone who knows they don't know? They're leaning in. They want to understand.

Honestly, it's often easier to work with someone who has no financial knowledge at all. That way, you're teaching them from scratch—rather than having to help them unlearn what they think they know. *And unlearning? That's often the hardest part.*
— *Debbi-Jo Horton, CPA*

"

The Story of the Gas Tank—A Lesson in Awareness

Let me tell you a story that changed everything for me. It's a story about a night when I learned a simple but profound lesson about awareness and preparedness.

As a teenager, I was driving my dad's truck home late at night. The truck was a bit fancy for its time—dual fuel tanks, a feature I didn't fully understand. I was cruising along, feeling confident, making good time. I had a curfew to make and didn't want to be late. Suddenly, the engine started chugging, coughing, and then it...just.. died. I coasted to the side of the road, heart pounding. It was a cold night, and I was miles from home.

No cell phones back then, so I had to hike to the only farmhouse I could see from my warm truck, knock on a stranger's door at almost midnight, and ask to use their landline. When my dad answered, he was calm and straightforward:

"You've got a second tank. There's a toggle switch under the dash. Flip it, and you'll be fine."

I found the switch, flipped it, and just like that, the engine soon roared back to life. I got lucky that night—nothing bad happened. But the lesson stayed with me: sometimes, the solution is right there, waiting to be flipped on. You just have to know where to look.

That night, I realized that the most critical switch in my life and business was awareness. Just like my truck had a second tank I didn't know about, my business had financial insights I was ignoring. And ignoring them could cost me everything.

The Second Tank—A Personal Revelation

Fast forward a few years. I was sitting at my desk, staring at my laptop, on yet another Zoom call with a new bookkeeper. I'd been through this before— overcharged, underinformed, embarrassed that I didn't understand my own numbers. My business looked successful from the outside, but behind the scenes, I was white-knuckling my way through financial fog.

The bookkeeper pulled up my profit and loss statement on the screen. I nodded politely, trying to follow along as she explained the figures—profit, margin, net income. But honestly, they might as well have been in a foreign language. I was pretending to understand, while inside, I felt lost, overwhelmed, and a little ashamed.

Then she asked a question that changed everything:

"What are your monthly goals—not just for the business, but for your life?"

I froze. The room went silent. That question hit me like a ton of bricks. I'd never really considered it before. I was so busy chasing revenue, paying bills, and trying to keep everything afloat that I'd lost sight of what I truly wanted.

And in that moment, I realized that I'd been running my business in a kind of financial fog—reacting to what the numbers said, but not really understanding what they meant for my life.

I started talking. Slowly at first, then with more confidence. We connected the dots between what I wanted, what it would cost to get there, and what my current numbers were actually telling me. For the first time, I felt a sense of empowerment. I wasn't just nodding along anymore—I was asking real questions.

And that shame I'd carried? It began to melt away.

The lesson? Just like flipping the switch in my dad's truck, I had access to a second tank all along. I just didn't know how to turn it on.

That moment opened my eyes to a fundamental truth: Financial awareness is the key to clarity, confidence, and control. When you understand your numbers, you know where you stand. You can make informed decisions, set realistic goals, and navigate your business with purpose.

If your business is like that truck, then financial awareness is the switch that keeps everything running smoothly. Without it, you're running on fumes, hoping to make it to the next station. But with awareness, you're in the driver's seat, able to see the road ahead clearly. And that's right where you need to be.

I don't believe most people want to be left in the dark—especially when it comes to something that controls so many facets of their lives.

When you help a client understand their bookkeeping and financials, you don't just teach them numbers—you give them power. You help them see the inner workings of their business. *And that's how real confidence is built — Yahweh Khao Sok*

No matter what your financial reality, confidence is built by letting the numbers see the light of day, not by keeping them tucked away in the dark. But if looking at your business finances head on feels a lot easier said than done, know that you aren't alone.

Section 2: Why Many Entrepreneurs Avoid Their Numbers

I get it. Digging into your financial data can feel intimidating—almost scary. The numbers seem cold, confusing, and overwhelming. You might think, *"It's too complicated,"* or *"I don't want to face the truth,"* or even, *"I don't know where to start, and I am so embarrassed."*

But avoidance only leads to uncertainty and stress. It's like ignoring the gas gauge when you're driving—eventually, you'll run out of fuel, and that's when the real trouble begins.

Many entrepreneurs fall into the trap of hoping their business will just "work out." They ride the wave of momentum, trusting their gut, and avoiding the spreadsheets that tell the real story. They think, *If I just keep pushing, I'll get there.* But that's like driving blindfolded.

The bottom line is that your business needs to support itself and your personal life. You need to be clear about exactly what you want, how much it costs, and what it's going to take to get there. You need a plan. And that plan needs to work on paper first. If the numbers don't work on paper, it won't work in real life. Don't waste your hard-earned money guessing.

See your numbers as your best allies. They reveal the truth of your business, highlight areas of strength, and show you where improvements are needed. They are the dashboard of your enterprise. Know them like the back of your hand, and trust them to direct you where you need to go.

Section 3: An Important Mindset Shift—Learning to Trust the Numbers

One of the most important mindset shifts you can make as a business owner is to stop fearing the numbers and start trusting them. Numbers don't lie. They don't play games. They aren't emotional. They simply reflect what *is*. And that's a powerful thing—because when you know where you are, you can confidently decide where to go next.

Most people avoid looking at their finances because they're afraid of what they'll find. They worry that the truth will confirm their worst fears—that they're behind, they're failing, or they're not "good" with money. But what if the opposite were true? What if the numbers, once understood, could become your greatest allies?

Just like that night in my dad's truck, there comes a moment in every entrepreneur's journey when the engine sputters. You feel stuck, uncertain, maybe even panicked. But then, you remember the switch. You flip it. And the engine roars back to life.

This chapter is about finding that switch in your own business. It's about trusting that when you engage with your numbers, something will come alive. That clarity will replace confusion. That momentum will replace hesitation.

You don't have to be a financial expert to understand your business. You just have to believe that the tools are already there...and that you're capable of using them.

Flip the switch. Trust the numbers. The engine will ignite.

Section 4: Creating New Habits: Useful Practices for Understanding Your Numbers

The foundation of financial awareness is simple but powerful: understanding your current financial situation. This means knowing your income, expenses, profits, and cash flow.

Many entrepreneurs avoid this step because they think it's complicated or boring. But it's actually the most crucial part of the journey. Without this understanding, every other step is guesswork.

Your first action is to take a clear-eyed look at your finances. How? By thinking about your budget in a new way.

The Role of a Budget—And Why Rigid Constraints Aren't Serving You

Many people think of budgets as restrictive, limiting, or punitive. And for some, they are. But at its core, a budget, when approached correctly, is a tool for awareness, not punishment.

A traditional budget says, "This is how much you have, and this is how much you can spend." It's reactive, often restrictive, and can feel like a prison. It doesn't inspire; it deflates.

Instead, consider the benefits of taking a more proactive approach that says, "This *is what I want, this is what it costs, and here's my strategy to get there.*"

In this way, you can imagine a budget as a GPS for your finances. It shows where you are now, but it also helps you plan your route to where you want to go. It's a living document—something you review regularly and adjust as needed.

Making Your Money Work for You

The key is not just tracking your numbers but understanding them deeply. How much are you earning? Where is that money going? What's your profit margin? Are there expenses you can cut or optimize?

Once you understand your numbers, you can identify patterns to uncover what's serving you and what's not. You can see where to cut costs, where to invest, and how to grow your income.

The Practice of Regular "Coffee Dates" with Your Numbers

One of the most effective habits you can develop is setting aside time each month to review your finances. Scheduling these "coffee dates" with your business creates dedicated, intentional time to sit down without interruption, look at your financial reports, and assess your progress.

Before this meeting, do a quick gratitude practice. Write down three things you're grateful for in your business. This shifts your energy from scarcity to abundance and reminds you of your wins, big or small.

During your review, answer these critical questions:
- *What's my current financial position?*
- *Am I on track with my goals?*
- *Where are my biggest expenses?*
- *Are there hidden costs or leaks?*
- *What adjustments can I make for next month?*
- *Do I need to adjust my goals in light of new information or changes in context?*

This process helps you stay proactive, rather than reactive, and keeps your finger on the pulse of your business. Remember, when you are brave enough to look at the numbers head-on, you can trust them as an ally to work in your favor.

Section 5: The 5 Financial Success Principles

By now, you've started to flip the switch. You're no longer avoiding your numbers—you're beginning to understand them through regular routines that help you build familiarity with and trust in them. You've started looking at your finances with fresh eyes, perhaps even curiosity. You've taken the first brave steps toward clarity.

But awareness alone isn't the goal. What you do next is what creates transformation, and that transformation comes from following the 5 Financial Success Principles. These aren't just tips—they're enduring truths. They'll help you make confident decisions, set aligned goals, and build a business that supports the life you want.

Think of these as the core filters for every financial decision you make going forward.

1. Know What You Want

Clarity is the starting point. Without it, you're just spinning your wheels.

If you don't know what financial success looks like for you, how will you recognize it when you get there? Most entrepreneurs say they want to "make more money," but that's not a goal—that's a hope. And hope is not a strategy.

Clarity Creates Power.

Imagine getting in your car and driving without a destination. You might cover a lot of miles, but you won't get anywhere specific. Your finances work the same way. When your goals are vague, your strategy will be too, and that makes consistent progress almost impossible.

Instead, get precise. Define what success looks like in your business and your life.

Do you want...
- *A certain monthly income?*
- *A cushion in your savings account?*
- *To be debt-free?*
- *To work fewer hours and have more free time?*
- *To be able to afford certain luxuries or ways of life?*

There's no wrong answer. But there *is* a wrong approach: not answering at all.

We talked in the last chapter about the power of making your goals measurable in order to ensure accountability and action. To do this consistently and effectively, use the **SMART framework** to give your goals the solid structure they need to be useful to you:
- **S**pecific: What exactly do you want?
- **M**easurable: How will you track it?
- **A**chievable: Is it realistic based on your current resources and stage of business?
- **R**elevant: Does it align with your values and priorities?
- **T**ime-bound: When do you want to achieve it?

Here are some examples of SMART goals:
- "I want to earn $15,000 in monthly profit within the next 12 months."
- "I want to save $20,000 by next July for my dream vacation."

- "I want to reduce my work hours to 30 per week while maintaining my current income within the next two quarters."

When you name a goal clearly and specifically, you bring it into reality. You move it from a thought to a target. And once it's a target, you can start planning around it.

Don't skip this step.

It's tempting to jump straight into action—launching offers, signing clients, cutting costs—but until you know what you're aiming for, all that action may not get you closer to what matters most.

These SMART goals are your compass. As we continue with the rest of the Financial Success Principles, you'll learn how to turn these goals into results.

2. Know How Much It Costs

You can't build a plan around blurry math. Strategy requires precision.

Now that you've clarified your financial goals, it's time to connect them to reality. This is where your vision becomes measurable and actionable. Outline in detail the costs associated with reaching your goals. Those costs may come in the form of time, money, or energy—all of which represent real trade-offs that must be considered when determining if your goals are something you're willing to make the aligned sacrifices to achieve. Be honest with yourself here to avoid setting goals that require actions you aren't willing or able to take.

Understanding Costs: A Deeper Dive

Let's say you've set a goal to earn $15,000 in profit each month. That's a powerful start. But now comes the next question:

How much does it cost to run your business and life?

If you don't know this, your target income number is floating in space. You need to ground it in real, tangible numbers that reflect your actual lifestyle and business needs.

Start by breaking your expenses into two categories:
- **Fixed expenses**: These are predictable monthly costs that don't change much: rent or mortgage, insurance, software subscriptions, payroll, phone bills, utilities.

- **Variable expenses**: These fluctuate depending on your activity level or season: advertising, travel, client gifts, continuing education, and event fees.

And don't forget to include personal expenses if your business is your primary source of income. This includes your home budget, groceries, medical expenses, savings, and any other expenses required to maintain your life outside of work.

You also need to factor in two often-overlooked categories:

- **Taxes**: Set aside 20–30% of your gross income (depending on your structure and location).
- **Investments**: What are you reinvesting back into your business or saving for future opportunities?

Ask yourself:

- What are my essential expenses each month, both business and personal?
- Where can I reduce or renegotiate costs without sacrificing value?
- What expenses are investments that will help me grow faster or work smarter?

For example, if you want to hire a virtual assistant, don't just tell yourself you "can't afford it." Look up the actual cost. Is it $25 an hour? $600 a month? What could that support free up for you to generate more revenue? Maybe that hire makes room for you to bring in an extra $2,000 per month—suddenly, the math makes sense.

If you want to launch a new offer, research the tools you'll need, from design software to email platforms to potential ad spend. Know the number. The clearer you are, the more strategic your next step will be.

Tip: Keep a **running list of all your expenses** in one place. Review it monthly during your "coffee date."

- Are you paying for subscriptions you don't use?
- Is there software that duplicates another tool?
- Could you bundle services or negotiate a lower rate?

Cutting unnecessary costs isn't about being stingy—it's about being intentional. It frees up money that can be reinvested or saved toward your bigger goals.

Mindset Shift:

Instead of saying, *"I can't afford that,"* ask:

"What must I do to create the funds I need for this?"

That single shift—from *lack* to *possibility*—is one of the most empowering things you can do as a business owner. Money doesn't respond to fear. It responds to focus, clarity, and aligned action.

By looking closely at the exact costs associated with reaching your goals, you will have laid the foundation necessary to profit from and grow your business in sustainable and smart ways.

3. Know Your Numbers

Tracking your income, expenses, and cash flow is the heartbeat of your financial health.

You've clarified your goals. You've figured out what it costs to live and operate the business you want. Now comes the part many entrepreneurs avoid — looking at the numbers themselves.

Here's the truth: You can't build a sustainable business if you're afraid to look at your finances. You don't need to love spreadsheets or become an accountant, but you *do* need to build a relationship with your numbers. They are the clearest, most honest feedback you'll ever get.

Tracking for Success

This is where a lot of business owners stumble. They get busy. They don't know where to start. Or they look at a Profit & Loss statement and feel like they're reading a foreign language.

But understanding your numbers is non-negotiable. Why? Because numbers tell a story. They reveal where you're thriving, where you're bleeding cash, and where you might be sitting on an untapped opportunity.

This doesn't mean obsessing over your bank account balance every day. It means **regularly reviewing** a few key financial reports that paint the full picture of your business.

Your primary financial statements include:
- **Profit & Loss Statement (Income Statement):** Shows how much revenue you've brought in, what it cost you to earn it, and what's left over. This tells you whether your current business model is profitable.

- **Balance Sheet:** Provides a snapshot of your financial position. It lists your assets (what you own), liabilities (what you owe), and equity (your net worth in the business). It's especially helpful for tracking debt and overall stability.
- **Cash Flow Statement:** Tracks how cash is moving in and out of your business over a specific time period. It answers the question: *Do I actually have the money I need to pay my bills right now?*

If you have a bookkeeper or accountant, review these together. If not, there are user-friendly tools (like Wave, QuickBooks, or FreshBooks) that can help you generate these reports even if you're not a numbers person.

And remember, your numbers are not there to shame you. They're there to support you. When you treat them with respect and curiosity, they become one of the most powerful tools you have for building a profitable, purpose-driven business.

4. Act As If

Behavior influences reality. Confidence is a habit before it becomes a result.

This principle of building confidence through behavior isn't about faking it until you make it. It's about *living* in alignment with the business you're building, even before the results show up.

When you act as if you're already successful, you train your brain, your behavior, and others around you to move in that direction. You begin to make decisions from a place of stability, not fear. You begin to carry yourself like a CEO, not just someone who's trying to "figure it out." You embody the success you desire.

All of this leads to a palpable shift in posture, mindset, and decision-making that changes the course of your business.

If you really want to run a profitable, sustainable business, then start by asking, *"How would I show up if I already had that?"*.

Here's what acting "as if" can look like in your business:

- **Paying yourself first:** Treat your salary as non-negotiable, not optional. You are your business's most valuable asset.
- **Investing in your growth:** Education, coaching, tools, or a team member who helps you stay focused are all valuable investments, not expenses, when chosen wisely.

- **Making confident pricing and marketing decisions:** Stop underselling your offers. Price based on the value you provide, not on what you think someone can afford.
- **Avoiding scarcity-based thinking:** Let go of the urge to hoard or panic. Scarcity shrinks. Strategy expands.
- **Setting boundaries:** Decide what kind of business owner you want to be and what you will no longer tolerate, whether it's inconsistent payment terms, overworking, or constantly second-guessing yourself.

Success is a collection of habits, not just outcomes. When you behave as someone who believes in their business, others start believing in it, too. You'll be amazed at how quickly momentum builds from there.

Tip: Small, consistent behavior shifts reinforce your identity as a successful entrepreneur.

- **Dress the part.** You don't need a designer wardrobe—just wear what makes you feel focused and powerful.
- **Speak with confidence.** Even if you're unsure, own your voice. The more you practice, the more natural it becomes.
- **Decide with authority.** Successful people don't know everything, but they trust themselves to figure it out, allowing them to make tough decisions with relative confidence.

When you act as if abundance is your default setting, you begin attracting opportunities, partnerships, and decisions that match that energy. And soon, the life and business you've been envisioning won't just be a goal, it'll be your new normal.

5. Take Inspired Action

Awareness is powerful—but action is transformational.

You've done the work to flip the switch. You've faced your numbers, clarified your goals, and begun to shift your mindset. Now comes the most important part: **doing something with what you know**.

Financial clarity without action is just interesting information. Real change happens when you **move from knowing to doing, from insight to impact.** Ultimately, moving from knowledge to results is about taking *deliberate*, *aligned*, and *purposeful* steps. Not because you feel pressured, but because you now have the clarity to make decisions with confidence.

Rest assured that you don't need to overhaul your entire financial life overnight. In fact, small steps that are taken consistently are the most sustainable and powerful.

What does inspired action look like? It might be:
- *Raising your prices by 10% to reflect your value.*
- *Setting up an automatic transfer to a tax savings account.*
- *Cancelling unused subscriptions and reinvesting that money into something that actually moves the needle.*
- *Finally, enrolling in the financial course you've been eyeing.*
- *Hiring a bookkeeper or virtual assistant to free up your energy.*

Each step you take becomes proof to yourself that you're in motion. It is proof of concept that you are capable, in control, and building something real.

Section 6: The Transformational Power of a Money Mindset Makeover

Back in high school, I was an athlete. My days were filled with practices, games, and just enough studying to get by—but makeup? Not exactly a top priority. But prom was coming, and for that one special night, I wanted to feel beautiful. The only problem? I had no idea how to apply makeup and no one who could teach me.

So my best friend Kari and I did what any two hopeful, slightly clueless athletic girls would do: we headed to the mall.

We landed at one of those sleek department store makeup counters, where a woman with flawless makeup greeted us like royalty. She invited us into tall, salon-style chairs and promised to show us exactly what to do. We were certain we'd walk out glowing.

Here's what we didn't anticipate:
- Makeup was *so* expensive, and we could each only afford *one* product.
- The artist only applied makeup to half of our faces and expected us to mirror the other half ourselves.

Her side looked polished, balanced, like a magazine cover. Our sides? Well... think "drunk clown meets Picasso." We walked out of that mall with mismatched cheeks, uneven eyeliner, and a very real sense that we were not quite as ready for prom as we'd hoped.

But here's the lesson that's stuck with me: transformation takes more than watching someone else do it. You have to learn the technique, practice the skill, and be willing to face the messiness before you master it.

A money mindset makeover works the same way. You can read the books, listen to the experts, and follow the influencers—but at some point, *you* have to pick up the brush and apply it to your own life.

You have to face the awkward first attempts and the inner critic. But if you keep showing up, if you keep adjusting, eventually you learn how to create something that feels authentic—and beautiful— to you.

If you've been operating from a place of scarcity—believing there's never enough and feeling like you're always behind—then this chapter is your call to shift. It's time for a money mindset makeover.

I'm talking about the kind of makeover that isn't just about feeling or looking better, it's about thinking differently, so you *act* differently. When you change how you see money, you change how you manage it. (Remember that from Chapter 1?)

So, how do you keep that new mindset alive, day after day? How do you move from a single shift in perspective to a consistent practice of financial growth?

Here's how to begin:

- **Start with gratitude:** Every time money flows in, say "thank you." Appreciate the abundance already present in your life.
- **Reframe your thoughts:** Instead of "I can't afford that," try asking, "How can I afford that? What's the strategy?"
- **Visualize success:** Picture yourself confidently managing your finances, paying yourself, and proactively investing in growth.
- **Affirm abundance:** Try simple affirmations like "Money flows easily to me," or "I am a master of my finances."

This shift from lack to abundance creates a whole new energetic space in your business and your life. When you believe there's enough—enough clients, enough money, enough opportunity—you start noticing doors opening where before you only saw walls.

And then? Then, you begin to become the hero of your own story.

Section 7: CEO Thought Leadership: Why Financial Awareness Is the CEO's Superpower

Financial awareness isn't about spreadsheets or perfection. It's about presence. It's about having a clear, honest understanding of where your business stands and where you want it to go. And most importantly, it's about using that insight to lead with purpose. Most entrepreneurs are running on instinct and grit, but the moment they tap into their numbers, something shifts. They gain access to clarity, stability, and decision-making power they didn't realize they had.

When you make financial tracking and regular check-ins a consistent habit, you stop reacting and start leading. You move from emotional decision-making to strategic action. You become the kind of business owner who leads with data, not doubt.

That's when the real transformation begins.

As you commit to financial mastery, setting measurable goals, reviewing your reports, and acting with intention, you begin to notice tangible changes:

- You *understand* your cash flow.
- You *confidently* raise your rates.
- You *intentionally* invest in growth.
- You *trust* yourself more.

These aren't just wins. They're turning points. Each one builds a stronger foundation. Over time, what once felt intimidating becomes second nature. You start to feel not just capable, but empowered.

The truth is, financial awareness is one of the most overlooked leadership skills in business. But the entrepreneurs who embrace it? They don't just stay afloat, they thrive.

So here's the invitation:

- Make financial awareness your non-negotiable.

- Lead from a place of knowledge, not avoidance.
- And watch how your numbers begin to tell a new story, one of growth, confidence, and real control.

Because when you master your money, you don't just run a business.

You lead it.

Section 8: Your Call To Action: Crossing the Financial Threshold to Write Your Own Hero's Journey

Every business owner reaches a moment that changes everything: a threshold where you stop hoping and start leading. This is the point at which you transition from instinct to intention.

That's where you are now.

You've moved from avoidance to awareness. From guessing to knowing. And while this transition might feel awkward or humbling, that discomfort is a sign of growth.

On the other side?

- **Clarity** in your decisions
- **Confidence** in your leadership
- **Control** over your path

You're no longer a passenger. You're in the driver's seat, with your dashboard lit and your direction is clear.

This is your turning point. Take a deep breath. Set your intention. Move forward with purpose.

Because now? Now, financial awareness is your superpower.

Top 5 Takeaways from Chapter 2: Financial Awareness

1. Your Numbers Are Not the Enemy – They're Your GPS

Financial awareness isn't about judgment; it's about guidance. When you begin tracking income, expenses, and cash flow, you gain clarity and direction. Your numbers help you navigate your business with confidence, rather than relying on guesswork.

2. Flipping the Switch Starts with Trust

Just like flipping that dual-fuel tank switch in my dad's truck, financial clarity begins when you trust the system and yourself. Numbers aren't vague or emotional. They're reliable and trustworthy signals that guide your next steps.

3. The Five Financial Success Principles Are Your Filters for Every Decision

These principles transform financial confusion into strategy. They give you a repeatable process to make smart, aligned money decisions.

1. *Know What You Want*
2. *Know How Much It Costs*
3. *Know Your Numbers*
4. *Act As If*
5. *Take Inspired Action*

Never underestimate their power to guide and support you.

4. Small Habits Create Big Shifts

The simple act of a monthly "coffee date" with your finances can change everything. Regular check-ins reduce anxiety, deepen understanding, and strengthen your decision-making muscles. Progress builds through presence and consistency.

5. Financial Mastery Is a Journey—Not a One-Time Fix

You don't need to be perfect to lead your business well. You just need to be present. Financial awareness is about ongoing practice, not perfection. Every time you choose to check your numbers, ask better questions, or shift your mindset, you're building lasting leadership.

Chapter 3:
Defining YOUR Vision of Success and Moving From Vision to Impact

Section 1: Success Isn't One-Size-Fits-All

I'm not really that into makeup, and if I'm being honest, not all that into clothing either. But I do enjoy looking nice, and I try. In the evenings, I love scrolling through Pinterest for outfit inspiration. You know, something that looks *just right* on the model. (Because it will look just the same on me, right?!)

I especially enjoy it when I have a stage I am getting ready to step onto or a trip I am going to be taking. I LOVE looking for just one or two special outfits.

And so I order an outfit or two, convinced that they will be a fashion home run for me. Except, more often than not, they aren't. Almost always, that piece that looks amazing on the rack (or on my friend Kari) looks totally wrong on me.

There was this one outfit I was absolutely sure would be my new go-to. Flowing linen pants, a cropped sweater, gorgeous heeled shoes—the works. I envisioned myself strolling into a chic coffee shop looking like a trendy and together lifestyle blogger.

But when I tried it on? Let's just say I looked less like "effortless chic" and more like "confused gardener." I've learned this lesson the hard way more than once. What looks good on someone else doesn't always work for me, and vice versa.

Why? Because style isn't one-size-fits-all. What flatters one person might not flatter another. It depends on your shape, coloring, height, and a dozen other personal factors.

And the same is true for success.

Two people can earn the exact same income and experience completely different realities. One feels abundant; the other feels trapped. One travels the world, works a four-day week, and sleeps peacefully. The other works weekends, dreads payroll, and secretly resents their business.

This isn't about how much money they make. It's about how their money works for them. Financial success is personal. The goal of this chapter is to help you define *your* version of success, not just financially, but in terms of freedom, security, and fulfillment.

I had two clients, Sam and Jordan. Both earned around $150,000 annually. Sam had a lean, flexible business, low overhead, and time to coach his daughter's soccer team. He reinvested with intention and built a retirement plan aligned with his actual dreams. Jordan had a big team, a fancy office, and zero peace. Every success felt hollow. Why? Because his business wasn't aligned with his values.

Success isn't about what you earn. It's about how well your life reflects what you value.

————————

Section 2: An Important Mindset Shift: You Don't Have to Want What They Want

We've all absorbed a story: "Success means making more. Bigger house. Bigger business. Bigger everything." If that's your dream, go for it. But you're allowed to want something else. You're allowed to want *enough*.

Success might look like scaling to 7 figures or working 25 hours a week and taking Fridays off. It might mean leading a national team or working solo with no meetings and minimal stress.

The real shift? Success isn't a finish line. It's a feeling. When you define it on your terms, you stop performing and start building.

Let's dive a little deeper and clear up some common financial myths. Have you ever told yourself:

- "I'll be successful when I make six figures."
- "Owning a big house means I'm financially secure."
- "Retirement is the ultimate goal."
- "I just need a little bit more, and then I'll relax."

How much, really, is "a little bit more?"

These ideas are easy to chase, but they're not always rooted in personal truth. Too many entrepreneurs are following a version of success that doesn't actually resonate with who they are.

The result? Burnout. Guilt. Confusion. A quiet voice asking, *"Is this really it?"*

Real financial success isn't about a number. It's about:

- **Freedom**: to live on your terms.
- **Security**: to make confident decisions.
- **Alignment**: between your values and your reality.

When your version of success is clear, decisions get easier. You stop undercharging. You stop overcommitting. And most importantly, you start building from a place of personal power.

Before you create your next financial goal or business milestone, ask yourself these critical questions:

1. **What does financial success look like for me?** Debt freedom? Passive income? A portfolio that grows quietly while you live freely? There is no one right answer.
2. **What kind of lifestyle do I want to create?** Remote work? Early retirement? Long weekends with your family? Let your money support the life you actually want.
3. **How do I want to use my money to create security?** Think savings, insurance, and investments. Security lets you take risks from a place of strength.
4. **What impact do I want my finances to have?** Think legacy. Do you want to build generational wealth? Fund causes? Hire and support others?
5. **What will financial success allow me to do that I can't do now?** This is where dreams are made. What becomes possible when you're no longer stuck in survival mode?

We'll spend more time later in the chapter formulating your answers to these questions, but for now, know that these questions are more than prompts. They are the roadmap to developing a clear vision of what success means to YOU.

Section 3: CEO Thought Leadership and Why You Must Define Success for Yourself

In business, we talk a lot about goals, performance, and growth. But rarely do we pause to ask a foundational question: *What does success actually look like for me?*

The absence of a personal definition of success is one of the most common reasons entrepreneurs plateau or, worse, build a business they no longer enjoy.

Defining your vision isn't just a reflective exercise. It's a strategic imperative.

When you have a clear vision of success, your decision-making improves. You're no longer distracted by trends, peer pressure, or the endless pursuit of "more." Instead, you focus on what matters most to you—whether that's freedom, impact, financial security, or a specific lifestyle.

This chapter introduces a critical framework for aligning your business with your life: the Three Pillars of Financial Success. Wealth & Security, Lifestyle & Freedom, and Impact & Legacy aren't abstract ideals. They're practical areas where money creates meaning. When these pillars are balanced and clearly defined, they become your compass for strategic growth.

Without this clarity, business owners often chase success that looks good on the outside but doesn't feel sustainable on the inside. The result is burnout, misalignment, and missed opportunities.

The most effective business strategies are built around a clear personal vision. The most resilient entrepreneurs are those who know exactly what they're building and why.

Define success on your terms. Align your business accordingly. And revisit that definition often. Because success isn't static. It evolves as you do.

And yet, this is easier said than done when we live in a culture that tells us that success looks just one way. For example:

- *"I'll be successful when I hit six figures."*
- *"If I own a big house, I've made it."*
- *"Success is when I can finally retire."*
- *"I just need to make a little more, and then I'll be happy."*

Sound familiar?

These ideas sound like success, but they're often built on *external* expectations, not internal alignment. Too many entrepreneurs adopt someone else's definition of success because it's what's praised, what's visible, or simply what they've been told they *should* want. The result? A lot of high-achieving professionals who feel burned out and confused quietly ask themselves, *"Is this really it?"*

Here's what I've learned from working with hundreds of business owners:

1. Financial success isn't about the number—it's about what that number allows you to do.

True success comes from the freedom to live on your terms, the security to make decisions without fear, and alignment with how you want to feel and what you want to create.

When your definition of success is clear, your decisions get sharper. You know what to say yes to and what to walk away from. You stop undercharging because you understand both your value and your goals. You stop overcommitting because you know what "enough" actually looks like.

Most importantly, defining success puts you in the driver's seat. You stop riding along in someone else's version of achievement and start steering toward a life and business that feels fulfilling now, not "someday."

This is where you belong—not reacting to what happens, but taking the lead. Not waiting around but taking action and building something that matters. On your terms, with clarity and purpose.

Confidence is the foundation for everything—even money.

I used to work as a waitress, getting paid in cash. My sister helped me build a budget: car payment, insurance, savings... but the last part never happened. I never deposited the money into the bank. If I made $500 that week, I felt like I had $500 to spend—because I physically had it in my hands.

That mindset stayed with me until someone finally taught me that money isn't just about what you earn—it's about what you do with it. And more importantly, that *money can give you freedom, but only if you're confident enough to manage it.*

True financial power isn't about having it all—it's about knowing you can create more when you need to. That confidence is what frees you. — *Lana Kinberg*

2. You must define what success means for you—deeply, personally, unapologetically.

Because here's the truth: most people are chasing goals that someone else gave them. They don't OWN those goals; they are just borrowing them.

They're following numbers that sound impressive, building lifestyles they don't enjoy, and measuring their worth by someone else's scoreboard. And even if they reach the top of that mountain, they're often exhausted, confused, or quietly disappointed when they get there.

But not you. You're going to do it differently.

This is all about YOU and YOUR vision. No one else's. And it's going to be worth every bit of effort it takes to bring it to life.

Believe it's possible.

If something feels too far outside your realm of possibility, you're less likely to believe it's achievable. That's the key — *you don't have to be sure it's going to happen, but you do have to believe it's possible.* We're not taught that enough. *The moment you don't think it's possible, you've already surrendered to failure.*
— *Debbi-Jo Horton, CPA*

Section 4: The Three Pillars of Financial Success

Now that you've taken the time to begin to envision a life and aligned financial goals that are truly your own, it's time to anchor those big dreams into a practical structure, something you can build financial plans around. That's where the Three Pillars of Financial Success enter the picture.

The Three Pillars are the *core areas where money shows up and creates meaning in your life.* When your goals and plans allow these three to be in balance, success starts to actually *feel* like success for you and not just look like it on paper.

1. Wealth & Security

This is your financial foundation. It's about:

- **Savings**: Emergency funds, opportunity funds, future-you funds.
- **Debt freedom**: Not owing anyone. Keeping what you earn.
- **Investments**: Building income that works even when you're not.
- **Stability**: Knowing that if life throws you a curveball, you've got a cushion and confidence.

This pillar isn't flashy, however, it is powerful. It gives you the safety to take risks and the freedom to dream bigger.

When you have wealth and security, you're not operating from fear or desperation. You're building something with a strong foundation, one that can weather storms and still move forward.

For many entrepreneurs, this is the piece that gets skipped in favor of flashier goals like scaling or six-figure months. But those goals mean little if they're built on shaky ground.

Wealth and security might look like:

- Setting up automatic savings each month.
- Paying off high-interest debt.
- Opening a retirement account—even if it starts small.
- Making sure your business has at least 3-6 months of operating reserves.

This is about building a buffer, not just financially, but emotionally. When you're not constantly worried about survival, you can make smarter, calmer, more aligned decisions.

This is where real power begins.

2. Lifestyle & Freedom

This is where money meets meaning.

It's about designing your life intentionally, not someday, but now. That might include:

- A flexible work schedule that lets you take Fridays off.
- The ability to travel without guilt or financial strain.
- Early retirement or planning sabbaticals without stress.
- Doing work that excites you instead of drains you.
- Having margin time to enjoy your family, hobbies, or rest without hustle guilt.

Lifestyle & Freedom is the reminder that money isn't just for savings accounts and spreadsheets. It's for *living*. It's for cultivating presence, fun, and flow in your daily life, not postponing happiness until some distant milestone is reached.

This pillar asks, "What does an extraordinary, everyday life look like for you?"

Maybe it's sipping your morning coffee slowly on the porch, coaching your kid's soccer team, or working in the garden every afternoon. Maybe it's hopping on a plane every quarter or working remotely from a cabin by the lake.

There's no wrong answer, only your answer.

And the best part? This pillar can often be activated before your bank account "says" you're ready. Start building life rhythms and work habits now that mirror the life you're working toward. Small shifts add up.

3. Impact & Legacy

This is where your financial life expands beyond you.

It's about how your money creates change, both now and long after you're gone.

That might mean:

- Creating generational wealth for your kids and grandkids.
- Giving generously to causes that matter to you.
- Funding scholarships or programs in your community.
- Mentoring, investing in others, or building something that outlives you.

Legacy isn't just what you leave behind. It's what you live into every day.

It's the decision to use money as a force for good, not just a personal cushion, but a communal ripple.

It's remembering that success isn't just about what you can earn, it's about what you can empower. The values you pass on. The systems you influence. The opportunities you fund.

When all three pillars—**wealth, lifestyle, and impact**—are working together, that's when your vision becomes a movement. That's when success turns into *significance*.

That's when money becomes not just a measure of achievement but a tool for legacy.

A Story of Defining Vision and Building a Life with Impact

Meet Jasmine.

Jasmine was a second-generation entrepreneur running a successful bakery that her mother started in their small town. On paper, everything looked great—steady income, loyal customers, even press features. But Jasmine felt constantly stretched thin. Her mother still helped with the books, her husband was transitioning out of a corporate job due to burnout, and they had recently taken in her niece after a family emergency.

Everyone depended on Jasmine—employees, family, and community. And while she loved her business, she felt like she was always reacting. Never resting. Never clear. One night, overwhelmed by payroll stress and an unexpected bill for her niece's school needs, she realized this wasn't the version of success she wanted. It was someone else's definition and not hers at all.

That night, she pulled out a notebook and asked herself three questions:

- What does success actually look like for *me*?
- What do I want my *life* to feel like?
- What kind of *impact* do I want this business to have on those I love?

And slowly, a new vision emerged. One rooted in what we now call the Three Pillars of Financial Success:

1. Wealth & Security

Jasmine realized she needed financial safety, not just for her business, but for her family. Her first moves? She created a reserve fund for three months of payroll. She automated savings. She met with a financial advisor and set up retirement accounts for both herself and her husband. She let her mom officially retire from the books and hired a part-time accountant.

Now, when life happens, Jasmine has options. Cushion. Breathing room. Her confidence soared.

2. Lifestyle & Freedom

Next, Jasmine looked at her time. She loved baking, but hated the early mornings and late nights. She adjusted her menu, dropped the items that took hours to prep but weren't profitable, and started closing two days a week.

She restructured her schedule so she could walk her niece to school each morning and enjoy quiet coffee dates with her husband.

Freedom, for Jasmine, wasn't about taking months off to travel the world. It was about reclaiming moments that mattered, creating space in her days, not just her calendar.

3. Impact & Legacy

Then came the legacy piece. Jasmine wanted to teach teens how to cook and bake, just like her mother taught her. She partnered with a local nonprofit to start weekend workshops in her bakery kitchen. She now mentors three high schoolers each semester, giving them both job skills and life confidence.

Her niece recently told her, "I want to be like you, Aunt Jas."

That was it. That was the moment she knew: she wasn't just running a bakery. She was building a life.

A life where money served her, not the other way around. A life where her vision wasn't just an idea, but a compass for every decision.

When Jasmine aligned her business with the **Three Pillars of Financial Success,**

1. Wealth & security
2. Lifestyle & freedom
3. Impact & legacy

Everything shifted. Her stress went down. Her confidence went up. And her purpose, finally, was set in an intentional plan.

Let this be your encouragement: You don't have to follow someone else's version of success. You get to define your own.

And you get to build it one pillar at a time.

Section 5: The 5 Financial Success Principles

The **5 Financial Success Principles** we've explored in each chapter aren't just journaling prompts. They're anchors. When used with honesty and consistency, they'll help you define a vision that actually excites you—and shape your financial life to bring it into reality.

1. Know What You Want

Ask yourself, "What Does Financial Success Look Like for Me?"

(Remember, this is your definition—not a borrowed one.)

Forget the highlight reels for a moment. Close the tabs on "How I Made $500K in 5 Months" and tune into what feels good to *you*.

Do you want:
- Complete debt freedom and a simple lifestyle?
- A growing investment portfolio and multiple income streams?
- Enough passive income to take summers off with your kids?
- A multi-million-dollar business and a home in three time zones?

Each of those versions is valid. But they require very different business models, time commitments, and strategies.

Take Vanessa, for example. She left her corporate job and started a virtual consulting business. Within a year, she hit $100K and immediately felt like she was "supposed" to scale. But when she actually sat down and asked what *her* version of success looked like, she realized she was already there. What she really wanted was time, not expansion. She raised her prices slightly, reduced her client load, and reclaimed 10 hours a week to spend with her family, AND she gets to wear Disney shirts to her home office. This makes her smile every day!

Vanessa "got richer" not only in income but also in the work she was doing and the relationships she built with her new, ideal clients. She was able to really, really focus on the joys of her life and her family. And to her, that *was* success.

Your Reflection Prompt:

What would make me feel financially successful—regardless of how it looks to others?

2. Know How Much it Costs

Now, it's time to consider what kind of lifestyle you want to create and get specific about how much that actually costs.

Think BIG here and let your money serve your life, not the other way around. In other words, don't live within your budget, but instead, make enough money so you can live within your means and bring in the amount of money to make that happen. To do that, you have to know how much the life you want costs. That's your carrot.

It's one thing to make money. It's another thing to have a life you *actually enjoy living*. Remember, money is just a tool.

Your question now becomes, "What kind of life do you want to build with your money?"

Maybe you dream of:
• Working from your laptop in coffee shops across Europe
• Taking Fridays off to volunteer at your child's school
• Living in a tiny home by the lake with no debt and lots of margin
• Creating a business that pays you well and runs with or without you

Success isn't just about income—it's about *income that matches your lifestyle dreams*.

And this is where the magic happens: when your vision of success aligns with your daily life, you feel energized, not drained. You don't need a vacation from your reality. You've built one that feels right.

Your Reflection Prompt:

If I designed my ideal week, what would it include? And what kind of financial structure would support it?

3. Know Your Numbers:

Ask yourself, "How do I want to use my money to create security?"

(Because peace of mind is the most underrated flex.)

Ask most entrepreneurs what they want, and they'll say "freedom." But freedom without security is shaky ground.

Security is about creating a financial base that lets you breathe deeper. Things like:
• Having six months of expenses saved
• Building a retirement account that you *actually* contribute to
• Investing in real estate, stocks, or your own business growth

- Being insured, protected, and proactive, not reactive

It's not sexy. But it's solid. And it's often the difference between staying in business or crumbling under pressure when life throws a curveball.

Think about Maya, who ran a fast-growing online shop. Sales were booming. But when her husband had an unexpected health scare and she needed to step away for two months, she realized she hadn't set anything aside. No savings. No systems. No security. The stress was overwhelming.

She promised herself she'd never be in that position again. Six months later, she had a reserve fund, clear SOPs, and a business that could flex to life's changes.

Today, her husband is still sick. But Maya isn't making decisions from fear anymore. She's no longer operating on adrenaline or pretending things are fine when they're not. Her relationship with money has become grounded, thoughtful, and strategic. She sets boundaries. She plans ahead. She makes decisions with stability, not wishful thinking. She no longer indulges in pie-in-the-sky fantasies or minimizes what's needed. She's traded avoidance for alignment— and she's thriving.

Security is the silent partner of every sustainable business. Don't ignore it. In fact, become best friends with this important partner of yours.

Reflection Prompt: *What would financial safety look and feel like in my life right now? What do I need to build to create it?*

4. Act As If

Now that you've laid the foundation through wealth and security and cast a clear vision for the lifestyle you want your money to support, it's time to zoom out. Now, ask yourself, "What impact do I want my finances to have?" and then step into that vision, acting as if that were already the case.

(Because money isn't just for you—it's for the legacy you leave.)

What do you want your money to do beyond your own comfort and freedom?

Maybe it's:

- Paying for your child's education or caring for aging parents

- Donating to causes close to your heart
- Hiring team members and paying them generously
- Building a business that empowers others
- Investing in underrepresented entrepreneurs or your community

Money is powerful. It can build bridges, open doors, and heal systems when used with intention.

But here's where the mindset shift kicks in: don't just wish for that impact. Act as if it's already in motion.

Imagine your business five years from now. It's thriving. You've got the income, the infrastructure, and the influence. What are you doing with it? How are you showing up? Who are you helping?

Now, begin doing small versions of that today. That might mean donating a small percentage of your income now, even if it's $5. It could be mentoring someone in your industry. It might look like setting up a monthly giving plan, sponsoring a scholarship, or writing your mission down where you can see it daily.

"Acting as if" doesn't mean lying to yourself or pretending you've made it. That is an important distinction. It means stepping into the identity of the person you're becoming. It embodies and magnifies the leader, the contributor, and the changemaker you already are within.

Even if the bank account hasn't caught up yet. It will, because

Clarity plus action creates momentum.

You don't need to be a billionaire philanthropist to make an impact. You just need to decide what matters most — and start channeling your income toward that vision.

Reflection Prompt: *What kind of ripple effect do I want my money to create—this year, in five years, or even after I'm gone? If I truly believed that vision was already in motion, how would I act today?*

5. Take Inspired Action

Ask yourself, "What Will Financial Success Allow Me to Do That I Can't Do Now?"
(This is where the dream becomes real.)

Let's make it personal. Because the clearest way to define success is to visualize the freedom it gives you.

What could you do that you can't right now if money weren't an issue?

- Spend more time with loved ones?
- Say no to projects that drain you?
- Finally take that trip you've been putting off?
- Sleep at night without stress?
- Start the nonprofit you keep thinking about?

This is the fuel. The emotional "why" behind every revenue goal and every spreadsheet.

It's not about money for money's sake. It's about possibility. It's about what opens up when you're no longer in survival mode—when you're no longer making every decision based on fear, fatigue, or scarcity.

But here's the secret: you don't have to wait.

You can begin taking inspired action today.

That might mean:

- Declining one project this month that you know drains you, even if it pays well.
- Booking the weekend getaway that fills your soul, even if it's modest.
- Saying no with confidence and yes with joy.
- Creating a small, symbolic version of your dream life, even just one hour a week.

Inspired action is not just action; it's action that's aligned with your future self. It's saying, "I believe in that version of me *so much* that I'm going to take a step in her direction today."

Think of it as rehearsal for the life you're creating. Each choice you make with clarity and courage becomes a vote for your future.

And yes, there will be resistance. You'll hear old stories like, "I can't afford to slow down," or "I'll rest when things settle." But those are the thoughts keeping you stuck.

You don't have to overhaul your whole life to move forward. You just need to do one brave thing.

Start with that.

Reflection Prompt: *What's one thing I'd change in my life tomorrow if I were financially free and what's one step I can take toward that today?*

These **Financial Success Principles** questions are a true map to real wealth if you choose to dive into them with **honesty and vulnerability**. And remember, this isn't a one-time reflection. These five questions are tools you'll revisit as you grow, shift, pivot, and evolve. What success means to you at 35 may look different at 50. That's not failure, it's refinement.

So put them somewhere visible. Answer them again every week, every month, and every year. Use them to guide your financial strategy, your business goals, and your personal decisions.

Because when you define success on your own terms and build your life around that clarity, you don't just grow your income; you grow your impact. You grow your peace. You grow your life. And that's the point of the whole journey. That's YOUR version of success.

Section 6: Your Call to Action: Define YOUR Vision of Success by Creating Your Personal Financial Success Statement

Now that you've reflected, dreamed, and clarified, it's time to bring it all together and put a stake in the ground by creating your own Personal Financial Success Statement—a simple, clear summary statement of what success means, looks like, and feels like to you.

Moving forward, this statement will serve as your compass. It's your definition of "enough," your reason for building, your filter for saying yes or no.

And remember—this statement isn't about impressing anyone. It's about owning *your* values, *your* vision, and *your* version of financial success.

Here's how to create it.

Step-by-Step Process

1. Review your answers to the Five Financial Success Principles Questions.

2. Choose your top 2-3 priorities across the **Three Pillars of Financial Success** (wealth, lifestyle, and impact).
3. Write a simple, clear sentence that summarizes what financial success means for *you*.

Here are a few samples that might give you a starting point:
- "Financial success for me means having a paid-off home, a $1M investment portfolio, and the ability to work on my terms."
- "I will feel financially successful when I can retire at 55, travel four times a year, and fund my children's education."
- "My definition of financial success is living debt-free, working three days a week, and giving 10% of my income to charity."

Be sure to write it down. In fact, write it down now. Post it where you can see it. Revisit it monthly. Speak it out loud. Let it guide your next move.

A few important things to remember:
- Your statement will change, and that's good! It means you are learning and growing. Give yourself permission to revise your statement whenever needed.
- When you're just starting out, success might mean paying your bills with less stress. Later, it might be about scaling a team or creating passive income streams. And later still, it might be about impact, legacy, or freedom of time.
- Even with the best intentions, it's easy to get distracted. Here are three common traps that derail entrepreneurs from their true version of success—and how to stay out of them.

Trap #1: Comparing Your Financial Success to Others

Comparison is the thief of clarity.

Just because someone's business looks shiny on Instagram doesn't mean it's aligned, sustainable, or even profitable. Don't measure your life with someone else's yardstick.

Stay in your lane. Build what matters to you.

Trap #2: Accumulating Money Without a Clear Purpose

Money for the sake of money is a hollow pursuit.

If you don't define what you want money to do for you, it will become a scoreboard. And you'll always be losing, because guess what, my friend, there's always someone with more.

Let purpose drive your profits. Let vision drive your numbers.

Trap #3: Sticking to an Outdated Definition of Success

Sometimes, the version of success you're chasing is an old dream or someone else's altogether.

If you've outgrown your goals, update them. Don't let your business drag you into a life you no longer want.

You're allowed to evolve. In fact, you need to.

At the end of the day, success isn't just about the money. It's about what that money *unlocks*—freedom, choices, peace of mind, and purpose.

Your version of financial success is valid. It doesn't need to be louder, faster, or bigger to matter.

But it *does* need to be clear. Defined. Owned.

And that's just what you've done.

Now you can give yourself full permission to succeed—on your terms.

Top 5 Takeaways from Chapter 3: Vision to Impact:

1. Success is Personal, Not Prescribed

True financial success isn't about hitting arbitrary income goals or copying someone else's lifestyle. It's about aligning your money with your values, goals, and personal vision. You get to define what success means for you and that definition is the foundation of everything else.

2. The Three Pillars of Financial Success Are the Backbone of a Meaningful Financial Life

Wealth & Security, Lifestyle & Freedom, and Impact & Legacy are the three core areas where your finances need to align. When all three are in balance, you experience not just financial growth but a life of intention, confidence, and fulfillment.

3. A Clear Vision Drives Strategic Decisions

Jasmine's story illustrates how defining your personal vision can transform not just your business but your entire life. When you're clear on what you want, you can restructure your time, reallocate your energy, and build a business that works *for* your life, not against it.

4. You Can Design a Life You Love Now—Not "Someday"

Freedom and fulfillment aren't reserved for retirement. By intentionally designing your schedule, values, and systems today, you can create space for joy, presence, and peace now—even while growing your business.

5. Your Money Has the Power to Multiply Your Impact

Financial success isn't just about stability. It's about contribution. From mentoring to giving back, from family to community, your money can be a vehicle for lasting change. When you build with purpose, your vision can ripple out far beyond yourself.

Chapter 4:
The Power of a Plan – Why Every Business Needs a Business Plan

Section 1: The Cost of Building Without a Plan

Would you ever leave $30,000 to $60,000 lying around for just any-one to pick up and walk off with? Of course not, but did you know that is what the average home builder pays for "extras" added in after the home building project has started?

If you fail to plan, you plan to fail.

Let's start with a truth you already know but might be ignoring: *It's far easier to build something right the first time than to go back and fix it.*

This is true whether you're building a house... or building a business.

When my husband and I built our home, we had a breathtaking lake view—and a vision to match it. We designed a great room with giant windows to soak it all in. In our minds, it was going to be the perfect place to relax, entertain, and feel connected to nature every single day.

But we made a smart move early in the process: before committing to anything, we laid cardboard cutouts on the floor where our furniture would go. We wanted to visualize how the space would actually function.

And that's when we discovered a problem.

Once seated, our line of sight didn't hit the lake—it hit the *deck railing.*

Our dream view? Blocked.

We realized that if we didn't make an adjustment *now*, we'd be sitting in that beautiful room every day, feeling frustrated and dis-appointed. So, we paused the project. It wasn't convenient, but we adjusted the design to raise the windows and preserve the view we fell in love with.

That change probably saved us a lifetime of regret.

But it didn't stop there.

We also made the mistake of placing the refrigerator on the oppo-site side of the kitchen from the garage. Every grocery trip meant tracking mud across our freshly cleaned floors—arms full, boots dripping, cursing under our breath.

It was only after living in the space that we realized how inconve-nient it was. We'd sacrificed function for aesthetics.

And it cost us time, effort, and extra work—all things that could've been avoided with better planning.

How Home Builders Budget for Mistakes

Here's the thing: our experience wasn't unique.

Home builders know that mistakes and mid-project changes are part of the process, and they budget for them. On average, homeowners spend an extra 10–20% of the total construction cost on changes, upgrades, or late design corrections.

That's $30,000–$60,000 in unexpected costs on a $300,000 build.

Even professional builders add 10–15% markups on change orders because they know how disruptive last-minute changes are to a project. Whether it's moving a wall, fixing cabinets, or adjusting plumbing, it all adds up fast.

The farther along you are in the build, the more expensive the fix.

And here's the kicker: most of those costs could be avoided with a better blueprint upfront.

Now Apply That Lesson to Business

If you wouldn't build a house without a blueprint, why would you build a business without one?

Yet that's exactly what so many first-time business owners do.

They launch fast, fueled by passion and possibility. They pick a name, build a website, create some offers, and start bringing in clients.

It's exciting...until it's not.
- They realize their pricing isn't profitable.
- Their services are too custom to scale.
- Their schedule is maxed out.
- Their vision is lost in the chaos of doing all the things.

They've created a business that technically works, but doesn't function well. Just like a house with the fridge in the wrong place.

Without a plan, all those little inefficiencies, frustrations, and mismatches *compound*. And fixing them later? That's where the real cost comes in.

Signs You're Building Without a Plan

Still unsure if this applies to you? Here are common red flags:
- You keep reinventing your offers every month.
- You're not sure what your packages actually *include*.
- You haven't paid yourself in weeks or maybe even months.
- You say yes to clients out of fear, not fit.
- You're always busy, but your income doesn't reflect it.

You can't explain your business model clearly in one sentence.

If more than two of these apply, you don't need to work harder. You need a better plan.

Tell Yourself the Truth Faster

There's a saying that's saved me more than once: "Tell the truth faster." Translated, that means you really aren't being honest with yourself.

If it doesn't work on paper, it's not going to work in real life. And if something already feels off, it's only going to get worse as you grow.

Why is knowing the truth so empowering?

Here's a scenario I see all the time:

Someone says, *"I want a virtual assistant, but I can't afford one."*

My next question is always, *"How much does a virtual assistant cost?"* More often than not, they have no idea.

They're basing their decision on an assumption, not on data.

Once we sit down and look at the numbers, they often realize the cost is far less than they expected. Or they realize it's not affordable *right now,* and that's just as valuable. Now they can build a plan to make it happen.

Knowing the truth sets you free. It gives you clarity. You can create a strategy rather than letting limiting beliefs drive your decisions. If you're not careful, those limiting beliefs will stop you from ever taking action.

That's why your business plan isn't just a luxury. It is your "True North", your lifeline. It's the tool that helps you catch the view-blocking deck railing before you build the wall. It's the plan that helps you put the fridge in the right place the first time.

Your business plan shows you:

- What you're building and why
- Where the friction lives in your current setup
- How your vision, systems, and values align (or don't)
- What needs to shift before it gets expensive to change

Growth Without a Plan = Expensive Mistakes

Here's the part no one likes to admit: **You will make the same mistakes at $1 million that you do at $100,000 unless you fix them.** It's true!

If you underprice your services now, you'll still be under-earning later. If your operations are messy now, they'll be chaotic at scale. If you're unclear about your vision now, no amount of revenue will bring clarity.

All that changes is the number of zeros.

In construction, change orders are expensive. In business, unplanned growth is even more costly because you lose more than money. You lose time. Energy. Confidence.

Here's an important mindset shift you need to make to be the successful business owner you dream of being:

A Business Plan is a Practical Tool—Not a Pretty PDF

A business plan is your guide to success. It's not just a document but a dynamic strategy for growth. It isn't about writing a dry 40-page document to impress a banker.

It's about designing a business that *actually supports the life you want.*

- A business that flows.
- A business that earns profit without burnout.
- A business where you *love the view,* not resent the path you took to get there.

In the rest of this chapter, we'll show you how to build a business plan that's functional, flexible, and rooted in your *actual* goals, not just the ones you saw online.

We'll walk through:

- The core components every business plan should include
- What makes a plan "living" vs. locked

- How to make decisions today that support the business you want tomorrow
- How to apply the Financial Success Principles to your Business Blueprint

Because here's the truth: The best time to make a smart plan is before the foundation is poured.

But the second-best time?

Now.

Section 2: Building a Plan That Works (For You)

Every business plan begins with a dream.

For me, it started on a napkin.

Literally.

I was sitting at a business conference surrounded by bold ideas, big thinkers, and too much hotel coffee when I grabbed a napkin and started scribbling. I sketched out what would eventually become my first business. It wasn't a pitch deck or a spreadsheet. It was a few circles and lines that captured something real: a vision.

When I got home, I took that napkin and turned it into a mind map. That mind map became a linear outline. Then I added structure, numbers, ideas, questions, and clarity. That messy napkin evolved into my first real business plan. And guess what?

It worked.

Not because it was perfect, but because it gave me direction.

Here's what I've learned since:

A business plan is not something you write once and check off on some magical "Business To-Do" list.

It's a living document; your first go-to when things get uncertain, confusing, or messy.

You'll refer to it often in the beginning:
- When you're making your first offers

- When you're setting prices
- When you're deciding who to work with
- When you're trying to stay focused instead of overwhelmed

As you grow, build systems, and become more established, you may check it less frequently, but it never loses its value.

That's why this chapter matters.

Let's start drafting a business plan that actually works.

One that reflects *your* vision.
    One that supports the kind of life and impact you're here to create.

One that helps you build with confidence, not guesswork.

This isn't about writing something perfect.

This is about designing something *intentional*.
    Let's begin with the foundation as we dive into the key components of a strong business plan.

Section 3: The Core Components Every Business Plan Should Include

Forget the corporate-style binders that no one reads. The best business plans are built to be used and revisited, not just admired.
    At its core, a powerful business plan answers **seven** essential questions:

1. What do you do, and why does it matter?

This is your **mission and purpose.**
    What problem are you solving?
    Who are you solving it for?
    And why is this the work you're uniquely called to do?
    Don't just describe what you sell, explain what you stand for. This is the emotional heartbeat of your business. It's what you'll come back to in every hard season.

2. What do you believe in?

This is your values section. What are the non-negotiables in how you do business?

For example:
- Do you value transparency and direct communication?
- Do you believe people come before profit?
- Is equity a part of your hiring or service strategy?
- Do you stand for sustainable growth, not hustle culture?

Your values shape how you operate, how you lead, and how you make decisions under pressure. A business without values is a business without a compass.

3. Who is your ideal client, and what do they need?

Don't settle for surface-level demographics. Get specific about their mindset, pain points, and desires.
- What are they struggling with that you can solve?
- What transformation are they craving?
- Why are they seeking someone *like you*?
- And just as important—who is *not* your ideal client?

The more clearly you define who you're for, the easier it becomes to create offers, content, and experiences that truly resonate. This is how you attract dream clients instead of energy-draining ones.

4. How does your business make money?

This is your **revenue model.** List out your products, services, packages, or programs. Define your pricing. Know your margins.

Ask yourself:
- What are your high-leverage offers?
- What's recurring vs. one-time?
- How many units, clients, or sales do you need to meet your financial goals?

If you don't know how your business generates sustainable income, you don't have a business; you have a hobby that pays (sometimes).

5. What systems support your delivery?

This is your **structure.**
- How do you deliver your service or product?

- What happens once a sale is made?
- What tools, tech, or team members help you fulfill your promise?
- Is it a hands-on service or a self-paced course?
- Do you rely on contractors? Automation?
- Is your backend chaotic or streamlined?

Systems make your business *work* without working you into the ground. They create consistency, reliability, and freedom.

6. What does success look like for *you*?

This is your **vision.** Forget everyone else's milestones. What do *you* actually want?

- Do you want to make six figures working part-time?
- Do you want to grow a team or stay solo?
- Do you want location freedom, creative freedom, or financial independence?

Define success on your own terms, or you'll spend your energy chasing someone else's dream.

7. What's your runway and what are your risks?

This is your **reality check.**

- How much time or money can you invest before this business needs to be profitable?
- What roadblocks do you anticipate?
- What will you do if things go off track?

A strong plan doesn't just dream—it prepares. When you name your risks upfront, they lose their power to derail you.

Why These 7 Questions Matter

These aren't just prompts. They're pillars. They help you stay rooted when you want to quit and flexible when it's time to pivot.

When you build your plan around:

- What you do,
- What you believe,
- Who you serve,
- How you earn,
- How you deliver,
- How you define success, and

- How you will adapt...

You're not just building a business. You're building a business that fits your life.

And when you find that kind of alignment?

Your energy, your marketing, your offers, and your joy will all fall into place.

_____

Section 4: The 3 Most Common Business Plan Mistakes And How to Fix Them

Mistake #1: Designing Without Living in Mind

In Homebuilding

In homebuilding, it's easy for homeowners, especially first-timers, to get swept up in the excitement of Pinterest boards and HGTV reveals. They start picking out backsplashes, dreaming about light fixtures, and debating paint swatches long before they've nailed down a solid floor plan.

The focus shifts to finishes before function, which often leads to costly design flaws. Kitchens end up with beautiful counters but no practical storage. Bedrooms lack closets. Open floor plans become echo chambers that feel more like gymnasiums than cozy gathering spaces. The home may look stunning in photos, but day-to-day living reveals the cracks, both literally and figuratively. What's missing is intentional planning, rooted in how the space will actually be used.

In Business

The same misstep shows up in business. Entrepreneurs, eager to launch, often skip the deep work of aligning their model with how they truly want to live and work. They say yes to every client, chase trends, and create offerings that sound good, but demand more time, energy, or overhead than they can sustainably give.

The business may impress on the surface: a polished website, a stacked calendar, and glowing testimonials. But underneath, it's exhausting. It doesn't fit their life. It lacks the systems, boundaries, and clarity needed to grow with purpose. Just like a poorly laid-out home, a business that prioritizes appearance over alignment will eventually need renovation.

The Fix

Design your business the way an experienced architect designs a home, *starting with how you want to live in it*.

Before you worry about branding colors or clever offer names, ask yourself the foundational questions:

- Do I want a full client roster, or do I crave spaciousness in my schedule?
- Do I prefer deep 1:1 work, or does the energy of teaching groups light me up?
- How many hours a week do I *actually* want to work—and how does that match the reality of what I'm building?

Remember, clarity and intentionality matter most in the planning stages. Don't "Pinterest" your business by focusing only on what looks good or what other people are doing. Just like a dream kitchen with no drawers becomes a daily frustration, a business that looks impressive but doesn't support your life will eventually become a burden.

Your business needs to be functional, sustainable, and designed around your values, energy, and goals. It's not just something to show off. It's something to live and work in every single day. Build accordingly.

Mistake #2: Rushing the Planning Phase

In Homebuilding

Some first-time builders are eager to "just get started." They're excited, motivated, and ready to see progress, so they rush into action. However, in their haste, they often bypass critical steps, such as skipping permits, overlooking plumbing and electrical systems, or downloading generic floor plans from unverified websites without considering whether they align with the land, local codes, or their own lifestyle. It feels productive in the moment, but it proves to be costly later.

Eventually, those early decisions catch up with them. The home construction stalls during inspections. Walls have to be torn open. Fixing what was missed becomes expensive, stressful, and time-consuming, often costing far more than it would have to slow down and plan it right the first time.

In Business

The same pattern shows up in business. Business owners dive in with passion, ready to launch the next big thing. But in the rush to get moving, they often skip foundational work. They put out offers without testing whether there is real demand. They skip over financial forecasting, assuming revenue will work itself out.

They say "yes" to opportunities without stopping to ask, "How will this actually work for my schedule, my team, my life?" The result is a reactive business held together with duct tape, last-minute decisions, and sheer determination. It may survive for a while, but it won't scale. And it definitely won't feel sustainable.

The Fix

Slow down to speed up. Lay the groundwork *before* you build. Just like a contractor wouldn't pour concrete without a blueprint, you shouldn't build a business without clarity.

Ask yourself:
- What's my offer, and how do my services or products work together strategically?
- Who am I for, and just as importantly, who am I *not* for?
- How will I consistently earn a living, and how will I reliably and sustainably pay myself?

Good planning reduces work. It prevents costly pivots. And most importantly, it builds a business with a stable foundation, one that you can grow and thrive in for years to come. Because a rushed beginning might feel like momentum, but a well-laid plan? That's real power.

Mistake #3: Not Consulting the Right Experts

In Homebuilding

DIY can be tempting, especially when budgets are tight and confidence is high. With endless YouTube tutorials and step-by-step blogs, many homeowners convince themselves they can figure it out as they go. They try to tile their own showers, install cabinets, or even navigate code compliance without professional guidance. What starts as a bold cost-saving move often ends in frustration: misaligned finishes, hidden structural issues, or projects that stall at inspection because they weren't built to code. Instead of saving money, they end up paying double to fix avoidable mistakes and sometimes risk safety in the process.

In Business

Business owners do the same thing. Driven, scrappy, and proud of their resourcefulness, they take on everything themselves. They write their own contracts using free templates from the internet. They manage their own books, guessing their way through accounting software. They avoid hiring coaches, strategists, or branding professionals telling themselves they'll figure it out **eventually.**

The problem?

"Eventually" often comes after a lost client, a tax penalty, or a branding misstep that confuses rather than converts. By the time they reach out for help, the damage is already done, time is lost, *and cleaning it up is far more costly than getting it right from the beginning.*

Delaying expert input doesn't just slow your progress. It introduces risk, creates unnecessary stress, and often keeps you stuck in amateur mode long after you're ready for something more.

The Fix

Surround yourself with support and expertise. You don't need a full team overnight, but you *do* need people who've been where you're going. Build a circle of trusted professionals: a legal advisor, a financial expert, a business coach, a branding strategist—whatever your current stage calls for.

Hire slowly, but hire smart. Know your own gaps, and fill them intentionally. Ask questions. Collaborate. Seek out those who see what you can't and know what you don't.

And don't be afraid to outsource what drains you. Just because you *can* figure something out doesn't mean you *should*. Your time is better spent in your zone of genius, meaning doing the work only you can do.

You don't get extra credit for doing it all alone. You just get exhausted. Sustainable success isn't about being the hero of every department. It's about building a business that's smart, supported, and scalable.

You'll go further and get there faster when you stop trying to carry it all by yourself.

Section 5: The 5 Financial Success Principles

Now that you understand the core components of a strong business plan and some of the pitfalls to avoid, it's time to layer on our 5 Financial Success Principles to help us create the strongest plan possible.

Here's a quick review of the 5 Financial Success Principles that we've seen in each chapter:

1. **Know What You Want**
2. **Know How Much It Costs**
3. **Know Your Numbers**
4. **Act As If**
5. **Take Inspired Action**

Look familiar? Good!

Now, let's explore how to apply each of these directly to your business plan.

1. Know What You Want

Clarity is the foundation of any good plan.

Before you list your services or set your pricing, stop and ask:
• What do I want this business to do for me?

- What kind of work lights me up?
- What kind of clients do I want to attract?
- What kind of hours and income do I want?
- What kind of life do I want to wake up to five years from now?

Be specific.

"Financial freedom" isn't a plan.

But "Work 30 hours a week, take Fridays off, and earn $12,000/month"—that's something you can reverse-engineer and build around.

A business built without a clear vision is like building a house with no blueprint, no budget, and no idea what you want it to look like when it's finished. You end up with walls in the wrong place, windows facing the wrong direction, and a layout that doesn't match your life.

It might look good on the outside, but functionally? You're frustrated and constantly rearranging your "furniture" just to make it work.

I've seen this happen over and over: business owners build businesses that impress other people... but exhaust them. Why? Because they didn't take the time to truly consider what they want before setting their vision.

Mini Story:

A coaching client once told me, "I want to scale."

It sounded like she was ready to grow fast. But when we dug deeper, what she really wanted was to simplify by reducing her hours and working with fewer, higher-quality clients. Her version of scaling wasn't *more*. **It was *less, but better.***

That moment shifted everything for her. She stopped chasing someone else's version of success and started designing a business that felt right for her life, her energy, and her goals.

Don't build a castle if what you really want is a cabin.

You're the architect of your business plan so start with a vision that actually reflects what you want and how you want to live.

2. Know How Much It Costs

It's time to get real about the numbers.

Before you build anything, you need to know what it's going to take *in money, time, and energy.* Most business owners skip this part or delay it until the books are a mess and their pricing isn't keeping up with their growth. But that's like building a house and ordering tile, cabinets, and windows without measuring a single thing.

Builders don't wing it. They measure, budget, and price accordingly. Your business is no different.

Here's what you need to know to build a financially sound business:

✔ Your monthly fixed costs

Things like:
- Software and subscription
- Insurance and licensing
- Office expenses or workspace costs

✔ Your variable costs

These are the expenses that fluctuate depending on your workload or season:
- Freelancers and contractors
- Materials, shipping, and client deliverables
- Marketing spend

✔ Your ideal salary
- What do you want to pay yourself, not just to scrape by, but to live the life you want?

The one thing I wish someone had told me when I started my business?

Pay yourself first.

That simple principle changes everything. — Debbi-Jo Horton, CPA

✔ Your tax savings and profit goals

Don't just aim to "break even."

You need to build in profit *on purpose,* not hope it shows up later. When you're clear on these numbers, you can price with confidence, not comparison, emotion, or fear.

Pro Tip: Use the Reverse Calculator Method

Let's say your goal is to earn $8,000/month. Your business expenses total $2,000/month. That means you need to bring in $10,000/month just to hit your income goal.

If your signature offer is $2,500, then you need four clients per month to meet that goal. That's your starting point. Now your marketing, scheduling, and systems can be built with clarity, not guesswork.

Too many entrepreneurs build emotional businesses, but not financial ones.

You can't hit a target you haven't defined. So define it.

Build a buffer for unexpected expenses. If 2020 taught us anything, it's that you never know what's coming. Planning for emergencies helps you stay resilient.

And pay yourself. Too many entrepreneurs neglect this step.

- If you're a sole proprietor or LLC, pay yourself through an owner's draw.
- If you're an S-Corp, you're required to pay yourself a reasonable salary.

Talk to your tax professional to make sure you're following the rules.

Include your financial benchmarks in your business plan. Don't leave them out because they feel intimidating.

You wouldn't build a home without a budget. Don't build a business that way either.

Knowing what it costs to *run* your business and what it takes to *reach* your goals is the difference between spinning your wheels and making strategic, profitable decisions.

3. Know Your Numbers

You wouldn't build a house without a measuring tape. Don't run your business without metrics.

Track:
- Revenue (monthly and by offer)
- Profit margins
- Hours worked vs. income earned

- Conversion rates (consults to clients)

This isn't about perfection. It's about progress.

Mini Case Study:

One solopreneur realized she was spending 70% of her week on a $500/month offer that drained her. When she ran the numbers, she restructured to a $2,000 offer she enjoyed more and hit her income goal with half the effort.

Data reveals what your emotions may overlook.

Scaling Magnifies Your Mistakes—Another Reason to Know Your Numbers

I've worked with business owners generating $1 million in revenue and others bringing in $100,000 a year. I can honestly say that the problems at $1 million can be *worse* than at $100,000.

Why?

Because they didn't fix the fundamental issues.

They grew their revenue, but their expenses ballooned, their systems didn't scale, and they were still making decisions on gut instinct instead of data.

If you don't fix your foundational issues early, they don't go away. They get *bigger*.

As one of my mentors once said, "You grow zeros."

$100 problems become $1,000 problems, which become $100,000 problems.

If it doesn't work on paper, it won't work in real life.

Full stop.

You can dream, hustle, and manifest all you want, but without numbers, it's just noise. Avoiding your finances doesn't protect your progress; it delays your growth. Most business owners don't underprice because they lack strategy. They underprice because they're still questioning their worth.

But here's the truth: a plan without numbers is just a wish. You don't need to be perfect with your bookkeeping or become an overnight financial expert. You just need to be honest. Honest about what you need, what you're spending, and what it'll take to build the life you're working so hard for. Financial clarity isn't about pressure—it's about power. It's your permission to stop guessing and start leading.

4. Act As If

This is the mindset shift that changes everything.

Imagine you're building a home meant to last 100 years. You wouldn't just eyeball the frame or guess where the load-bearing walls should go. You'd plan carefully. You'd act like it matters, because it does. The same principle applies in business. If you want something strong, sustainable, and built to last, you have to lead with intention from the start.

Start showing up like the CEO you're becoming. Build systems now, even if they're simple. Put financial boundaries in place and stick to them. Raise your prices when your business plan and your value say it's time. You don't need to fake it. You need to function like it.

If your vision is a streamlined, six-figure business that supports your lifestyle, don't wait until you hit the milestone to act like it's real. Step into that identity now. Own your role as the leader of your business. Show up with the mindset, habits, and boundaries of the future version of you — the one who's already arrived.

Don't wait for permission. You're the boss. Act like it. Lead from vision, not from fear. When you start making decisions from where you're going, instead of where you feel stuck, you move faster, more confidently, and with far greater alignment.

You've got this. Step into your next level now.

Step Into Your Role as CEO—*today.*

This isn't about faking it until you make it. This is about functioning *as if* the business you want already exists—and letting your decisions reflect that level of intention and leadership.

Start showing up like the CEO you're becoming:

- Build systems now, even if they're simple
- Use professional language, processes, and documentation
- Set financial boundaries—and enforce them
- Raise your prices when your business plan shows it's time
- Schedule regular reviews (monthly or quarterly) to track your plan
- Use clean proposals, polished client onboarding, and organized tools — even if no one else sees them but you
- *The way you treat your business teaches the world how to treat it, too.*

Adopt Decision-Making Habits That Match Your Vision

Just like a builder selects materials based on the house they're building, your decisions should reflect the business you want, not the one you're afraid to outgrow.

Ask yourself:

- Do you want to build a **tight-knit family business?**
  - ▶ Prioritize personal connection, flexibility, and deep client relationships.
- Do you want to build a **scalable company or a national brand?**
  - ▶ Focus on systems, automation, hiring frameworks, and brand consistency.

Either path is valid. But both require **intentional choices** from Day One.

Final word on Acting As If: This principle isn't about pretending. It's about aligning.

It's about choosing to operate today with the clarity, confidence, and boundaries of the business you want to lead tomorrow.

You don't need to wait to be successful to behave like a leader.

You become successful because you behave like one.

5. Take Inspired Action

Ultimately, plans are meaningless without action. Business plans are used for building businesses and not just stared at. Use your business blueprint as a springboard, not a security blanket.

Every week, choose one step that moves you closer to your vision. One action. One adjustment. One bold decision.

Sometimes that action will be strategic, such as in raising prices, launching a new offer, or investing in support. Other times, it will be deeply personal as in trusting yourself more, saying no, or stepping into greater visibility.

Progress isn't found in the perfect plan.

It's found in the consistent, aligned actions that bring your plan to life.

What Does *Inspired* Action Look Like?

Inspired action is not frantic. It's not hustling for the sake of feeling productive. It's action rooted in clarity, purpose, and momentum.

Examples of inspired action might include:
- *Launching a new offer that reflects your current values and capacity*
- *Raising your rates after reviewing your profitability metrics*
- *Offboarding a misaligned client to make space for the right ones*
- *Hiring a VA to reclaim your time and elevate your systems*
- *Creating content that speaks directly to your ideal client's needs*
- *Saying "no" to an opportunity that doesn't fit—even if it's tempting*

Inspired action is courageous. It's creative. It's often uncomfortable.

But it's how you move from intention to impact.

The Cost of Inaction

One of the biggest threats to your business isn't failure, it's drift.

Drift happens when you're busy but not aligned.

When you're working hard but not checking the map.

Waiting six months to review your plan might mean:
- You *miss opportunities* that were ready for you
- You *miss warning signs* that your business model needs a pivot
- You keep doing things that no longer serve your vision

A house without regular maintenance starts to fall apart. A business without regular check-ins does the same.

Create a Check-In Culture
(Even If You're a Team of One)

High-performing businesses don't operate on autopilot.

They operate on *awareness*.

Make it a habit to check in with your plan, your metrics, and your mindset.
- *What's the most aligned step I can take this week?*
- *What decision have I been avoiding that would move me forward?*
- *What is no longer serving me—or my business?*

Write it down. Then do it.

Section 6: What Makes a Plan "Living" vs. Locked

Let's get one thing straight:

A business plan should never be carved in stone.

One of the biggest misconceptions business owners, especially new ones, often carry is that their plan needs to be perfect and finalized before they can move forward. It's a common misconception that success solely belongs to those who meticulously draft their plan. But that mindset will trap you.

A rigid plan will box you in. A living plan will grow with you.

Here's the thing: there's a big difference between a locked plan and a living plan. Or, put another way, your business plan needs to be living and breathing, just like you (kinda). Let's break that down.

A *locked* plan assumes you know everything upfront: your exact audience, every offering, your pricing model, and your team structure. It's rigid, linear, and doesn't leave much room for experimentation, pivots, or the inevitable surprises of real business. It may feel safe, but it's often out of sync with how businesses actually grow.

A *locked* plan is like a museum display. It might look good, but it's untouchable—frozen in time, detached from your current reality.

A *living* plan, on the other hand, evolves with you. It's structured but not stiff. It includes goals, strategies, and numbers, yes, but it also leaves space for feedback, iteration, and the lessons only action can teach. It's reviewed often, refined regularly, and rooted in reality.

A living plan can be compared to a garden. It starts with intentional design. But it needs watering. It needs pruning. It needs space to grow in new directions as the seasons change.

In reality, your business will evolve in tandem with you. Your clients will surprise you. The market will shift. You'll discover strengths you didn't know you had and drop ideas that once felt central.

A living plan honors all of that. It's not about being uncommitted. It's about being responsive.

So, don't write your plan in stone. Write it in pencil. Just make sure you *keep writing*.

Here's what each one looks like in action:

✖ Locked Plans:
  • Are written once, then ignored, never to be looked at again

- Contain rigid goals and outdated assumptions
- Collect dust in a drawer or get lost in your Google Drive
- Create guilt ("I'm off-plan... I must be failing."
- Focus more on how the business *should* work than how it actually *does*
- Often written to impress others rather than guide yourself

✖ Living Plans:
- Are reviewed and revised regularly, monthly at first, quarterly as you grow
- Adapt to your experience, feedback, and market shifts
- Reflect your current goals, not just your past vision
- Empower decisions rather than restrict them
- Keep your mission and values at the center
- Help you pivot with purpose, not panic

A Real-World Example: The Planner Who Had to Pivot

I once worked with a new entrepreneur named Rachel. She launched a personal relationship coaching business with a tight, clean business plan—one she had spent six months perfecting before announcing her services.

The plan included group coaching offers, a detailed launch calendar, and a robust content strategy based on teaching budgeting.

It looked amazing on paper. But three months in, she was exhausted.

Her audience didn't want help budgeting. They wanted help *earning* more. Her content wasn't converting, and the group program felt like a mismatch for her coaching style. But she clung to her plan because she thought changing it meant she had failed.

When we sat down together, I asked her one simple question:

"Is this business plan helping you—or holding you hostage?"

That broke something open.

We mapped out a new version of her plan, one that focused on private coaching around income growth strategies—what her clients were *actually* asking for. She simplified her model, increased her rates, and finally felt aligned.

That's the power of a *living* plan.

Your business will grow. *Your plan should, too.*

Think of your business plan like a GPS. Initially, you rely on it constantly. You don't know the route yet. Every turn feels unfamiliar. You check it every few minutes to make sure you're on track.

But eventually, you become more confident. You learn the terrain. You start trusting your instincts.

Still, when there's construction, a detour, or unexpected roadblocks? That GPS is your lifeline.

Your business plan should be the same: something you refer to when the path gets confusing, not something that limits your ability to adapt.

My Own Pivot Story: From One-to-One to Many

When I first started my business, I was offering one-to-one services only. It felt natural because that's what I knew from my previous career. I built my entire plan around this model: pricing, offers, schedules, all of it.

But a year in, I hit a wall. I was burned out, overbooked, and completely maxed out on time. I realized I hadn't created a business. I'd recreated just another job.

I went back to my plan. I looked at the original napkin sketch, the mind map, and the numbers. And I gave myself permission to pivot.

That's when I started working with a business coach on my business plan, and it changed everything. I had reached a tipping point in my business. What had once felt exciting now felt overwhelming. I was stuck in a cycle of one-to-one work, burning out while trying to serve everyone personally. Through coaching, I began to see the power of scalable offerings—courses, group programs, and frameworks that let me serve more people without sacrificing my time or sanity.

But here's the key: that growth didn't happen because I pushed harder. *It happened because I took a step back and updated my business plan.*

I got clear on my values. I redefined who I wanted to serve. I mapped out new income streams that actually aligned with my life and energy. Coaching helped me stop reacting and start designing with strategy, structure, and support.

If you're at a crossroads in your business and wondering what's next, that might be your signal to pause, not to quit, but to refocus your plan and recommit to your vision.

How to Keep Your Plan "Living"?

So, how do you keep your plan dynamic, relevant, and alive?

Here are four practical strategies:

1. Set regular review points.

In the beginning, revisit your plan monthly. Make the switch to quarterly reviews as you become more stable and popular.

Each time, ask:
- What's working?
- What's not?
- What needs to evolve?
- What do I need to consider next

Pro tip: Schedule "CEO time" once a month to review your plan. Put it on your calendar like a meeting. Don't wait for a crisis to prompt you to review your plan.

2. Track real data.

Let your numbers speak. Monitor your revenue streams, conversion rates, client feedback, and time spent on tasks. Let this information *inform* your next decision.

And remember: What gets measured gets managed. What gets ignored gets expensive.

3. Update your vision and values as you grow.

You may shift your niche, your goals, or your delivery model. That's not failure. It's maturity. Your plan should reflect the business you're *running now*, not the one you imagined two years ago.

4. Use your plan as a filter, not a rulebook.

When new opportunities come your way such as speaking gigs, partnerships, new services, ask:
- Does this align with my mission?

- Does it serve my ideal client?
- Does it move me toward my vision—or just add noise?

The clearer you are about your plan, the more confidently you can make a focused and aligned decision and confidently say "Yes!" or "No!" Remember, say NO to the good opportunities so you can say YES to the great opportunities!

How to Make Decisions Today That Support the Business You Want Tomorrow

Your business doesn't become successful all at once. It becomes successful one decision at a time.

That means the choices you're making *right now*—how you price your offers, who you choose to work with, what you say yes to, and what you let go of—are shaping the business you'll be running six months, one year, or five years from today.

The future version of your business is being built in your everyday choices.

A Zoom Call with my Coach Barbara

I'll never forget a Zoom call I had with my coach Barbara.

Yes—that Barbara.

We were chatting on a scheduled Zoom call, and I was feeling stuck. I had reached a point where I was juggling multiple offers and too many projects, and I wasn't sure which direction to take next. I was worried that if I cut anything out, I'd be leaving money on the table. I was overwhelmed, but afraid to let go.

Barbara listened to me lay out all the options. Then she leaned in, smiled, and said something like:

"Build the business you want to have, not the one you're afraid to lose. And let me tell you that you can't build it on leftovers. You gotta be all in."

It hit me like a lightning bolt.

The truth was, I was making decisions based on fear: fear of missing out, fear of disappointing people, and fear of choosing the wrong thing. But Barbara's words helped me shift my perspective.

Instead of asking, *What's working right now?* I started asking, *What will still be working for me in three years?*

That simple mindset shift changed everything.
The Problem with "Now" Thinking
It's easy to make decisions that only solve today's problems.

- You take on a misaligned client because the cash flow is tight.
- You underprice your services just to close the deal.
- You keep doing everything yourself because it's faster than training someone.

But "now" thinking traps you in survival mode.

If you want a business that gives you freedom, stability, and long-term growth, you have to start thinking like the future version of yourself — the one who's already built it.

Think Like the CEO You're Becoming

Here's the question that can transform your daily decision-making:

"Would your 'Future You' be grateful for this decision, or would she be cleaning up after it?

Start applying that question to everything:

- Your schedule: Are you designing your week for sustainability or burnout?
- Your pricing: Does this reflect your value or your fear?
- Your clients: Are you building a dream roster or a stress portfolio?
- Your offers: Do they scale or trap you in a time-for-money cycle?
- Your systems: Are they duct-taped together or ready to support growth?

Your Plan = Your Filter

This is where your business plan becomes your secret weapon.

When you're clear on your mission, your values, and your vision, you can filter every decision through that lens:

- Does this opportunity align with my purpose?
- Will this move me closer to my ideal lifestyle?
- Is this a short-term fix or a long-term solution?

It stops being about what's shiny or urgent. It starts being about what's aligned and strategic.

Real-Life Application: Saying No to Say Yes

After that call with Barbara, I made one of the hardest (and best) decisions of my career: First, I quit my full-time job, which was scary, as it was a steady paycheck and more importantly, steady medical insurance. I said "No" to the good.

Then, I said "yes" to growing my business. I cut out an entire service line that was bringing in revenue—but draining my energy. It looked good on paper. But it didn't fit the future I wanted to build. I was wanting to scale up —but I was creating my own bottleneck.

It was scary. But it freed me up to build the things I *really* wanted—scalable programs, better client experiences, more creative space. Within months, my income went up, my hours went down, and my impact expanded.

Not because I did more. Because I did less, intentionally.

Expert Insight from Barbara

Here's one more gem from Barbara I'll never forget:

"The best business owners aren't the ones who do everything. They're the ones who make bold decisions early and trust themselves and their team to figure it out."

That's what this part of your business plan is about: Designing a decision-making framework you can trust. This framework should not only support the business you're building, but also the life you're here to live.

Section 7: CEO Thought Leadership: Bringing It All Together

When you create a well-structured business plan informed by the 5 Financial Success Principles, you stop running a business by default and start leading one by design.

And from there?

Everything changes.

- Your *offers* start aligning with your energy and values.
- Your *pricing* reflects your worth, not your fear.
- Your *calendar* makes space for your life, not just your work.
- Your *decisions* serve your long-term vision, not just today's pressure.

Because here's the truth:

Your business isn't just here to generate income. It's here to build the life you actually want to live.

You're not hustling in circles anymore. You're not guessing your way forward. You're not trying to fit someone else's version of success.

Instead...
- You're building from a place of purpose.
- You're leading with vision, not reaction.
- You're using your business as a tool for impact, alignment, and financial freedom.

This is how modern entrepreneurs rise—not with hustle, but with clarity.

Not by working more, but by building better.

Not by chasing success, but by *defining it—and building toward it with intention.*

The market will change.

Your clients will change.

You will change.

The strongest businesses aren't the ones with the prettiest plans.

They're the ones whose plans evolve with purpose.

So go ahead.

Write your plan in ink, but keep the eraser nearby. If it's messy, that means it's real.

Because the real magic isn't in getting it perfect. It's in building something that can grow with you.

———————————

Top 5 Takeaways for Chapter 4: Why Every Business Needs a Plan

1. Your Business Plan Is a Living Document, Not a One-Time Task

A rigid, set-it-and-forget-it plan will only box you in. A *living* plan evolves with your growth, allowing you to pivot, refocus, and make strategic decisions based on what's real, not just what was imagined early on.

2. Clarity Comes Before Strategy—Know What You're Building

Don't start with tactics. Start with vision. Define what you want your business to do for your life. Get specific about your goals, values, ideal clients, and the kind of work that lights you up. Don't build a castle if what you really want is a cabin.

3. Financial Foundations Are Non-Negotiable

Know your costs. Track your numbers. Price for profitability. Your business isn't just a passion project—it's a financial engine. Understanding your break-even point, profit margins, and key performance indicators (KPIs) empowers you to lead with confidence.

4. Act Like the CEO You're Becoming—Not the Freelancer You Used to Be

Show up today as the leader of the business you want tomorrow. Build systems, set boundaries, and make intentional choices that reflect where you're headed, not where you're starting from.

5. Plans Only Work if You Do—Take Inspired, Consistent Action

Review your business plan monthly. Celebrate what's working and adjust what's not. Don't let drift, delay, or perfectionism keep you stuck. A strong plan + small, courageous steps = serious momentum.

Chapter 5:
Starting Your Business With a Solid Foundation

Disclaimer: The content in this chapter is for educational and informational purposes only and does not constitute legal or financial advice. Business structure requirements vary by state and country. Please consult a licensed attorney or tax advisor to determine what structure is right for your specific situation.

"

Growing up, money wasn't something we talked about much in my family—

and when we did, I wish I had listened more. Now, as a 1099 profes-sional, the biggest lesson I've learned is this: I'm my own boss. I am responsible for my success—or my failure. That realization changed everything.

I had to build resilience on every level—emotional, physical, spiri-tual—and I had to stay passionate. It's like planting a garden. You don't harvest tomorrow. You keep showing up, watering it, trusting that eventually, you'll eat. — *Rodolfo Gargioni*

"

Section 1: Why Business Structure Matters

If you've been following along, you've already cast a bold vision for your business. In the last chapter, we walked you through the process of drafting your business plan to help support and guide your dream.

But back to our building metaphors. What good is a blueprint for a house if you don't pour the concrete?

Yes, we're circling back to the part of the process that usually comes first in real construction—the foundation. And no, you didn't miss a step. The reason we held off until now is that most business owners start with action but forget to plan, and then they forget to protect what they're building.

Now that you've visualized the house (your business, complete with a solid business plan), we can get it grounded (the legal and financial structure).

We get it. You didn't start your business because you love paper-work. You started it because you had a vision, something you wanted to build, share, and serve. But here's the truth that every business owner eventually learns: without structure, your vision has no foundation.

Think of your business like a house. The foundation isn't the sexy part. No one takes Instagram selfies with the concrete slab. But if it's not done right, everything else is at risk.

In business, *your legal and financial structure is that slab.* Get it right, and you can build anything. Get it wrong, and the cracks will show up when you least expect them.

This chapter is about laying that foundation. We'll walk you through the key business structures, decode the myths surrounding LLCs and S-Corps, and help you make informed, strategic decisions that support your long-term goals, both legally and financially.

And yes, we'll talk about taxes. But more importantly, we'll discuss building a business that *endures.*

By the end of this chapter, you'll understand the differences between common small business structures, why structure matters legally and financially, and how to confidently choose the best framework for where you are now and where you want to go.

Let's Start With a True Story

I once received a call from an FBI field agent regarding a fraud investigation. My heart dropped. In that split second, my brain raced through every movie I'd ever seen where an innocent person ends up behind bars. I envisioned my bank accounts being frozen, my name being tarnished, and years of struggle to clear my name. It sounds dramatic, but when you're under the spotlight (and you have a companion who is just a bit paranoid), your mind doesn't care about logic. It cares about survival.

My husband, who's been in high-level business for years, gave me firm advice: "Don't tell them anything. Be vague. Stay calm."

That was the plan. At least, it was for the first minute.

Then the agent said something that shook me to my core: "I think you may be part of the problem."

Cue the panic. I swung hard in the other direction and started talking—probably more than I should have. I explained everything, in way too much detail, desperate to prove I had nothing to hide. Of course, I hadn't done anything wrong. But someone I had partnered with—someone I worked for as an independent contractor—had and she filed false charges under my licensure.

It won't matter who has you in their scope—the FBI, the IRS, or a disgruntled client. If your business isn't built on a solid legal foundation, you risk more than just stress. You risk your reputation, your finances, and your future.

I learned two life-changing lessons that day:

1. I am highly motivated to avoid legal trouble. I now pay good money to make sure my legal ducks are in a row. Because no amount of income is worth risking everything.
2. I'm much more selective about who I do business with. Legal structure isn't just about protecting your money. It's about protecting your name, your livelihood, and your peace of mind.

So, let's dive into what a business structure actually is, and it matters.

Your business structure determines:
- Legal liability
- Tax treatment
- Administrative requirements
- How others (clients, banks, partners) view your business

A common misconception is that your business structure doesn't matter much until you're making "real money." But the truth is, structure protects you from the start and sets you up to grow. Just because you aren't where you plan to be doesn't mean you don't need a solid foundation on which to build your dream. Progress still needs protection. And if you're building something meaningful, you can't skip the groundwork.

And if you're tempted to skip over the task of determining your business structure out of fear or intimidation, don't let the desire to do this "perfectly" hold you back from doing it at all. You can start out simply, then adjust and refine as you move forward and gain confidence.

Let's go back to Alex for a moment, a case study we examined in earlier chapters. She was a brilliant graphic designer who turned her side hustle into a full-time business almost overnight. Her calendar filled with clients, and money began to flow in. But she didn't file any paperwork. She thought, "I'll form an LLC later...when I'm making real money."

Six months in, a client accused her of copyright infringement and threatened legal action. That's when Alex realized the harsh truth: she had no legal separation between herself and her business. Her personal savings, her car, and even her apartment were potentially on the line. The fear was overwhelming, not just because of the claim, but because she hadn't built any protection around the thing she worked so hard to create.

Don't wait for the storm to start before you build the shelter. Structure is the difference between panic and peace, between scraping by and scaling with confidence.

Start With These Non-Negotiables

Regardless of what structure you ultimately choose for your business, these two basic steps are essential for anyone serious about being seen and treated as a professional:

1. Apply for an EIN (Employer Identification Number)

This free ID from the IRS allows you to open a business bank account and avoid using your Social Security number on tax documents like W-9s. It's one of the easiest steps—and one of the most important.

2. Open a Business Bank Account

No exceptions. No "I'll do it later." Separate your funds from day one. This isn't just about clean bookkeeping—it's about protecting your LLC status and presenting yourself as a professional entity.

Remember, how you treat your business is how others will treat it, too.

You're not just starting a side hustle. You're building something that matters. So lay the groundwork like you mean it.

You're the boss. Start acting like it.

Section 2: Overview of Common Business Structures

Before you can build upward, you need to know which kind of legal and financial footing you're standing on. This section gives you a clear, side-by-side comparison of the four most common small business structures.

Each structure comes with its own level of complexity, liability protection, tax treatment, and paperwork. The goal here isn't to pick the perfect one forever—it's to make the most aligned choice for where you are *now*, with an eye toward where you're going.

Table 5.1: Overview of Common Business Structures

Structure	Description	Pros	Cons	Best For
Sole Proprietorship	An individual running a business without formal setup	Easiest to start, no extra filings	No liability protection	Hobbyists, early-stage side hustles
Single-Member LLC	A legal entity separating personal and business assets	Liability protection, flexible taxes	State fees, annual paperwork	Solo entrepreneurs, freelancers, and consultants
Multi-Member LLC	LLC with two or more owners	Shared responsibility, flexible structure	Needs operating agreement, shared liability	Partnerships, joint ventures, family-run firms
S-Corporation (S-Corp)	A tax status for LLCs or corporations	Potential self-employment tax savings	Requires payroll, compliance, extra filings	High-earning, stable, service-based businesses

Pro Tip: You're not just choosing a structure—you're choosing how the government, banks, and partners will see your business. Make it count.

You can see from the chart above that choosing the right business structure isn't just a formality; it's a foundational decision that affects your taxes, your liability, and how others perceive your business.

Whether you're starting simple with a sole proprietorship, protecting your personal assets with an LLC, or planning for tax optimization with an S-Corp, each path comes with trade-offs. The key is to choose a structure that matches your stage of growth, risk tolerance, and business goals, not someone else's shortcut. Start simple, stay legal, and evolve as you grow.

Section 3: Deep Dive: LLC vs. Sole Proprietor

For many business owners, one of the most strategic early moves may be forming a single-member LLC—depending on their location, goals, and risk profile. You can technically file on your own, but I highly recommend hiring an attorney to ensure it's done correctly the first time. The registration process isn't just red tape. It serves as your primary safeguard and first line of defense.

Here's why: as soon as you're doing anything that involves liability, such as working with clients, delivering services, or selling a product, you need to separate yourself from your business legally. A single-member LLC does exactly that. It ensures that if something goes wrong (and we hope it never does), any legal claim goes after your business, not your personal assets.

But here's the catch that most people don't talk about...

An LLC isn't magic. You still have to act like a business owner. That means zero blending of personal and business funds. No "just this one time" using your business account for lunch. No paying personal bills from your LLC. Courts look at both your documentation and your behavior. If business and personal finances are mixed, a judge may disregard the LLC's protection — a concept known as 'piercing the corporate veil.' It's something you never want to experience.

Now, let's break it down clearly.

What is an LLC?
- LLC stands for Limited Liability Company
- It protects your personal assets if your business is sued
- It allows for pass-through taxation (your profits are taxed on your personal return)

What Is a Sole Proprietorship?
- It's the simplest business structure with no legal separation between you and the business
- Easy and free to start, but it offers no personal protection

- You take on all the risk and all the liability

We've talked a lot about starting your business as a Single-Member LLC. But can you start your business as a sole proprietor?

Sure. For many, that's the simplest entry point. It's not perfect, but it's legit and it gets you moving. You can always restructure later. The most dangerous thing is waiting until it's perfect before you begin.

But if you do decide to go the LLC route from the beginning, you've got choices to make:

- Do you want to remain a Single-Member LLC?
- Are you forming a Partnership LLC with someone else?
- Do you want one parent LLC with multiple DBAs underneath?

These decisions matter, but they're not final. Business is fluid. You can revise your structure down the line—and yes, it may cost a bit in paperwork or filing fees, but that's a small price to pay for clarity as you grow. Nothing is set in stone. This is your business, and it should evolve with you.

Pro Tip: Even if you start as a sole proprietor, obtain an Employer Identification Number (EIN) and open a separate business bank account. It builds legitimacy and sets the stage for growth and structure.

Another consideration to take into account when determining your business structure is to think through the financial implications of each structure type. The table below outlines which financial factors are required for each business structure.

Table 5.2: Financial Foundations by Structure Type

Task	Sole Prop.	LLC	S-Corp
EIN Required	Optional	Yes	YES
Separate Bank Accounts	Strongly Advised	Required	Required
Payroll Setup	No	No	Required
Separate Tax Return	No	No	Yes
Legal Protection	None	Yes	Yes

The Importance of Structure: A Real-World Example

Jenna was a passionate ACT and SAT prep coach who started tutoring high school students on evenings and weekends. What began as a small favor for a neighbor quickly snowballed. Word spread, and before she knew it, Jenna was juggling six clients a week, making more than her day job.

But Jenna never formalized her business. No LLC, no separate business bank account—just cash, personal checks, and a few casual contracts with parents.

Everything changed when a parent accused her of promising score improvements that weren't delivered. The accusation turned into a demand for a refund, and when Jenna pushed back, the parent threatened legal action. Because she was operating as a sole proprietor, there was no separation between her business and personal life. Her bank account, her car, and even her apartment lease were suddenly in the conversation.

Jenna had to hire a lawyer, refund the money, and rebuild her credibility, all while wishing she had taken steps early on to protect what she was building. Had she formed an LLC, she would've had more credibility, clearer boundaries, and, most importantly, legal protection.

That's the power of separation and why structure is not optional.

Section 4: When (and Why) to Avoid Rushing Into an S-Corp

S-Corporations are often sold as the ultimate "tax hack" for entrepreneurs. Scroll through business forums or listen to enough financial podcasts, and you'll hear the same advice on repeat: "Switch to an S-Corp and save thousands on taxes." But the truth is far more nuanced—and rushing into an S-Corp too early can cost you more than it saves.

Let's set the record straight. This isn't about jumping on a trend. Making a decision that suits you, your business stage, and your financial reality is crucial.

Ask Yourself These 3 Questions Before Electing S-Corp Status:
- Are you consistently earning at least $75,000 in annual net profit?

- Are you prepared to run payroll, file quarterly reports, and manage more complex tax filings?
- Do you have a reliable tax advisor (not just TurboTax or a well-meaning friend)?

If you answered "no" to any of these, it's time to pause.

Red Flags That Scream "Not Yet":
- You're a solopreneur with unpredictable revenue
- You're reinvesting most of your profits into the business
- You're unclear about how payroll or distributions even work

These aren't deal-breakers, but they're signs that the S-Corp might be premature. Let's break down the real reasons to wait.

Myth-Busting the S-Corp Hype

1. The Payroll Trap

Once you elect S-Corp status, you're required by the IRS to pay yourself a "reasonable salary." That means:
- Setting up and running payroll
- Withholding and remitting employee taxes
- Filing quarterly and annual payroll reports

If that sounds like a lot, it's because it is. And if you're still a one-person show, that administrative load can quickly bury you. Many business owners are surprised to learn that "simple" payroll software doesn't automatically handle compliance. It still requires oversight, careful timing, and accuracy. One mistake can lead to IRS penalties or interest.

That's why it's essential to inform yourself about exactly what each payroll provider offers—and what they don't—when adding payroll to your organization. You need to ensure that whatever provider you choose will file your payroll taxes for you and submit all required state and federal reports on the correct schedule for your specific business requirements. And be sure to check out two or three in detail. What one colleague may highly recommend, another colleague may strongly dislike. The action – and the choice is

The most important thing to remember: use a professional payroll provider. Whether you choose one of the big-name companies or a reputable local provider, the key is to avoid calculating taxes by hand or submitting reports manually. Doing so opens you up to unnecessary compliance issues and penalties—costly mistakes that far outweigh the relatively minimal cost of hiring a professional payroll service.

2. The Self-Employment Tax Myth

Yes, S-Corps can help you save on self-employment taxes, but only if you're generating significant profit. If you're making under $75,000 a year, the costs of payroll services, additional tax filings, and accounting help often outweigh the savings. Think of it like buying a luxury car to save on gas. It only makes sense when you can afford the car and all the maintenance.

3. The Distribution Loophole Illusion

A popular myth goes like this: "Just pay yourself a low salary and take the rest in distributions to avoid payroll tax." Sounds brilliant, right?

Not so fast. The IRS closely monitors this practice. If they determine your salary is unreasonably low, they can reclassify distributions as wages, hit you with back taxes, and penalize your business. Once the IRS flags you, it can lead to ongoing audits for years to come.

4. Administrative Overload

S-Corps require a separate tax return for the business. You'll also need to:

- Maintain corporate formalities (like meeting minutes)
- Track shareholder distributions
- Possibly issue K-1 forms to members

If you're still building your systems or don't have professional support, these tasks can become complicated quickly. Mistakes here aren't just inconvenient. They're potentially expensive.

5. Limited Flexibility for Losses and Deductions

Early-stage businesses often experience lean years or reinvest heavily in growth. In an S-Corp, you lose flexibility in how losses and deductions can be claimed, which means your tax position may be less favorable during tough periods.

Real Talk: Reversing an S-Corp Election Is No Joke

One of the most overlooked facts about S-Corps is this: once you elect the status, it's very difficult to reverse.

- You need IRS approval to change your designation.
- You might face tax consequences or timing restrictions.
- You may be stuck with the structure for years.

This isn't a "just try it out and see how it goes" decision. It's a legal election with long-term consequences.

Reminder: Build for Growth, Not for Trends

Too many entrepreneurs are being sold S-Corp status as a silver bullet. It's not. It's a tool, and like any tool, it only works if you're using it for the right job at the right time.

Before making this leap, consult a tax professional, such as a tax planner or tax strategies, not just someone who files returns, but someone who truly understands your goals, your numbers, and your business stage.

Because the real goal isn't just to save money. It's to build something that lasts.

Real-Life Application: When the Right Structure Saves Thousands

Let me share something I've seen too many times over the past six years.

I've met hundreds of entrepreneurs who are driven, brilliant people, and also who had *no idea* how they were actually filing their taxes.

Here's the quick test: If you're signing multiple tax returns or putting your signature on behalf of an entity, you're not a sole proprietor. You likely have an LLC, S-Corp, or C-Corp. And if you don't *know* which one, it's time to find out. Fast.

And here's the sad part: Many of those same business owners were structured as S-Corps when they shouldn't have been.

They weren't consistently making enough to justify the administrative burden. They weren't paying themselves properly. A different setup could have prevented the stress, penalties, and wasted money they were dealing with.

My personal recommendation is to avoid an S-Corp if you're not consistently generating at least $30,000/month in profit, but again, make sure that you seek the advice from a tax professional, because every business has its own individual dynamics that lead to the decision to make that decision.

Now, a quick point of clarity: In some parts of this chapter, you'll see $75,000/year referenced as a benchmark. That figure is often cited as a best practice. However, when I share my personal rule of thumb, you'll notice the bar is set much higher. Why the discrepancy? It comes down to the difference between common recommendations and lived experience.

Ultimately, the decision (and the positive or negative consequences) is yours. Do your research. Reflect on where you are, where you're headed, and how quickly you want to get there. To help you think it through, here's a case study to consider.

Case Study: The $30K Per Month Rule

Kim was bringing in $60,000/year. Her bookkeeper encouraged her to switch to an S-Corp. She did.

However, this is what is "cost" her to make the switch:
- She had to hire a payroll service
- Her quarterly reports were missed
- She was fined for not taking a reasonable salary

Savings on taxes: $2,000

Total costs and fines: $4,500

Lesson: Structure should match your stage, not your ambition.

You don't need complexity. You need clarity.

Section 5: The 5 Financial Success Principles

As you've likely learned by now, filtering each decision through the 5 Financial Success Principles enables you to make the best, most strategic decision possible for your business. Let's filter our decision around business structure through them

Let's break them down them down again, this time as we consider business structure:

1. Know What You Want

This is where clarity starts in determining the best structure for your business. What kind of business are you building?

- A side hustle that supports your household income?
- A boutique firm with a small, focused team?
- A scalable business with partners, employees, or even future franchise plans?

Your vision shapes your structure. And your structure shapes everything else—your taxes, your legal protections, even how you brand and fund your business.

If you're staying small and lean, there's nothing wrong with remaining a sole proprietor. Just keep things clean: open a separate bank account, use accounting software, and treat it like a business.

If you're growing, it's time to think bigger. That might mean forming an LLC, drafting a partnership agreement, or planning your structure with future growth in mind.

The point is: be intentional. Where you want to go determines what you need to build now.

2. Know How Much It Costs

Every choice in business has a price tag—some up front, some down the road. Your business structure affects your finances in multiple ways:

- A sole proprietorship is simple and cheap to maintain.
- An LLC offers more protection but may have state fees and compliance requirements.
- An S-Corp might save on taxes, but only if your profit justifies the added costs of payroll and compliance.

Before you make any decisions, calculate the true cost, not just the setup, but the ongoing time, energy, and money needed to maintain that structure.

3. Know Your Numbers

You can't make good decisions if you don't understand the reality of the numbers behind each structure option, as well as the operating numbers of your business. How these two work together will help determine which structure is best.

Before you even open your digital doors, take time to:
- Check local regulations and licensing requirements.
- List every start-up cost, such as licenses, website, software, inventory, insurance, and equipment.
- Forecast your monthly operating expenses, such as subscriptions, tools, rent, utilities, and staff (even if the staff is just you).
- Add a buffer for surprises. Because there will be surprises.

Then, build a simple forecast. Nothing fancy—just a 12-month spreadsheet that includes what you expect to spend and earn. Revisit it monthly. Update it as you grow. Ensure that your numbers support the business structure you've chosen, and vice versa.

4. Act As If

Act like a legitimate business from Day One—even if you're still working from the kitchen table.
- Open separate bank accounts
- Track business income/expenses
- Pay yourself
- Set aside for taxes
- Personal account

Yes, it's a bit of a hassle. But integrity matters.

If you buy office supplies and groceries in the same Walmart trip, use separate payment methods. That small act reinforces the mindset that your business is real and that it deserves structure and discipline.

When you physically transfer money from your business account to your personal account, it becomes real. You feel the reward of earning through your business. You earned that.

Plus, when tax season rolls around, you'll be grateful that your business records are clean, clear, and separate. No hunting through Venmo statements or sorting Amazon receipts from personal purchases.

5. Take Inspired Action

Get the advice. Ask the questions. Make the appointment.

One of the biggest traps new business owners fall into is analysis paralysis. They don't act because they don't know what to do.

But asking a question IS taking action.
- Meet with an accountant who understands small business.

- Talk to a business attorney—yes, even just for an hour.
- Avoid cookie-cutter services that sneak themselves in as your business's registered agent or owner.

Build real relationships with professionals who will grow with you. As your business scales, your financial and legal needs will evolve. Make sure your advisors evolve with you.

And remember: your job is not to know everything. Your job is to build a team that helps you know what matters.

When in doubt, take the next step. Get clarity. Get help. Get moving.

Section 6: Tools to Build With Confidence

Building a solid business foundation isn't just about making the right decisions. It's about using the right tools to stay organized, prepared, and protected. Whether you're still researching your business structure or already knee-deep in client work, these tools will help you work smarter, not harder.

You don't need to guess your way through this. With a few key checklists and templates, you can move from confusion to clarity and make decisions based on facts, not fear.

✔ Comparison Guide: Sole Proprietorship vs. LLC vs. S-Corp

This simple, side-by-side breakdown shared earlier in the chapter gives you a clear view of each structure's:

- **Tax treatment**
- **Legal protection**
- **Ongoing compliance requirements**
- **Best fit depending on your stage of business**

Use this guide to confidently choose the structure that matches your goals. This isn't about what your friend did or what's trending online — it's about what works for *you*.

✔ Cost Planning Worksheet

Wondering what your business will really cost you? A cost planning worksheet template isn't hard to find, but can help you:

- Map out your startup costs (licenses, filing fees, software, equipment)
- Forecast your next 12 months of fixed and variable expenses
- Plan for one-time and recurring costs

Seeing it all on paper not only helps with financial planning—it also builds the muscle of thinking like a business owner. You'll know what's coming, and you'll make smarter choices because of it.

✔ Financial Setup Checklist

This is your essential "do-this-first" list. No fluff—just real steps that signal: *I run a real business. I treat it like one.*

- **Apply for an EIN**: It's free through the IRS and lets you separate your business identity from your personal one.
- **Open separate business bank accounts**: Keep your income, taxes, and expenses clean.
- **Choose accounting software**: Wave, QuickBooks, or even a simple spreadsheet will do.
- **Identify your fixed and variable monthly expenses**: Get a grip on what you're spending.
- **Create a tax savings account**: Contribute monthly so tax season doesn't sneak up and crush you.

These tools won't just keep you compliant. They'll build your confidence. Knowing your numbers, understanding your structure, and having a plan doesn't just protect you. It *empowers* you.

Business is unpredictable. But when you have the right tools, you stop reacting and start leading.

Section 7: CEO Thought Leader Insight—Why Structure Matters Beyond Legalities

Most entrepreneurs think of structure as legal paperwork or tax filings. But visionary leaders know it goes deeper. The real power of structure is that it creates *clarity,* not just for the IRS or the bank, but for your brain.

When your structure is unclear, you hesitate. You second-guess. You stop yourself from growing because something feels off. But when the foundation is solid, your mind relaxes. You make sharper decisions. You think bigger.

Here's the CEO truth: Structure is what allows your creativity to flourish without chaos. It's the container for your vision. And it's one of the highest forms of leadership—building something so clear that others can confidently step into it.

Want to be taken seriously as a leader? Start by structuring your business like a leader.

Does growth sometimes feel scary?

Of course.

Is it worth doing, anyway?

Absolutely.

In business—and in life—you're either growing or you're dying.

There is no staying the same. Growth is exhausting but necessary. You're not as good as your best day, and you're not as bad as your worst. You have to constantly check in: Where are you in your financial and entrepreneurial journey? Are you dreaming, or are you setting goals? A dream lives in your head. A goal lives on paper.

The difference? Action and mindset.

Positive self-talk has been one of the most powerful tools in my journey. Every single day, I remind myself, 'You're the best.' Even when I don't feel like it. Even when things go wrong. Every obstacle is just another roadblock God gave me to overcome.

Speak it into existence—and it will become real. That's how I went from zero to hero. Because life is about abundance.

If you wouldn't talk down to a flower or insult a block of ice, why would you do it to yourself? Science shows that speaking kindly to water molecules creates beautiful crystalline patterns. Plants grow stronger when spoken to with love. You are no different. Always bring value before asking for value. Always seek relationships before transactions. And always keep growing. — *Joseph Lombardi*

99

Section 8: Your Call to Action—Structure is Strategy

With this knowledge in hand to build your confidence and push you forward, it is time to do your own research into potential business structures and either pick one (if you're just starting out) or update/adjust your structure if your business is already operating but you know it is time to make a structural change.

Ultimately, you don't build structure because it's fun, flashy, or on-trend. You build structure because it gives your business—and your vision—the foundation it deserves. Every form you file, every account you separate, every process you document is an act of protecting your future.

Creating structure is about more than taxes or compliance. It's about integrity.

Structure is how you honor the work you're pouring into your business. It's how you protect your creativity, your time, and your income from being derailed by avoidable mistakes. When you structure your business with intention, you're not just building for today. You're preparing for tomorrow—for the growth, the challenges, and the opportunities ahead.

Yes, these decisions can feel technical. And yes, at times they can feel overwhelming. But underneath all of that, structure is self-respect. It's a signal to the world and to yourself that your business matters. That you're not just winging it. That you're building something real, something that's here to stay.

So choose clarity over complexity. Choose protection over pressure. Choose the structure that aligns with your values and supports your growth.

Because this is your business. Build it like it matters—because it absolutely does.

Top 5 Takeaways from Chapter 5: Business Structures 101

1. Structure Is Protection, Not Paperwork

Your business structure isn't just a formality — it determines your legal liability, tax obligations, and how the world sees your business. Even if you're just starting out, structure matters from Day One.

2. Waiting to "Make Real Money" Is a Risky Myth

Many entrepreneurs delay forming an LLC or creating legal separation because they think they're "not there yet." But one legal challenge or tax issue can jeopardize everything — your savings, your reputation, even your future income.

3. Real-World Experience Underscores the Need for Structure

From FBI investigations to client lawsuits, this chapter highlights how skipping structural steps can lead to high-stakes consequences—even if you've done nothing wrong. The stories aren't scare tactics. They are real lessons from the field.

4. Progress Still Needs Protection

Starting small is fine. Staying unstructured is not. Whether you're side hustling or scaling a firm, treating your business like it matters means building in systems that protect it as it grows.

5. Structure Reflects Self-Respect and Vision

Choosing the right business structure isn't just a technical step. It's a declaration that your work is valuable, your future is worth protecting, and you're building something meant to last.

Part 2:
Stepping into Success

In Part One, we laid the groundwork for business success by redefining your relationship with money and developing a clear financial vision of your journey.

In this section, we'll teach you how to implement financial strategies that bring your vision to life. By embracing forecasting, you'll focus on growth and adaptability, leaving behind restrictive budgets in favor of empowering financial planning. You'll discover how effective bookkeeping and consistent accounting safeguard profits and alleviate stress while providing the clarity necessary to make informed financial decisions. The tools and systems outlined in this part of the book serve as your pathway to traction and success, enabling you to make informed choices that drive profitability and stability. Here, vision transforms into action.

Chapter 6:
Ditch the Budget, Embrace Forecasting

Section 1: Finding Focus in Your Finances

When I was eight, I thought binoculars were magical. I LOVED how I could see things with magnification that I couldn't see with the naked eye. I'd grab them off the windowsill, throw the loop over my neck, and dash outside, convinced I could spot anything—an eagle in the trees feeding eaglets, people drinking wine in a boat on a lake, or the neighbor's dog playing with a ball three blocks away. But I was always in such a hurry that I'd lift them to my eyes without checking which end I was looking through.

Half the time, I'd end up staring at a blurry, distant version of the world—everything smaller, farther, and more confusing than before. I'd squint, adjust, and wonder what was wrong.

Then I'd flip them around and suddenly, everything snapped into place. The bird was right there. The leaves had detail. The world felt clear and close and possible again.

I've come to realize we treat our finances the same way.

We're so eager to get clarity, to make smart decisions, to "see what's going on," that we grab whatever financial tool is nearest and hope it helps. For most people, that tool is a budget. (I mean, be honest, how many budget apps have you tried?) We zoom in, get hyper-focused on every dollar, every line item, every latte—and still feel confused and constrained.

But just like those backward binoculars, budgeting often gives us the wrong perspective.

Budgeting zooms in too tightly.

You see the transactions. You obsess over categories. You try to control every inch of your financial world. It feels like you're managing your money, but really, you're stuck reacting to the past.

Flip it around, and you get forecasting.

Suddenly, you're not stuck in what was. You're looking toward what could be. Forecasting helps you keep the big picture in focus. It's about building a plan around your vision, not your limitations. It's proactive, not reactive. It is strategic, not restrictive.

It's the tool that helps you say, "Here's what I want. Here's what it will take. And here's how I'll get there."

In this chapter, we're going to flip the binoculars around. We'll explore why forecasting is the key to financial clarity, how it empowers you to lead your business with confidence, and why it works better—especially for business owners—than traditional budgeting ever could.

If budgeting has ever made you feel boxed in, forecasting will help you breathe a sigh of relief.

Let's adjust your focus and show you what's possible when you look forward with intention.

Section 2. Budgeting vs. Forecasting: The Difference, and Why It Matters

Let's clear something up right away: budgeting and forecasting are not the same thing. Yes, they both deal with money. Yes, they both involve planning. And yes, they both have a place in a financially healthy business. But how they operate and, more importantly, how they look and *feel*, couldn't be more different. Remember the binoculars story? The same thing applies here.

A **budget** is like a financial snapshot. It tells you where your money *should* go based on your *current financial situation*. It's typically built on past data and organized into categories like rent, payroll, software, and supplies. The main goal is to stick to the plan, stay within the lines, and avoid overspending. It's structured. It's clear. But it can also be rigid and confining.

For business owners, especially those in seasons of growth, experimentation, or transition, a budget can start to feel like trying to run a marathon in shoes that are two sizes too small. Technically, you can move forward, but it's uncomfortable, and it limits your range. Budgeting can be useful for stability and control, but it's not always the right tool for momentum and expansion.

PROS of Budgeting:

- ✔ Great for managing expenses
- ✔ Offers guardrails for overspending
- ✔ Helps maintain discipline
- ✔ Useful for fixed, predictable income

CONS of Budgeting:

- ✘ Often backward-looking
- ✘ Can feel restrictive and rigid
- ✘ Doesn't adapt well to change
- ✘ Focuses on limitation, not opportunity

Forecasting, by contrast, is more like using a GPS than a paper map. It's dynamic, flexible, and future-focused. Instead of saying, "Here's what you have," forecasting asks, "Where are you going and what might happen along the way?" It enables you to project revenue, estimate expenses, and explore multiple scenarios based on your goals, rather than just your current reality. As your business grows or shifts, your forecast can adapt right alongside it.

This approach opens the door to intentional decision-making. Forecasting helps you answer important questions like:

- *Can I afford to hire someone this quarter?*
- *What happens if I raise my prices?*
- *If I invest in marketing, how soon will I see a return?*

The answers to these questions aren't guesses (or at least, they shouldn't be!). They're informed possibilities grounded in real numbers. While forecasting won't give you guarantees, it will give you clarity, direction, and the ability to make smart moves with confidence.

PROS of Forecasting:

- ✔ Future-focused and growth-oriented
- ✔ Adapts to changes in business and market
- ✔ Encourages vision and long-term strategy
- ✔ Builds financial confidence and clarity

CONS of Forecasting:

✖ Requires regular updates
✖ Can be uncomfortable if you're not used to numbers
✖ Not 100% predictable (but neither is business!)

Why Knowing the Difference Matters

Most business owners don't start their business because they love spreadsheets. They start with a vision—freedom, flexibility, impact, legacy. But somewhere along the journey, money begins to feel more like a source of stress than a tool for growth. Financial decisions become reactive. Budgeting becomes the default, and dreams get buried under invoices, uncertainty, and a constant sense of "not enough."

That's why understanding the difference between budgeting and forecasting isn't just a technical distinction; it's a leadership shift. Budgeting keeps you in a defensive stance. You're constantly working to stay within limits, avoid mistakes, and tighten the belt. It's about managing scarcity — shrinking to fit what's already there.

Forecasting, on the other hand, invites you into an offensive mindset. It helps you look ahead, identify opportunities, and build with intention. It allows you to adapt to change, test new strategies, and prepare for what's next. When you budget, you're asking yourself, *"Can I afford this?"* When you forecast, you're asking, *"What would it take to make this happen?"*

One keeps you stuck in what's not possible. The other unlocks creative thinking about how to bring your vision to life.

In today's fast-paced business environment, agility beats rigidity. Your business is constantly evolving. So is your life. And your finances should evolve too. Forecasting gives you a dynamic, living relationship with your money. It helps you anticipate cash flow dips before they derail your plans. It gives you the confidence to say yes to opportunities, not because you're guessing, but because you've planned for them.

Knowing the difference between budgeting and forecasting empowers you to lead instead of react. You stop trying to "make do" with what's in front of you and start guiding your business toward what's ahead. You go from being a financial passenger to being the financial pilot.

This one shift, this deeper understanding, can change everything: how you make decisions, how you grow, and how much ownership you feel over your financial future. Forecasting puts you back in control, not by limiting you, but by showing you what's truly possible.

Let's dive more deeply into the differences between forecasting and budgeting.

Budgeting vs. Forecasting: What's the Difference?

Table 6.1. Budgeting vs. Forecasting

	Budgeting	**Forecasting**
Focus	Past and present	Present and future
Mindset	Restriction and control	Vision and adaptability
Primary Question	"Can I afford this?"	"What will it take to achieve this?"
Approach	Fixed plan, tight categories	Flexible, evolving projections
Best For	Stability, fixed income, expense control	Growth, goal-setting, and strategic planning
Feelings	Confined, limited	Empowered, proactive

The big idea here?

Budgeting helps you survive. Forecasting helps you grow.

Forecasting is more than just a financial tool. It's a mindset shift. While budgeting often comes from a place of limitation and control, forecasting invites you to lead with possibility. It shifts your thinking from *"How do I stay within my limits?"* to *"How can I grow intentionally?"* This mindset prioritizes clarity over confusion, adaptability over rigidity, and vision over fear. It allows you to move from reaction to strategy, from scarcity to opportunity.

At its core, forecasting isn't about restriction. It's about creating the space to grow with confidence. It's about a game-changing mindset shift that can change the course of your business in the best ways.

Section 3: Tina's Story —The Four-Cup Glass of Water

Tina was a natural. She had that rare mix of passion and purpose—an expert in her field with a heart for service and a gift for connecting with clients. Her business got off to a strong start, with new referrals coming in and glowing testimonials piling up. On the outside, everything looked like a win.

But on the inside? Tina was overwhelmed. Despite the steady income, she never felt secure. She'd celebrate a great month, only to find herself short on cash two weeks later. She wasn't being careless. She was simply pouring everything into her work and hoping it would all balance out.

The problem wasn't income. It was structure.

Tina's financial flow had no rhythm, no buckets, and no clear plan. The money came in and flowed right back out—into software subscriptions, last-minute tax payments, grocery runs, and occasional client gifts. She didn't know what she could afford or whether she was even truly profitable.

And she's not alone. Many business owners find themselves in a similar situation, working hard and producing good work, yet constantly second-guessing their financial situation. That's where I like to introduce one of my favorite forecasting tools.

It's not fancy. But it's powerful.

I call it the **Four-Cup Glass of Water.**

Your money is like water. If you don't have a container, it spills. That's the simplest way to explain why so many business owners, especially purpose-driven ones, feel like they're working nonstop yet barely staying afloat. They're pouring income into a leaky system.

Imagine this: You have a pitcher full of water. That pitcher represents your monthly revenue. If you try to pour that water out without any cups underneath, it will go everywhere. A little here, a little there. And suddenly, your pitcher is empty—and you're left wondering where it all went.

But what if you had four cups, each clearly labeled, ready to receive what you poured?

That's what forecasting is. It's the process of giving your money a destination before it disappears.

And when you pour with purpose, you can lead your business (and your life) with clarity and control.

Here's how the Four-Cup Method works.

Cup 1: Taxes—20%

The first cup is for taxes—the one too many business owners try to ignore until it's unavoidable. Taxes are inevitable, and the best way to avoid stress is to prepare as you go.

Forecasting for taxes means setting aside a percentage of every dollar you earn. I recommend starting with 20%. If your situation is more complex, work with an accountant to adjust it, but whatever you do, don't skip this step.

Planning for taxes in advance removes the panic, builds discipline, and puts you in control of your year, not at the mercy of tax season.

Cup 2: Yourself + Investment—10%

This cup is often overlooked, especially by business owners in the early stages of their business. But let me be clear: if your business can't pay you, it's not working.

Set aside 10% of your income to pay yourself, invest in your future, or build a reserve. This money might go toward retirement, savings, or even a dream vacation that reminds you *why* you do what you do. It's not just about the money; it's about honoring your value.

Forecasting here means baking this amount into your monthly plan, not treating it as leftover or "someday" money. You are the engine of your business. You must receive payment. Without exception.

Cup 3: Yourself + Personal Life—40%

Life costs money. Groceries, housing, insurance, kids, the occasional night out—this cup covers it all. One of the biggest mistakes business owners make is mixing personal and business finances without any boundaries. That's a fast track to burnout and resentment.

Forecasting helps you determine what your life *actually* costs and builds that into your income goals. If you know you need $4,000 a month to comfortably run your household, then you can work backwards and figure out how much revenue your business needs to generate.

This cup brings reality and aspiration together. It connects your business plan with your life plan. which is exactly what many entrepreneurs are craving.

Cup 4: Business Expenses—30%

This cup powers your operations. Think of everything it takes to keep your business running: software, contractors, team members, marketing, supplies, rent, and more.

This is where forecasting really shines! Instead of guessing what you can afford or falling into the trap of reactive spending, you create a living plan. If you want to launch a new product, run an ad campaign, or hire help, you'll know in advance what's feasible.

Some months, this cup might need to expand. Others, it might shrink. Forecasting helps you manage that fluidity without losing control.

Building Your Forecast with the Four-Cup Method

Let's move from metaphor to method. Here's how to turn this idea into a working forecast for your business:

Step 1: Set Your Revenue Goal

Start with the top. What's your target revenue for the month or quarter? Let's say you want to bring in $12,000 this month. That's your pitcher of water.

Step 2: Apply the Four-Cup Percentages

Using the structure above:
- $2,400 → Taxes (20%)
- $1,200 → Pay Yourself / Investment (10%)
- $4,800 → Personal Life (40%)
- $3,600 → Business Expenses (30%)

Already, you can see how the money flows. But we're just getting started.

Step 3: Reverse-Engineer the Revenue

Forecasting isn't just about where the money goes. It's about how to earn it in the first place.

Ask yourself:
- How many clients do I need to hit that revenue?
- What packages or offers will get me there?
- What marketing actions do I need to take to generate that income?

This is where forecasting becomes powerful. You're not guessing—you're designing.

Tina's Forecast in Action

Let's bring it back to Tina.

Once she adopted the Four-Cup Method, she began forecasting her revenue and expenses monthly. She used a spreadsheet, tracked her actuals, and reviewed her cups every four weeks.

The results?

Her tax panic disappeared. She started consistently paying herself. She stopped second-guessing business purchases because she had a plan in place. And perhaps most importantly, she felt in control of her money for the first time in years.

Forecasting gave her permission to stop hustling blindly and start building with purpose.

Tips to Make Forecasting Stick

1. **Create a simple spreadsheet** with income targets and your four cups.
2. **Check in weekly or monthly** to track progress and update projections.
3. **Adjust as you grow.** The percentages are a starting point, not a rule.
4. **Use forecasting to test ideas.** Want to hire someone? Run the numbers first. Thinking about a retreat or new product launch? Forecast the cost and revenue potential.

Forecasting is like stretching before a workout. It prevents injury and improves performance. Once you build the habit, it becomes second nature.

Remember: Pour with Purpose

The Four-Cup Glass of Water isn't about perfection, though. It's about purpose. It's about giving your money structure so it can support your life and business, rather than control them. Forecasting has nothing to do with being good at math and everything to do with being a thoughtful steward of what you're building. It's about intention, clarity, and ownership.

So take a deep breath. Grab your pitcher. Set up your cups. And pour with purpose. Because money without a plan spills.

But money with a vision? That flows exactly where it needs to go.

Section 4: The Power of Forecasting: What the Experts Say

Forecasting isn't just another finance tool. It's one of the most valuable strategies you can adopt to lead your business with clarity and intention. And it's not just us saying that. Experts across the financial, strategic, and business development sectors agree: forecasting is the key to the difference between constantly reacting and confidently leading.

Clarity in the Chaos

"Forecasting brings clarity to chaos."

It's a quote you'll hear from countless business leaders and financial experts. Why? Because forecasting turns a reactive business into a proactive one. It gives you a roadmap not just for where your business *has been*, but for where it's *going*. You're not waiting for a cash crunch or last-minute tax surprise to force your hand. You're preparing in advance. You're leading on purpose.

From Confusion to Confidence

According to multiple business growth platforms, one of the biggest benefits of forecasting is that it completely transforms how you manage your cash flow. Instead of crossing your fingers and hoping that your bank account will cover your next move, you're looking ahead and setting realistic income goals, mapped out expenses, and accounting for future investments.

Forecasting lets you ask smarter questions:
- *What do I need to earn to hit my goals this quarter?*
- *What happens if I lose a client—or land a bigger one?*
- *Can I afford to hire or launch right now?*

You're not guessing. You're planning.

Proactive, Not Reactive

This is the shift that turns business owners into CEOs.

When you rely on budgeting alone, you're always working with what's already happened. You're reacting to the past by trying to fix, trim, or recover. Forecasting flips the script. It's future-focused. It helps you lead your business with forward momentum.

Experts strongly encourage scenario planning as part of the forecasting process. This means running multiple versions of your financial future:
- **Baseline** – What you *expect* to happen
- **Best-case** – If everything goes better than planned
- **Worst-case** – If revenue dips or challenges arise

This kind of strategic thinking doesn't just prepare you. It strengthens you. When change comes, you don't flinch. You pivot.

Forecasting Fuels Strategy

Forecasting doesn't just help you manage your finances. It aligns them with your vision; that's why so many advisors, consultants, and financial analysts are vocal about its importance. It helps you turn long-term dreams into short-term actions.

Want to grow your team? Forecast it.

Thinking about a big launch next year? Forecast the timeline and investment.

Curious if your pricing supports your lifestyle? Forecast the margins.

When you forecast consistently, your finances stop being a stressor and start becoming a decision-making tool.

Real Business Advantage

Not surprisingly, many industry reports show that businesses that actively forecast outperform those that don't. The reason is simple: they're more agile. They make faster, more strategic decisions. They're not afraid of change. They're ready for it. And they know what growth *actually* costs before they pursue it.

In times of uncertainty, forecasting becomes even more valuable. It keeps your footing steady when the ground shifts. It lets you navigate dips, slowdowns, or unexpected expenses without losing momentum—or your peace of mind.

Bringing It All Together

Forecasting isn't about perfection. It's about intention. It doesn't require a finance degree or a crystal ball. It requires a willingness to look ahead, to plan for possibilities, and to lead with confidence.

When you build forecasting into your monthly rhythm, you stop reacting to your numbers and start using them to shape your future. Experts agree: if you want to grow with purpose, scale with strategy, and avoid the burnout of always playing catch-up, forecasting is your next best move.

Section 5: The 5 Financial Success Principles

From Theory to Action: The 5 Financial Principles That Make Forecasting Work

Forecasting is more than just a spreadsheet. It's a decision-making tool, a mindset, and a map. But to use it well, you need a few guiding principles to steer you. Our 5 Financial Success Principles will help you move from *"I hope this works"* to *"Here's how I'm going to make it happen."*

1. Know What You Want: Vision-Driven Financial Goals

If forecasting is the process of looking ahead to plan your future, knowing what you want for the future is a prerequisite to forecasting well. Before you ever open a spreadsheet, pull up a dashboard, or punch numbers into a forecasting tool, you need to answer one fundamental question (if you haven't already):

"What do I want my life and business to look like?"

We've encouraged you to ask this question at multiple points already in this book, and that's because most business owners skip this step. They jump straight into numbers without defining the *why* behind them. But forecasting that isn't anchored in your vision is just another version of budgeting. To create a meaningful forecast, you need clarity on what you're building.

If you can't speak clearly about what your vision of success looks like, or you don't have it written down and posted in a place you can see it (remember that action item from part one?), then do that now. No tool or tactic can replace clarity of vision. Period.

From Vision to Milestones

Once you know where you're headed, you can begin to turn that vision into measurable milestones through forecasting. Let's say you want to increase your revenue by $120,000 this year. That's your *destination*. Your first step is to break that goal into smaller checkpoints: $10,000 per month, or about $2,500 per week.

But don't stop there.

Next, ask the strategic questions:
- *How will I bring in that $10,000 each month?*
- *Do I need to raise my prices?*
- *Do I need to sell more of my current offer, or create a new one with higher margins?*
- *Can I serve more clients without burning out?*
- *Will I need to hire help or invest in automation?*

This is where forecasting becomes more than math—it becomes *strategy*.

Reverse Engineering Your Revenue

Let's say your main offer is a service package priced at $2,000. To hit $10,000 in revenue, you need five clients per month.

Simple, right?

But now forecast around that goal:

- *Do you currently have five leads per month converting?*
- *Do you have the capacity to serve five clients without sacrificing quality or health?*
- *What happens if one client backs out or delays payment?*

With forecasting, you're no longer guessing. You're building a roadmap from real data.

If the math doesn't work? You adjust the plan, not the dream.

Play the "What If" Game

One of the most powerful ways to apply this principle is through scenario forecasting. This means forecasting three versions of your financial plan:

1. **Best Case:**

   What if everything goes right? Your marketing lands, your new package takes off, and you bring in $15,000/month. Can you handle it? Do you need to hire? Where will the overflow go—toward taxes, savings, or expansion?

2. **Base Case:**

   Your plan works as expected. You hit $10,000. Expenses are stable. This is your operating benchmark.

3. **Conservative Case:**

   What if a launch flops or you only bring in $6,000 this month? Do you have a buffer? What gets cut? Can you flex into something else to supplement the dip?

This kind of mental rehearsal helps you respond instead of react. It gives you a decision-making head start. You're not surprised—you're already prepared.

Don't Forget Lifestyle Goals

Forecasting isn't just for business growth—it's for life design.

Let's say part of your vision includes:

- Taking off two months each year
- Paying off debt
- Saving for a down payment
- Spending more time with your kids

Those are *financially driven lifestyle goals*. And they deserve to be built into your forecast just as intentionally as your business goals.

So ask:

- *How much income do I need to live the way I want?*
- *How much do I need to save or invest each month to meet personal milestones?*
- *If I want time freedom, what has to shift in my pricing, offers, or delivery models?*

This is how you move from hustle to harmony.

A Quick Forecasting Example

Tasha's Vision:

She wants to work only four days per week, take two 2-week vacations per year, and increase revenue by $60,000 annually.

Step 1: Break it down. $60K ÷ 12 = $5,000/month increase.

Step 2: She offers coaching packages at $2,500. She needs two more clients per month.

Step 3: Forecast: Can she support two more clients without overworking? If not, she raises her price to $3,000. Now, she only needs one to hit her goal.

Step 4: She runs three scenarios:

- Best case = signs three clients = $9,000
- Base case = signs two = $6,000
- Low case = signs one = $3,000
- With this data, Tasha can now plan content, create leads, and build capacity, all based on a vision, not a guess.

The Takeaway

"Know what you want" isn't just good advice. It's the foundation of meaningful forecasting. Your vision determines your numbers.

Your numbers drive your strategy. And your strategy creates your outcomes.

Without a clear vision, you're just plugging numbers into a spreadsheet. With one, you're building a roadmap that connects your ambition with your daily actions.

Start there—start with *why*. Then let forecasting show you *how*.

2. Know How Much It Costs: Anticipate the True Costs of Growth

Once you know *what* you want and have forecasted how to get there, the next step is figuring out what it's going to *cost* to make that happen. This is where many business owners stumble. We become so focused on achieving big income goals that we forget to factor in the real cost of getting there.

Forecasting isn't just about revenue. It's about resources — how much time, energy, and money you'll need to bring your vision to life.

Growth Comes with a Price Tag

Say you want to bring in an extra $100,000 this year. That sounds great on paper, and you could forecast ways to get there, but what are the real costs required to actually make it happen? Will you need to increase your marketing spend? Invest in new software tools or a course platform? Hire a second assistant or bring on a designer to help execute your vision?

Forecasting helps you look beyond the top-line number and into the true cost of growth. It allows you to map out what it will take to create, support, and deliver that extra revenue *before* you commit to it. Instead of chasing numbers blindly, you're making informed decisions based on what success will realistically require.

Remember: Ramp-Up Costs Are Real

Here's something people forget: most growth costs money *up front*.

If you're launching a course, hiring help, or opening a new location, you'll likely have a few months of investment before you see a return. Those are called **ramp-up costs**, and they matter when you're building in costs to your forecasting.

Example:
• Course platform: $900

- Design & branding: $1,200
- Ads: $3,500
- Assistant: $4,800

Total upfront cost: **$10,400**

Forecasting helps you see this in advance and decide if you need to adjust pricing, delay your launch, or pre-sell your offer to reduce risk.

Forecast What It Takes to Hire

Thinking about hiring? It's an exciting step—and often a necessary one—but it comes with more than just a paycheck. Before you bring someone on, you need to ask: What will it *really* cost?

Beyond salary, there's training time, onboarding processes, tools, equipment, software access, and sometimes even increases in payroll taxes or benefits. If they're client-facing, you might also need to account for additional support, supervision, or quality control during their ramp-up period.

Many entrepreneurs underestimate the full cost of hiring until they've already said yes—and by then, the financial strain has already set in. Forecasting gives you the chance to test it all before you commit. You can build a model that reflects the short-term ramp-up and the long-term return. Does your revenue need to increase to support the hire? Can you sustain the cost if growth takes longer than expected?

Forecasting doesn't just answer the question, *"Can I afford to hire?"*—it answers the more important one: *"Can I afford to hire wisely and sustainably?"*

Bottom Line: Costs Matter in Reaching Your Vision

Dreaming big is important. But bringing that dream to life takes more than passion. It takes planning. And that planning begins with forecasting the true cost of growth. You have to know your numbers, anticipate the investment, and make adjustments *before* you're overwhelmed.

Because guessing your way through growth will eventually burn you out. Forecasting your way through it? That's how you lead with clarity, confidence, and control.

3. Know Your Numbers: Cash Flow Is King

Even profitable businesses can run into serious trouble if the cash doesn't show up when the bills do. That's why forecasting and cash flow tracking must go hand in hand. Profitability looks great on paper, but if the timing of income and expenses doesn't align, you can still find yourself unable to make payroll, cover rent, or fund a new initiative.

Forecasting helps you bridge that gap by revealing not just *how much* money is coming in, but *when*.

A well-built forecast allows you to anticipate when revenue will land and when your obligations are due. It offers a bird's-eye view of your financial flow, so you can identify potential shortfalls weeks or even months in advance. That means fewer financial "surprises" and more strategic decisions. You're no longer reacting to emergencies. You're preventing them before they ever start.

And here's the best part: forecasting isn't a set-it-and-forget-it tool. It's a living, breathing document designed to evolve with your business. At the end of each month or quarter, revisit your projections. Compare your actual numbers to what you planned. Did you hit your revenue targets? Were your costs in line with expectations, or did something spike unexpectedly? What trends are emerging that should inform your next moves?

When you treat forecasting as an active part of your business operations—not just a one-time spreadsheet—you sharpen your instincts. You start seeing around corners, recognizing opportunities earlier, and adjusting faster when needed. Your confidence grows, and so does your capacity to lead.

To make forecasting truly effective, it's important to track a few key metrics consistently:

- **Gross Profit Margin & Net Profit Margin** – These show how efficiently your business is operating. Are you earning enough after covering direct costs? Is your bottom line healthy after all expenses?
- **Customer Acquisition Cost (CAC)** – This tells you how much it costs to bring in a new client or customer. If it's too high, your marketing strategy may need refinement.

- **Average Revenue per Client** – Are you maximizing the lifetime value of your clients? This metric helps you determine whether you're fully monetizing your services.
- **Operating Cash Flow** – This reflects the actual cash your business generates from day-to-day operations. It's your financial heartbeat, determining whether you have enough liquidity to keep the business running smoothly.

Together, these numbers tell the real story of your business's financial health and help you determine whether your forecast is grounded in reality or fantasy. The more you engage with them, the more accurate and powerful your forecasts will become. And over time, this habit of regular check-ins will build not just smarter strategies, but a stronger, more resilient business.

4. Act As If: Think Like a CEO, Even if It's Just You

Whether you're a solo founder or leading a growing team, it's time to step fully into your role, not just as the owner, but as the CEO of your empire. That mindset shift starts with how you treat your finances. You can't afford to wing it. You must act as if your business is a multimillion-dollar operation, even if you're still building it brick by brick.

Start by incorporating forecasting into your monthly financial meetings. This is your opportunity to sit down, review your forecasts, compare actual results to your expectations, reflect on what worked, and make thoughtful adjustments. These check-ins will give you insights that no marketing book or online course ever could, because they're rooted in *your* data. In your reality.

Treat your finances like they matter, because they do. When you do, your posture changes. Your energy shifts. You carry yourself with the clarity and confidence of a leader who knows where they're headed and how they're going to get there. And when others see that? They start to believe in your vision, too. Better clients come your way. New partnerships open up. Even potential investors take notice. People are drawn to businesses that feel stable, grounded, and intentional.

And here's some good news: you don't need fancy tools to start. Sure, there are robust platforms that can automate forecasts and generate gorgeous dashboards, but that's not what makes a business powerful. A basic accounting system plus a solid spreadsheet can take you farther than you think. You can forecast, track, and analyze with tools that are low-cost (or even free). What matters isn't the software you use. It's the consistency of *using it* that makes the difference.

Leadership isn't about reacting to what's happening. It's about planning for what's next. When you take your numbers seriously, you're not just managing a business. You're building something that lasts.

5. Take Inspired Action: Adapt and Adjust as You Go

Forecasting is only as good as your willingness to act on it. This is where many entrepreneurs get stuck. They create the plan... and never touch it again.

Don't let that be you.

Once you've set your recurring time to review your forecast, integrate reflection on these questions consistently:

- *Are we on track?*
- *What's changed in the market or in our business?*
- *Do we need to pivot?*

If demand spikes, forecast how you'll meet it. That might mean hiring, expanding capacity, or stocking more inventory.

If cash is tight, use your forecast to renegotiate terms, increase collection efforts, or secure bridge funding.

If sales are exceeding expectations, this is your cue to reinvest in marketing, team growth, or innovation. Opportunities get missed when you're only looking backward. Forecasting keeps your eyes forward.

Each new forecasting cycle presents an opportunity to refine, evolve, and *improve*.

Financial Leadership Starts With You

When your forecasts align with your actuals, celebrate because this means you've built a business with rhythm and clarity.

When they don't? That's your opportunity to learn. What shifted? What was misunderstood or overestimated? What systems need refining?

Forecasting is a tool of financial leadership. It's your chance to move from anxious guesswork to empowered action. It's how you stop spinning your wheels and start steering your ship.

So go ahead, ditch the budget, build the forecast, and chart the course. You've got this.

Section 6: CEO Thought Leadership—Own the Numbers, Lead the Vision

Let's get something straight: you don't need a boardroom to be a CEO. You don't need a C-suite title or a seven-figure business. If you're steering the ship meaning making the calls, holding the vision, you're already the CEO of your business. The question is, are you acting like it when it comes to your money?

True leadership doesn't just show up in your marketing, your mission, or your brand. It shows up in how you treat your numbers.

The most successful CEOs, whether they're running startups or billion-dollar companies, treat forecasting like a board-level tool. Not a budget scribbled in the margins. Not something they look at once a year at tax time. But a core part of their strategic leadership.

You don't need fancy software to start doing this. What you need is a rhythm—a financial operating cadence. Something simple, sustainable, and consistent.

It might look like this:

- **A monthly money meeting**: Block an hour on your calendar. Grab a coffee. Open your spreadsheet or dashboard. Review last month's actuals. Compare them to your forecast. Celebrate what worked. Investigate what didn't. Adjust for the month ahead.
- **A quarterly financial check-in**: Step back and zoom out. Are you on track for your revenue goals? Do your expenses reflect your growth plan? What trends are starting to emerge that you might need to address early?
- **An annual strategy review**: Look forward. What major investments, hires, launches, or pivots are on the horizon? Build those into your forecast. Don't be reactive—be ready.

This doesn't have to be overwhelming. It can be simple, powerful, and even *enjoyable*.

When you start treating your finances like a CEO, you start showing up differently. Your decisions become clearer. Your confidence grows. You speak with more authority in team meetings, pitch calls, and sales conversations. You stop playing small—because you're no longer guessing. You're leading.

And guess what? Others notice. Investors. Partners. Clients. When you run your business like a true leader, especially financially, you attract other high-level thinkers who want to work with someone operating at that level.

So here's your permission slip: you don't need to wait until your business is "big enough" to lead like a CEO. You lead now. With the spreadsheet. With the scratchpad. With the simple, powerful act of knowing your forecast and updating it regularly.

Because leadership isn't about perfection. It's about responsibility. About seeing the whole playing field and stepping up to make the next right move.

Treat your forecast like a strategy document, not an afterthought. Use it to cast vision, to test ideas, and to make brave decisions with clarity.

That's how real CEOs operate. And the truth?

You're already one of them.

Section 7: Your Call to Action—From Budget Stress to Forecasting Power

At this point, the truth is evident: budgeting has its place, but forecasting is the tool of top leaders. This chapter challenged the old narrative that financial planning is about limits and restrictions. Instead, you've learned that forecasting is about freedom, a forward-looking, values-driven way to lead your business and life with intention.

Where budgeting keeps you in the past, forecasting invites you to dream, plan, and grow. It's about turning vision into numbers, numbers into strategy, and strategy into results.

You've seen how forecasting:
- Helps you anticipate growth, not just survive expenses.
- Allows flexibility for changing seasons, hiring decisions, and business evolution.
- Gives structure to your income, just like a glass gives shape to water.
- Keeps your energy focused on creation, not just conservation.

By shifting from *"What do I have to work with?"* to *"What do I want to create?"—you've* stepped into a whole new mindset.

So, what do you do now?

Here's your call to action:

1. Pick your forecasting tools (template or software).
2. Set a time in the next week to complete the four-cup exercise.
3. Set a recurring "forecast refresh" meeting.

And remember, you don't have to have all the answers, just the courage to start asking better questions.

Because this isn't about playing small. It's about pouring your money with purpose into the business, and life, you're here to build.

Let's keep going. The best is yet to come.

Top 5 Takeaways from Chapter 6: Ditch the Budget, Embrace Forecasting

1. Budgeting is Static. Forecasting is Strategic.

A budget looks backward and focuses on restrictions. Forecasting looks forward, empowering you to make intentional decisions based on your goals, not just your limitations.

2. Forecasting Gives Structure and Flexibility.

Just like a glass gives shape to water, forecasting provides a container for your money. It helps you direct your income where it's needed, such as taxes, personal life, investments, and business expenses, all with structure and purpose.

3. The Mindset Shift Is the Real Win.

Moving from scarcity to strategy means you're no longer asking, *"What can I cut?"* Instead, you're asking, *"What can I build?"* Forecasting is about growth, not guilt.

4. You Don't Have to Guess—You Can Prepare.

From hiring decisions to seasonal slowdowns, forecasting helps you anticipate expenses and income before they happen, so you can act instead of react.

5. Forecasting is a Leadership Tool.

Whether you're solo or scaling, forecasting makes you think like a CEO. Monthly reviews, adaptable plans, and financial clarity give you the power to lead your business with confidence.

Chapter 7:
Taxes—Tactics and Deductibles

Section 1: Reframe the Fear—Why Taxes Are the Business Owner's Test

I remember the exact moment I opened the email.

It was March 5th. I was getting ready for my regular morning meeting with my Executive Peer Group, a business group of incredible women who are in business like me. This is a group where I feel I have friends and is something I always look forward to because it grounds me, resets me, and reminds me I'm not doing this whole business thing alone. But that morning started differently. Before I even poured my second cup of coffee, I sat down to check my inbox. Just a quick glance, I told myself, before I head out the door..

There it was.

Subject line: *Review Before Filing*

Amount owed: *$10,317*

I stared at it. For a moment, I think I actually held my breath. I hadn't set aside the money. I didn't even know it was coming. No warning. No mental prep. Just a five-figure punch in the gut.

Immediately, the internal narrative took over: "You should've known better." "How did you let this happen?" "You're supposed to be good at this stuff."

It wasn't just a tax bill. It was a shame. Guilt. That sick feeling that you've somehow failed at being a "real" business owner.

The Mindset Shift I Didn't Know I Needed

After seeing that number, I pulled myself together, got in the car, and went to my business group meeting, though, to be honest, I considered skipping. But I'm so glad I didn't. That meeting gave me a moment I'll never forget. One of the women in our group casually shared a thought that struck me deeply:

"If you're paying taxes, it means you're winning. You made a profit. That's not a problem; it's a milestone."

She didn't even say it directly to me, but it was *for* me. Suddenly, the entire narrative shifted. I wasn't in trouble. I was in a new season. The bill wasn't a punishment. It was proof that my business had grown. That I was doing it. That I was making money. The problem wasn't the number. The problem was that I hadn't planned for it.

That single line gave me a new lens: I wasn't bad at business. I just hadn't learned this part of it yet. And that's a very different story.

From Shame to Strategy

For years, I operated in reactive mode when it came to taxes. I told myself I'd figure it out later or that I didn't earn "enough" yet for it to really matter. I avoided my numbers more often than I'd like to admit, hoping that if I didn't look too closely, I wouldn't feel overwhelmed.

But avoidance is a costly coping mechanism. It doesn't protect you. It prevents you from growing. I wasn't intentionally irresponsible; I just hadn't built the systems yet. I hadn't developed the habit of checking in regularly, forecasting, or even asking better questions of my accountant.

That $10,317 changed all of that. It turned my tax process from something reactive and rushed into something strategic. Because here's the truth:

When you start looking at your numbers with clear eyes, even when you don't like what you see, you begin reclaiming power.

You move from shame into strategy. You move from crisis mode into CEO mode.

The IRS Isn't the Enemy

Let's just clear this up: the IRS isn't hiding in the bushes waiting to ruin your life over a misplaced lunch receipt.

They're not monsters. They're humans with jobs, just like you and I: jobs that involve interpreting tax law and ensuring businesses file their returns correctly. That's it.

For a long time, I operated under this vague fear of getting audited, as if the IRS was watching over my shoulder at every moment. I assumed that one wrong move would get me into trouble. But once I actually started reading up on what the IRS looks for, what red flags really are, and what counts as adequate documentation, I realized they just want clarity.

They want you to report what you earned, document what you spent, and file your paperwork on time. That's it. No drama. No fear tactics. Just structure.

The key is to stop dreading tax season and start mastering it. Because taxes, when planned for and understood, aren't just a burden, they're a strategic tool. Smart tax planning helps you keep more of what you earn, grow your business with confidence, and operate in peace rather than panic.

Every hero has their test, and taxes are yours. They force you to confront the uncomfortable: the numbers, the rules, and the systems you haven't set up yet. But stepping into that discomfort with strategy and support? That's what turns chaos into clarity. That's how you level up from freelancer to CEO.

You Don't Have to Be an Expert, But You Do Have to Take the Lead as the Business Owner

One of the biggest mindset shifts I made after that tax season was understanding that I don't need to be a tax expert, but I *do* need to lead like a business owner. I had been treating tax prep like an annual annoyance instead of an integral part of my company's rhythm. I wouldn't do that with client work or project timelines, so why was I doing it with something that literally affects every dollar I keep?

Leadership means stepping into the parts of business that aren't always fun or flashy. It means creating a structure that supports your future, not just your current survival. I still don't want to become a tax guru. But now I ask better questions. I track my income more regularly. I set aside money throughout the year instead of hoping I'll have enough in March. And that alone has made all the difference.

Every Choice Has a Consequence—What Will Yours Be?

I've learned that taxes are not a punishment. They're a reflection.

They reflect your growth. They reflect your systems. They reflect how seriously you're taking this business you've built from scratch. If you're paying taxes, that means you're earning. And if you're earning, you have something worth protecting, worth planning for, and worth stewarding well.

The real problem isn't taxes. It's avoidance. It's shame. It's waiting until you're in over your head to start asking for help.

But every moment offers a choice.

You can keep avoiding, or you can take ownership.

You can keep running, or you can reframe.

This chapter is about helping you make the shift I made, not by becoming perfect, but by becoming prepared.

Because once you stop fearing taxes, you start building a business that can truly thrive.

Section 2: Start Smart—What Business Owners Need to Know From Day One

If you're in the early stages of building your business, I want to tell you something I wish someone had told me: *you don't have to earn a certain amount of money to take your business seriously*. And don't **ever** let anyone tell you that you aren't a business owner until you make money. You don't need a six-figure income or a giant team or a wall of client testimonials before you treat this like a real operation. You just need to start making intentional, smart decisions—especially when it comes to taxes.

Because once you start accepting money for your services or products, you've crossed an invisible line. You're no longer dabbling. You're in business. And with that shift comes a responsibility that can feel overwhelming, especially if no one has walked you through it before.

Business Structure Setup—Keep It Simple, But Be Sure You Do It

An important prerequisite to understanding how taxes impact your business is to ensure you have a clear and established business structure within which you are operating. We reviewed business structure options in depth in chapter five, but let's provide a quick refresher here.

Most people start out as a sole proprietorship by default. That simply means your business income and expenses are reported under your own name and Social Security number. It's easy, it's fast, and it requires very little setup. But it also means you're personally responsible for everything your business does—good, bad, or otherwise.

A Limited Liability Company (LLC), on the other hand, adds a layer of legal protection between you and your business. It separates your personal and business assets, which can come in handy if something goes wrong. It can also lend credibility when working with clients or applying for business loans. You can still be taxed the same way as a sole proprietor unless you choose something different, but the setup signals to yourself and others that this is more than a hobby. You're building something real.

You don't need to hire a lawyer or create a board of directors to take this first step. Start small, but start officially. Register with your state, get your paperwork in order, and give your business the solid foundation it deserves.

By ensuring you have a clear (and appropriate) business structure, you set yourself up for success when tax time rolls around. This is business ownership 101.

First-Year Essentials—What You *Actually* Need

There's a lot of noise online about what you need to launch a business such as branding packages, color palettes, and a fancy website. But from a tax perspective, the essentials are much more practical. Here's what actually matters when you're starting out:

First, get an EIN—an Employer Identification Number. We've already talked about this, and I'm just doubling back. It's free from the IRS and serves as a unique identifier for your business, similar to a Social Security number. You'll use it when opening a bank account, signing contracts, or working with certain vendors. Even if you're a sole proprietor, having an EIN keeps your personal SSN off official paperwork. It's a small step that goes a long way toward protecting your identity and professionalizing your operation.

Next, open a separate business bank account. This isn't just a nice-to-have. It's essential. Mixing personal and business funds is a recipe for confusion, lost deductions, and potential audit risk. Keep your business income and expenses flowing through a dedicated account so you can track them cleanly and clearly.

You'll also want to choose a bookkeeping system that fits your style. That could be software like QuickBooks or Xero, or a spreadsheet if you're just getting started. The goal isn't perfection. It's consistency. You want to know where your money is going, what you're earning, and what your tax picture looks like long before April rolls around.

And finally, track your startup costs. Those early purchases, such as your laptop, software subscriptions, website domain, or that online course you took to improve your skills, may be deductible. Don't wait until you feel "official" to start recording your expenses. If it helped you launch, it matters.

Track Everything—Especially in the Beginning

I'll be honest: I didn't do this well in my first year. I kept most of my receipts in a box on the floor of my office, thinking I'd "deal with them later." Guess what? That time eventually came, and it was stressful, confusing, and more expensive than it needed to be. If only I had known how important it was to organize things from the beginning.

The earlier you start tracking, the easier everything gets. Create a system that works for you—maybe it's digital folders in Google Drive, maybe it's an app on your phone, or maybe it's a good old-fashioned binder. Just make sure you're saving receipts, invoices, and mileage logs. And don't assume your bank statement is good enough. It's not. You need actual records that show what was purchased, for what purpose, and when.

Make it a weekly or monthly ritual—ten minutes at the end of the week to upload receipts, review your expenses, and update your records. This one habit will save you hours of stress later and could save you hundreds or even thousands of dollars at tax time.

Quarterly Estimated Taxes—A Curveball You Can Avoid

Here's one of the biggest surprises that catches new business owners off guard: you don't just pay taxes in April. Once you're self-employed and earning a steady income, the IRS expects you to pay throughout the year in the form of quarterly estimated taxes.

If you expect to owe at least $1,000 in taxes, you're required to pay estimates on these four dates:
- April 15th
- June 15th
- September 15th
- January 15th (of the following year)

It doesn't matter if you're not incorporated or only working part-time. If you're earning self-employed income, you're responsible. Missing these payments won't land you in jail, but it *will* result in late fees and penalties and that's money that could've stayed in your account.

To stay on track, aim to set aside 25–30% of your income for taxes in a separate account. If you prefer more accuracy, you can use the safe harbor rule, which says that if you pay 100% of what you owed last year (or 110% if you made over $150K), the IRS won't penalize you, even if your actual tax bill ends up higher.

It doesn't have to be perfect, but it does need to be intentional. This is one of those things that's easy to ignore...until it isn't. Paying quarterly protects you from surprise bills and gives you more control over your cash flow. And as we've already said, control = clarity.

A Quick Note on The Hobby Loss Rule—And Why It Can Cost You Big

This is one of those tax rules nobody tells you about until it bites you—or in my case, nearly did. It's called the **Hobby Loss Rule,** and it's something every business owner needs to understand, especially in those early, messy, figuring-it-out seasons. That's exactly where I was. Like many business owners, the business I'm running today wasn't my first attempt at building something meaningful. I had dabbled in a few different directions, testing ideas, shifting services, and trying to find the right fit. I was passionate and driven but also still learning the ropes of business-building.

One tax season, I received a rather curt email and formal-looking PDF attachment from my accountant saying, "The IRS might consider what you're doing a hobby." I was stunned and a bit scared. I had paying clients. I was investing in tools, courses, branding—everything I thought a business owner was supposed to do. BUT, I was not showing any profit because my spending was more than what I was bringing in. I started doing my own research and learned that the IRS has very specific criteria they use to determine whether your activity qualifies as a business or a hobby. And if they classify it as a hobby, it's not good news.

Here's the kicker: if your work is seen as a hobby, you still owe taxes on your income, but you can't deduct your expenses. All those investments you made to try to get things off the ground—your website, coaching, software, training, and travel—they don't count. You end up paying tax on the money you earned *without* being able to offset it with the money you spent to earn it.

It felt like a gut punch. But I also realized how important it was to start treating my business like a business, not just in spirit, but in structure. That one conversation saved me a lot of stress and probably a lot of money down the road. If you're serious about what you're building, make sure the IRS can see that too.

So, what can you do to protect yourself from the Hobby-Loss Rule?

Well, the IRS decides if you have a hobby or a business by looking at whether you're actively trying to make a profit. That doesn't mean you have to be profitable every year, but you do need to be able to show that you're operating like a business. Do you advertise? Do you keep good records? Have you registered your business and opened a separate bank account? Do you shift strategies when things aren't working?

If you're showing up like a business owner—tracking your numbers, taking steps to improve your results, and treating your work seriously—you're usually in the clear. But if you're treating your business like a side hobby with occasional income and no real structure, you may lose the very deductions that could help you grow.

So yes, you can love your work. You can feel wildly passionate about it. But if you want the tax benefits of owning a business, you also need to show that you're building one.

Section 3: Deductions—The Laugh Test and Speed Limit Analogy

One of the most common questions I get as a business owner is this: "Can I write this off?"

And honestly? I get why people ask. The world of business deductions can feel like one giant gray area, especially when you're doing your best to follow the rules but also trying to be smart about what you claim.

The truth is, deductions aren't about gaming the system. They're about legally optimizing your tax liability.

That's it. The IRS actually *wants* you to take deductions, as long as you do it responsibly and can back it up. And thankfully, the rules for what qualifies are clearer than most people think.

What the IRS Looks For: The 3-Part Test

The IRS uses three basic questions to determine whether a business expense is deductible. If you're wondering whether something qualifies, this is your checklist:

1. Is it ordinary?

This means it's a common expense in your industry. For example, coaching may be ordinary for business owners but wouldn't make sense for a construction company unless it's industry-specific.

2. Is it necessary?

The expense doesn't have to be vital, but it does need to be helpful and appropriate for running your business.

3. Is it primarily for business?

If there's a personal benefit mixed in, the expense needs to be clearly tied to your business purpose. The *primary* function must be business-related.

If you can confidently answer "yes" to all three, you're probably in the clear.

Now, if you're unsure, here's a little exercise I like to use. Picture yourself sitting across from an IRS agent in a black suit. He opens your file, looks you in the eye, and says:

"We audited your account, and we see that you bought pencils. Can you explain why this is an ordinary, necessary business expense?"

If you can calmly respond, "Yes, I use them to write notes during coaching sessions, brainstorm client strategy, and take notes during calls," then you're good. If, however, your gut tightens and you have to reach for a justification, maybe don't take that deduction.

That's the rule: *If you feel uneasy explaining it, don't write it off.*

The Accountant Speed Limit Metaphor

When I asked my accountant about a questionable deduction years ago, he gave me a metaphor that stuck with me forever.

"My job is to tell you the speed limit is 55. If you go 60 or 70, I'm still in the car with you. But if you go 90, I'm out. You'll need to find another accountant."

It made perfect sense.

55 mph means completely safe, clearly documented, fully justifiable expenses. Think: business coaching, software subscriptions, mileage logs, or advertising costs.

70 mph is the gray area — maybe it's reasonable, but you'd better be ready to explain it.

90 mph is when you're stretching reality: personal spa days labeled as "client wellness," or a trip to Hawaii written off as "strategic planning." That's not just risky, it's an audit magnet.

The takeaway? Stay close to the speed limit. Use your deductions, but don't abuse them.

The Laugh Test (a.k.a. Don't Get Cute With It)

I once attended a tax training by Bob Jennings. He explained deductions with something called the laugh test. He said,

> "If a client asks me if they can deduct something and it makes me laugh out loud, the answer is probably no."

Let's play this out.

- Deducting your hot tub because it "helps you relax after work"? Ha! That's a no.
- Deducting your business coach because they help you grow and run your company better? Grin and nod. That's a yes.

Use common sense. If it sounds ridiculous to say out loud, don't try to squeeze it into your return. It's not worth the risk or the audit.

What You *Can* Deduct (That You Might Be Missing)

Here are some of the most commonly overlooked, yet completely legitimate, deductions:

- **Professional development**: Courses, conferences, certifications, masterminds, coaching
- **Marketing and advertising**: Website costs, business cards, social media ads, brand photos
- **Software and subscriptions**: Anything you use for your work — QuickBooks, Canva, CRM tools, etc.
- **Home office expenses**: If you work from home and use a specific space exclusively for business, you can deduct a portion of your rent/mortgage, utilities, and internet
- **Meals and entertainment**: 50% of the cost is deductible if it's a legitimate business meal (think: client lunch, not date night)
- **Business travel**: Flights, hotels, car rentals, gas, and even part of your per diem for meals
- **Health insurance premiums**: If you're self-employed and not covered elsewhere
- **Vehicle use**: Track your mileage for business errands and appointments—those miles count

A Wise Move: Building Your Own Deduction Strategy

If you want to get a handle on your deductions, one of the most useful things you can do is **create your own deduction strategy.**

Here's how to get started:

1. **Make a list of recurring business expenses.** Think of everything you spend money on regularly that directly supports your business. Include office supplies, subscriptions, marketing, professional services, and software.
2. **Run each item through the 3-part IRS test we mentioned just above:** Is it ordinary? Is it necessary? Is it primarily for business?
3. **Review your bookkeeping records.** Make sure you're actually tracking these expenses. Are they being categorized correctly? Are the receipts saved? If not, fix it now.

When your deductions are well-documented and intentional, they don't just reduce your tax bill—they give you peace of mind.

One Last Note on Itemized Deductions

You might remember hearing your parents talk about saving receipts for car tags, house tax, or medical bills. That used to be more common. But these days, especially in 2024 and 2025, the standard deduction is so high that it's rare for most people to itemize deductions on their federal tax return.

That said, don't assume it's a waste to keep those records. State tax laws vary, and some states still have very low standard deduction thresholds. *Always ask your accountant if it makes sense to itemize on your state return.* Sometimes, that little bit of effort can make a big difference locally, even if it doesn't matter federally.

Reflection Activity: Map Your Own Deductions

Before you move on, take 10 minutes to do this:
- Write down your top 10 recurring business expenses
- Run each through the 3-part IRS test
- Ask yourself: Would this pass the laugh test?
- Mark which ones are being tracked correctly, and which need attention

You don't need to be perfect. You just need to be intentional, and you need to get started.

When you master your deductions, you don't just save money, you build a business that's lean, smart, and audit-ready. And honestly? That kind of clarity feels just as good as the refund.

In fact, for me, it feels better. A lot better.

Section 4: Smart vs. Silly Spending—Don't Burn Dollars to Save Cents

There's a dangerous myth floating around in the business world, especially around tax time, and it sounds like this:

"It's a write-off, so it's basically free!"

Let me be the one to say what most people don't: no, it's not.

Spending money you didn't need to spend just to reduce your tax bill is still spending money. That deduction doesn't make it free. It just makes it *slightly discounted*.

Don't Spend $70 Just to Save $30

Let's say this as plainly as possible: if you buy a $100 printer in December just to get a deduction—and your current printer works just fine—you didn't save money. You spent $70 unnecessarily.

I see people do this all the time. It's tax season, and everyone's scrambling to reduce their taxable income. So they go out and buy gadgets, office chairs, expensive software, new clothes, or random supplies just to "get their expenses up." But what they don't realize is they're eating into their own profit.

Yes, that deduction will lower your tax bill. But it doesn't make the purchase wise.

You are allowed to be profitable. You are allowed to pay taxes. And you are allowed to save that money instead of blowing it on last-minute panic spending.

A business with a strong profit margin and a clear mission doesn't fear taxes. It plans for them—and spends with intention.

Reframing Write-Off Culture: More Is Not Always More

Somewhere along the way, "write it off" became synonymous with "do whatever you want." But write-offs aren't magic erasers. They're tools. And like any tool, they work best when used intentionally.

You're not building a business just to avoid taxes. You're building a business to create impact, freedom, stability, and legacy. That means spending money where it matters and learning to ignore the pressure to buy something just because someone on TikTok said it was "deductible."

Want a good rule of thumb? Before you buy something, ask yourself, *"Would I still want this if it weren't deductible?"*

If the answer is no, skip it. If the answer is yes, and it supports your mission, your client experience, or your long-term goals, then great! Buy it and document it properly.

So, before you click "add to cart," take a moment and zoom out. Ask:
- *Does this help me serve my clients better?*
- *Will this make my business more efficient, profitable, or scalable?*
- *Am I making this decision from a place of alignment or anxiety?*

Strategic purchases feel different. They're rooted in clarity, not fear. They serve your goals, not your guilt. They may still be deductible, but more importantly, they're *valuable*. They create ROI that goes beyond a tax break. That's what smart business spending looks like.

A New Way to Think About Profit

Of course, profit isn't the problem. Profit is the point. It's what allows you to breathe, to grow, to lead from a place of strength rather than scarcity. It's the sign that your business is healthy and your decisions are aligned.

So when you find yourself staring at your numbers and wondering how to lower your tax bill, don't let panic drive the conversation.

Instead of asking, *"How can I spend this money just to pay less in taxes?"* ask,

"How can I put this money to work in a way that strengthens my business and supports my long-term goals?"

That might mean saving. It might mean reinvesting in better systems or support. It might mean paying yourself more consistently.

But let the strategy serve the vision, not just the spreadsheet. Because the goal isn't to reduce profit. The goal is to use it wisely.

Section 5: The 5 Financial Success Principles

These **5 Financial Success Principles** are at the core of this book *and* at the core of how business owners educate themselves through financial clarity. The principles don't just help you make money— they help you use it wisely, plan proactively, and build something sustainable.

When you apply these principles specifically to your tax strategy, you shift from reacting at year-end to leading with purpose all year long.

Let's walk through them one by one, starting with the most fundamental.

1. Know What You Want: Plan for After-Tax Income

If you've ever set a revenue goal and still felt broke at the end of the year, this principle is for you.

It's easy to get caught up in topline numbers. We celebrate "six-figure businesses" and revenue milestones like badges of honor, but those numbers don't tell the full story. What actually matters is what you keep after expenses, taxes, and obligations are paid. That's the number that funds your life. That's the number that creates stability, peace of mind, and options.

If you're only planning for gross revenue, you're building your business on shaky ground. It's like budgeting based on your salary without accounting for taxes and deductions. You might feel like you're making progress until the bill comes due and there's not enough left over to move forward.

So let's flip the script.

Start by asking yourself this question:

How much money do I want to *actually* have in hand after taxes are paid?

Not **what you want to earn** on paper. Not **what sounds impressive** at a networking event. But **what do you actually need,** realistically and intentionally, *after taxes,* to sustain your lifestyle and fund your goals?

That number is personal. It might mean having $6,000 a month available after taxes to cover your living expenses, savings contributions, and business reinvestments. It could mean building in a profit buffer so you can take a guilt-free vacation. Or maybe it looks like setting aside $20,000 for a home renovation or finally hiring your first team member. Whatever it is, clarity around that number becomes your anchor; it grounds your strategy and reshapes your definition of success from flashy to sustainable.

The point is this: until you define the after-tax outcome you want, every financial decision is a guess.

Set Financial Goals With Taxes in Mind

So let's think this through. Do you want to reinvest in your business this year? Great! Make sure that's part of your net income plan, not just your top-line hopes. Hoping to max out a SEP IRA or solo 401(k)? You'll need to calculate what's left after taxes before you can commit those dollars. Trying to buy a home, fund college, or pay down debt? It's your after-tax income, not your gross revenue, that will do the heavy lifting. When you anchor your goals in what you actually have access to, your financial plan becomes more grounded, more realistic, and far more powerful.

By building your goals around after-tax clarity, you create a more honest, empowered financial roadmap. You stop chasing vanity numbers and start designing a business that truly serves you.

Practical Tip: Reverse-Engineer Your Revenue

Let's say your goal is to take home $100,000 after taxes this year. And your tax rate is approximately 25%. That means you'll need to **net** about $133,000 before taxes and probably **earn** closer to $180,000 to $200,000 in gross revenue, depending on your margins.

See how different that is from just setting a six-figure goal?

Reverse-engineering from your actual life needs, not your ego or Instagram comparison, effectively puts you in control. It allows you to price with intention, plan your cash flow, and enter tax season with peace of mind, rather than panic.

2. Know How Much It Costs: Understand Your Tax Liabilities and How to Minimize Them Legally

One of the most common (and painful) mistakes business owners make is underestimating how much they'll owe in taxes (i.e., one major "cost" of doing business). You're focused on growth, revenue, clients, and impact and then suddenly it's March, and you're staring at a surprise tax bill you weren't prepared for.

Understanding your full tax picture—federal, state, and even local—isn't just for accountants. It's for business owners who want to lead with clarity and protect their profits. You need to know what's coming so you can plan for it, not panic because of it.

Start by getting familiar with the tax brackets. Your income doesn't get taxed at one flat rate. It's taxed in ranges, or brackets. And while it's tempting to assume you're in a lower bracket to avoid overpaying, it's almost always better to estimate on the higher side. If you overpay, you'll get a refund. But if you underpay? You'll owe, and that can be financially and emotionally destabilizing.

In addition to understanding your brackets, take time to learn about common deductions and credits available to business owners. The IRS website might not be thrilling reading, but it is the most credible and up-to-date source of tax-related information. Don't rely on social media posts, chat forums, or that one video you saw from a stranger claiming to write off their entire vacation unless it's backed by actual tax law and verified by a licensed professional.

A Note on Tax-Saving Strategies

There are tax strategies designed to help you *legally* lower your tax burden. Retirement accounts, such as SEP IRAs or solo 401(k)s, allow you to defer taxes while investing in your future. Health savings accounts (HSAs), education deductions, and specific business credits can help reduce your tax bill *if you're aware of them and take advantage of them ahead of time.*

This is where working with a qualified tax professional makes a big difference. And not just any tax professional—one who understands your business model and your industry. A good accountant doesn't just fill out forms; they help you think strategically about how to structure your income, track your deductions, and plan for growth.

Think of it this way: every dollar you don't plan for is a dollar at risk. But every dollar you *do* plan for can be put to work, whether that's for reducing your taxes, reinvesting in your business, or building your wealth.

3. Know Your Numbers: Track Income, Deductions, and Credits Meticulously

We know we've said it many times before, but this one can't be over-stated: accurate, consistent bookkeeping is one of the most powerful tools you have as a business owner. Period. End of story. Not just because it helps you "stay organized," but because it protects your profit, unlocks deductions, and ensures you're paying what you owe and not a dollar more.

Let's be honest. Most business owners didn't start their business expecting to become bookkeepers. But the truth is, if you don't know your numbers, you can't make good decisions. And when it comes to taxes, that lack of visibility can cost you thousands.

The foundation of this principle is simple: what gets tracked gets optimized. If you're not tracking your income accurately, you might underreport and risk penalties. If you're not tracking your deductions thoroughly, you're likely leaving money on the table. If you're not regularly reviewing your financial reports, you'll miss opportunities to proactively manage your tax obligations, especially if your income fluctuates throughout the year.

Keep Your Records Clean and Digital

Start with a reliable accounting system. Whether it's QuickBooks, Xero, Wave, or another platform, the key is consistency. Your accounting software should help you categorize income and expenses, reconcile transactions, and generate reports that give you a real-time snapshot of your business's health.

But software alone isn't enough. You also need to maintain clear documentation for every deductible expense. That means uploading and storing digital copies of receipts, invoices, and any backup documentation that proves the business purpose of the purchase.

Let's be clear: your bank statement is not enough. It shows what was purchased, but not *why* and that's what matters most to the IRS. A receipt for a coaching program, a screenshot of an online course, or a travel itinerary tied to a conference all create a defensible paper trail that supports your deductions. Think of it as audit armor: boring to build, but priceless when you need it.

Make Reviewing Your Numbers a Ritual

You might be sick of hearing this by now, but your financial reports shouldn't be something you only look at once a year. They should be a regular part of your business rhythm. Monthly check-ins with your profit and loss statement, quarterly reviews of your income trends and expense categories but these habits give you a clearer view of your tax trajectory *before* tax season hits.

Why does this matter? Because your tax obligations shift as your revenue grows or contracts. A one-time project, a new offer that scales fast, or a seasonal dip—each of these can significantly affect what you owe. If you're only looking backward at the end of the year, you're already too late to make adjustments.

Avoid Overpaying (and Under-Tracking)

It's a common and costly mistake: overpaying in taxes simply because you weren't tracking expenses properly. Maybe you missed deductions. Maybe you forgot to log mileage. Maybe you let receipts pile up in a drawer. Those small lapses can add up to thousands in lost deductions and unnecessary tax payments.

But the flip side is just as true: tracking well can save you thousands. It's not just about getting it "right". It's about reclaiming your power as a business owner. Because when you know your numbers, you don't just survive tax season. You navigate it with clarity, confidence, and control.

4. Act As If: File Proactively and Avoid Last-Minute Panic

If you want to run a successful business, you have to start acting like a successful CEO—*now*. Not "when the money gets consistent.

" Not "once I hire a team." Right now. The way you show up for your finances is one of the clearest indicators of whether you're building a business or babysitting a side hustle.

And nothing exposes this faster than tax season.

Too many business owners treat taxes like a yearly panic button. They wait until the last possible moment, open a spreadsheet in dread, and whisper a prayer that it won't be as catastrophic as they fear. But that's not how CEOs operate. CEOs plan ahead. They act with intention. They don't just react to numbers, they use them proactively to make smarter decisions.

"Act As If" means adopting the habits of the person you're becoming. Do you want to be a confident, strategic, and in-control business owner? Then manage your taxes like one.

Start With Quarterly Habits

We've already talked about this earlier in our chapter. If your business is profitable, you're probably required to pay quarterly estimated taxes. And if you ignore them, you could face hefty penalties, not to mention that pit-in-your-stomach feeling when your tax bill blindsides you in April.

Acting As If you are already a successful CEO, use this approach: Build taxes into your cash flow. Set aside 25–30% of every payment into a dedicated tax savings account. Pay quarterly without hesitation. When tax time rolls around, you'll already have the money waiting. You'll feel like a boss, because you are one.

Filing Isn't Just Compliance—It's Strategy

Waiting until year-end to look at your numbers is like trying to steer a boat by checking the map once a year. Smart CEOs review financials monthly. They talk to their accountants *before* big decisions. They optimize deductions throughout the year, not just in the final week of March.

Tax laws shift, and your income will too. Staying informed, building a relationship with a trusted tax pro, and using financial reports to forecast your obligations will keep you in the driver's seat. That's how real leaders operate.

From Side Hustle to CEO

Filing proactively isn't about being "good with money." It's about stepping into the mindset and responsibilities of a business owner who's here for the long haul. When you treat your tax prep like a core part of your business strategy, not a once-a-year annoyance, you build trust in yourself and credibility in your business.

Side hustlers guess. CEOs prepare.

Side hustlers wing it. CEOs plan for growth.

You don't have to wait until your business hits a magic number to lead like a CEO. Start today. Build the systems now that you'll thank yourself for later. Take taxes seriously, not with fear, but with power.

When you *act as if*, you create the reality that follows.

5. Take Inspired Action: Invest in Expert Advice to Optimize Your Tax Strategy

If there's one thing that separates reactive business owners from empowered CEOs, it's this: they don't try to do it all alone, especially when it comes to taxes.

Sure, DIY tax software might seem convenient. YouTube videos and free webinars might offer bite-sized tips, but when it comes to optimizing your tax strategy, guessing your way through it is like flying blind. *It's not just risky, it's expensive.*

Inspired action isn't about doing more. It's about doing what matters, with support. That means investing in the expertise of an accountant, EA (Enrolled Agent), or qualified tax advisor who understands your business, your goals, and your growth trajectory.

Tax Planning Isn't a One-Time Task—It's a Year-Round Strategy

Hiring someone to help you with your taxes *once a year* is like seeing a personal trainer only after you've already injured yourself. Year-round tax planning, on the other hand, is like having a coach in your corner who is consistently spotting you and helping you train smarter, avoid missteps, and stay on track with your goals.

When you meet with a tax professional throughout the year, not just during tax season, they can help you:

- Adjust your estimated payments as your income shifts

- Track and maximize deductions while you still have time to act
- Plan major purchases or investments in a tax-savvy way
- Review any changes to tax law that could impact your business
- Make decisions *before* they become expensive mistakes

Yes, It Costs Money—But It Pays You Back

The right tax advisor won't just fill in the blanks on a form. They'll spot opportunities, flag blind spots, and give you a proactive plan that saves far more than their fee.

Think of it this way: a $1,000 investment in expert advice might save you $5,000 in taxes and prevent $10,000 worth of stress. That's not a luxury. That's a smart move.

And as your business grows, your tax situation becomes more complex. You'll encounter new thresholds, deductions, and responsibilities. Having a trusted advisor means you're never guessing. You're growing with guidance.

Don't Just File—Lead

This is your business. These are your numbers. You don't have to become a tax expert to take ownership of your financial future, but you do need to surround yourself with people who are knowledgeable in this area.

Taking inspired action means investing in support that empowers you to make informed, aligned, and strategic decisions. It's the difference between winging it alone and building something sustainable with intention. Saying, "I don't need to do this by myself," isn't weakness—it's wisdom.

Because the most successful entrepreneurs don't just pay taxes and hope for the best—they plan for them, prepare for them, and build businesses that grow in confidence. And they do it with the right people in their corner.

The Power of Financial Principles in Tax Strategy

Taxes aren't just about forms and deadlines—they're about alignment. When you apply the 5 Financial Success Principles to your tax planning, you move from reactive to proactive, from overwhelmed to in control.

You **know what you want,** so your tax strategy reflects your true goals, not just your gross income.

You **know how much it costs**, so you're prepared, not surprised, when obligations come due.

You **know your numbers**, so you can spot opportunities, reduce liabilities, and sleep better at night.

You **act as if**, stepping into your role as CEO, not someday, but today.

And you **take inspired action**, by getting expert support that turns confusion into clarity and growth.

Together, these principles shift your approach from stress and scarcity to confidence and power. Because when you treat your tax strategy like an extension of your business plan, not an afterthought, you don't just keep more of your money. You lead with intention. You build a business that lasts.

And you do it on purpose.

Section 6: DIY vs. Pro Help—A Time and Sanity Comparison

Let's face it: tax season sneaks up on us all. And when it hits, most business owners face the same decision: should I do this myself, or should I hire a professional?

At first glance, the DIY route seems like the smart, cost-effective option. But dig a little deeper, and the trade-offs become clear.

The DIY Route: Seemingly Cheap, Secretly Draining

Here's how a typical DIY process goes:
- 2+ hours gathering documents - longer if you're unsure what you need or have to dig through inboxes and drawers.
- Time to sign in or reset your password (because let's be real, when's the last time you used your login?)
- 1–2 hours navigating the platform, rereading rules, and second-guessing deductions.

- Mental gymnastics around things like:
  - Did the software apply the home office deduction correctly?
  - Can I file my state taxes differently from my federal return?
  - What happens if I get audited—will they help or charge me more?

Then there's the post-filing anxiety: "Did I do it right? Did I miss something important? Is this going to come back to haunt me?"

What if you get a letter from the IRS six months later? Will you pay again to have someone fix it? And how much will that cost both financially and emotionally?

DIY taxes may not cost you upfront. However, they come at a cost in terms of time, uncertainty, second-guessing, and potentially missed deductions. If that's a risk you're willing and able to take, there can be a place for DIY-ing it.

But you have to go into it with your eyes wide open.

A Case Study in Trying to Do It Alone

Remember my $10,000+ tax bill?

It was early March. I had finally sent in my tax documents, feeling a little behind but not too worried. Then the email hit my inbox: *"You owe $10,000."*

Cue the panic. I was distraught with worry. Paralyzed with shame. Beating myself up for making such a huge mistake.

Looking back, I realize that if I had an accountant in my corner, someone with whom I had built a trusting and long-term relationship, things could have gone much differently.

If I had had my own accountant to call on in that moment, I bet that situation would have gone more like this:

She would have looked at me calmly, kindly, and said, "Hey, did you put any money into an IRA yet?"

I probably would've blinked at her, caught off guard. "Wait—can I still do that?"

And she would've nodded.

"Absolutely. Even though it's too late in the year to go out and buy tax-deductible business expenses to help lower your tax burden, it's *not* too late to reduce your tax bill in other ways. You actually have until April 15th to contribute to an IRA or SEP IRA for the previous tax year."

At this point, I'd be leaning in, pen in hand.

"Okay... so how much can I contribute?"

"That depends," she'd explain. "The maximum contribution amount changes each year. If you have a SEP IRA, it's based on a percentage of your income. But let's say, for example, your income is $50,000 and the max you can contribute is $10,000. If you put in the full amount, that drops your taxable income to $40,000."

I'd pause, doing the math.

"And that could move me into a lower tax bracket?"

"Exactly," she'd say. "It could lower the amount of tax you owe *and* help you build long-term savings. It's a win-win."

Then she'd give me the step-by-step:

1. Tell your accountant how much you want to contribute.
2. They'll include that amount on your return.
3. Then you actually have until April 15th to make the deposit into your IRA or SEP IRA account.

Then, she'd gently remind me that if you say you're going to contribute and then don't, the IRS can penalize you. So don't claim it unless you really follow through.

All of this would have been productive, accurate, and useful advice to receive in my moment of panic. It would have changed the way I viewed the entire situation.

But more than that?

It would have changed the way I viewed myself as a leader. I would have felt empowered, not defeated. In the driver's seat, not just along for the ride.

That's the conversation I wish I'd had right after I opened that email and saw the $10,000 tax bill.

Here's my point in sharing this little story: you may have more options than you think if you have someone knowledgeable in your corner.

Ask the right questions. Stay calm. And yes, consider using an accountant. They can save you a great deal of heartache and worry. And for a business owner, peace of mind is often more valuable than gold.

So, what's it like to work with a pro?

The Pro Route: Strategic, Streamlined, and Sanity-Saving

Now let's talk about hiring a professional:

- 1–2 hours max to prep your documents (less if your Accountant gives you a checklist).
- 1 hour or less to answer questions, review the return, and sign.
- Confidence that your taxes are done right the first time, with every deduction optimized and no surprises waiting for you in the mail.
- Audit protection—a good tax pro will back up their work if questions come up.
- And the kicker? Their fee is typically tax-deductible next year.

You're not just buying a service. You're buying peace of mind.

You're reclaiming hours of your life. And you're investing in a long-term relationship with someone who sees the full picture of your business—and helps you plan accordingly.

You Get to Decide

There's no judgment here. If you love a good spreadsheet and feel empowered doing it yourself, great. If you'd rather delegate and free up your brain for higher-level strategy, also great.

But here's the truth: this isn't just about filing a form. It's about how you want to feel running your business.

Do you want to spend your energy worrying about line items and tax code? Or do you want to operate in your zone of genius and let a pro handle the rest?

At the end of the day, it's just a decision. One isn't right or wrong. It just depends on what kind of CEO you want to be.

But my two cents?

Proactive tax management protects both your profits and your peace of mind. When you plan ahead, you minimize liabilities, maximize deductions, and avoid the last-minute scramble that turns tax season into a crisis.

The best approach?

Collaborate with a tax professional who works closely with your bookkeeper. Together, they can help you build a smart, strategic tax plan that keeps you compliant and confident while ensuring you take full advantage of every benefit the tax code allows.

Tax Prep Checklist: DIY or Hiring a Pro?

No matter which path you choose, starting with the right prep makes everything smoother. Here's what you'll need:

Business Info
- EIN (Employer Identification Number) or Social Security Number (for sole proprietors)
- Legal business name and structure (LLC, S-Corp, Sole Prop, etc.)
- State and local tax IDs (if applicable)

Income Records
- All 1099-NEC or 1099-K forms
- Client payment reports (Stripe, PayPal, Square, etc.)
- Invoices and proof of income received outside platforms
- Interest income (1099-INT if applicable)

Expense Records
- Profit and loss statement (from bookkeeping software or spreadsheet)
- Receipts for major purchases and recurring expenses
- Home office expenses (square footage and total home size, utility bills, rent/mortgage)
- Business travel records (mileage log, airfare, hotel receipts)
- Meals and entertainment with business purpose documented
- Equipment and technology purchases
- Subscriptions and software tools

Tax Payments
- Quarterly estimated tax payment records (Form 1040-ES or confirmation receipts)
- Prior year's tax return (helpful for comparison)

Additional Considerations
- Retirement contributions (IRA, SEP IRA, Solo 401k)
- Health insurance premiums (if self-employed)
- HSA contributions

- Charitable contributions (if you itemize)
- Any pandemic relief (EIDL, PPP forgiveness, etc.)

If You're Hiring a Pro:

- Ask for a **prep checklist** (many provide this so use it!)
- Schedule your appointment early
- Bring questions about deductions, retirement, or upcoming financial goals

If You're DIY-ing:

- Block off at least 3 focused hours with no distractions
- Use IRS.gov for deduction rules (not social media)
- Double-check your numbers before filing
- Print or save a full copy of your return + confirmations

Final tip: Whether DIY or pro, keep your digital and paper records for at least **3 years**. Audits can go back that far, and organized records = peace of mind.

One Final Note: Ask the Right Questions (Because Your Tax Pro Should Too)

Here's something I wish more people knew: not all tax professionals ask the right questions. And sometimes, it costs you.

For example, I once told my tax firm that my phone bill was $2,500 *after* adjusting it to reflect only the business portion. But they didn't ask—they just assumed it was the full amount and reduced it again. That's a huge miss. What they didn't know (because they didn't ask) was that I'd already done the math.

Moral of the story?

Your tax preparer should talk to you. They should ask real questions, get to know your business, and not just plug numbers into a form. A collaborative relationship with your accountant, EA, or financial manager ensures that deductions are done right and that you're not leaving money on the table due to assumptions or miscommunication.

Think Carefully Before You DIY
(Unless You Truly Love Stress)

If you're still wondering if you should do your own taxes, my gentle (but firm) recommendation is that you don't.

The truth is, a good tax professional doesn't just fill out forms. They become part of your financial team. They help you uncover savings, stay compliant, and avoid stress. Yes, hiring them is a business expense, but it's also a tax-deductible investment in peace of mind.

You know what else is tax-deductible? Professional development. So, if you work with a business coach to shift your mindset, set goals, and move from vision to impact. Yep, that's a write-off. Hire a bookkeeper? Also, a write-off. And the purchase of this absolutely fantastic book, you are now holding in your hands? You guessed it! A write-off.

And the value of the time, confidence, and clarity they all bring to your life?

Absolutely priceless.

Section 7: CEO Thought Leadership on Retirement Planning—A Tax Strategy Superpower

If there's one financial tool that consistently gets overlooked by business owners—especially in the early years—it's retirement planning. But here's the truth: saving for retirement isn't just responsible, it's *strategic*. Done right, it becomes one of the most effective ways to reduce your tax burden today while building wealth for tomorrow.

You're not just putting money away for later. You're lowering your taxable income right now. Think of it like being your own employer match. Every dollar you contribute to a Traditional IRA, SEP IRA, or Solo 401(k) works double duty: it grows your future nest egg and reduces what you owe the IRS this year. It's a win-win.

Still think you "can't afford" to save for retirement? Let's reframe that. If you put just $60 a month into an IRA, you could reduce your annual taxes by about $250 and grow your retirement savings by

$720. That's not an expense. That's a strategic financial move. That's *leverage*.

Retirement Isn't Just for Later—It's a Smart Choice Today

I hear this all the time: "I'm embarrassed. I know I should be saving for retirement, but I just don't have the money."

Let's reframe that.

Imagine you're a W-2 employee. Most employers match your 401(k) contributions up to a certain percentage. It would feel foolish to leave that free money on the table, right? Let's say your paycheck is $1,000, and you contribute 3%. That's $30. If your employer matches it, you now have $60 going into retirement every payday. Over a year, that's $720 in *free* money.

Now, imagine you're the business owner. You can be your own match. Even setting aside $60 a month into an IRA doesn't just build your future — it can save you about $250 in taxes this year. That's nearly $1,000 gained between tax savings and retirement growth.

The best part?

You're doing it intentionally. You're choosing your outcome. Every decision comes with consequences, and when it comes to finances, you have the power to shape those outcomes.

Don't Forget the Deadline:

Remember, many retirement contributions, like IRAs and SEP IRAs, can be made up until April 15 for the *previous* tax year. So even if you're filing in March, you still have time to make a last-minute contribution that could lower your tax bill *and* potentially drop you into a lower tax bracket. Consult with your accountant *before* submitting.

Bonus Power Play: HSAs as a Retirement Vehicle

Another smart, often-overlooked retirement strategy? Health Savings Accounts (HSAs). These are not just for paying current medical expenses. They're one of the most tax-advantaged accounts available.

Here's why:

- **Triple tax benefit:**
  1. Contributions are tax-deductible.
  2. Growth is tax-free.
  3. Withdrawals are tax-free when used for qualified medical expenses.

After age 65, you can withdraw funds from an HSA for *any purpose* without penalty (though you will pay regular income tax if not used for medical expenses—making it act like a traditional IRA in retirement).

If you have a high-deductible health plan (HDHP), you may be eligible to contribute up to $4,150 per year (individual) or $8,300 (family) in 2025, with an additional $1,000 catch-up for those over 55. That's a huge opportunity to lower your taxable income *and* prepare for future healthcare costs, which, let's be honest, are often one of the biggest retirement expenses.

The Retirement Strategy Mindset

Don't think of retirement planning as something you "should" do someday. Think of it as part of your CEO strategy and something you "get to do" now. It's not about age. It's about being *wise*. Every dollar you save today helps create financial freedom, flexibility, and options down the road.

Even modest contributions add up, especially when they're part of a larger financial strategy that includes tax planning, business growth, and wealth building. Retirement accounts aren't just for later. They're for *leaders* and they work best when you start now.

Section 8: Call to Action: Choose Your Tax Journey

Every financial decision has a consequence. But here's the truth: when you know better, you do better.

Taxes aren't scary when you're prepared. They're not punishment. They're proof of profit. They're not theft. They're the price of success. If you're paying taxes, you're making money. And that's something to be proud of.

Taxes often feel like a burden, but in reality, they're a reflection of financial growth. The more your business earns, the more you'll owe, and that's not a sign of failure. It's a sign that what you're building is working.

Taxes are not the enemy. Confusion is. Avoidance is. Procrastination is.

When you shift your mindset from fear to strategy, everything changes. You stop scrambling in April and start planning in August. You stop asking, "How much will I owe?" and start asking, "How can I make every dollar work harder for me?"

That's the power of financial maturity.

You don't have to become a tax expert. But you *do* need to get organized. Track your expenses properly. Ask the right questions. Hire smart help. Build systems that work even when you're tired or busy.

The most successful entrepreneurs don't just pay taxes. They plan for them.

You have new tools. A new mindset. A new level of awareness. That means you're ready to make a different decision. So ask yourself: *"What happens six months from now if I do nothing?"* If the answer is fear, debt, or more of the same, then it's time to do something different.

Choose clarity over chaos.

Choose structure over stress.

Choose to lead your business financially, strategically, and intentionally.

So what's your next right step?

What can you do right now to change how taxes feel for you next year?

Maybe it's scheduling that tax planning call.

Maybe it's opening your books.

Maybe it's simply saving this chapter as a reminder that you're not behind — you're building.

Just don't wait. Your future self and those that your business serves will thank you.

———————

Top 5 Takeaways from Chapter 7: Taxes

1. Taxes Are a Strategic Tool, Not a Burden

Taxes aren't something to fear—they're a sign of business growth. When approached with clarity and planning, taxes can help you build wealth, fund retirement, and reinvest in your business. Reframe your mindset from avoidance to empowerment.

2. Know Your Numbers and Plan Proactively

Accurate bookkeeping and regular financial reviews are essential. Don't wait until tax season to scramble. Tracking income, deductions, and liabilities year-round helps you avoid surprises and make confident, informed decisions.

3. File Like a CEO—Not a Side Hustler

Treat your business like a business. Set aside money for taxes, file quarterly if needed, and work with professionals who understand your goals. Proactive filing shows you're leading, not reacting—and that mindset shift changes everything.

4. Smart Deductions Save Real Money

Use the IRS's 3-part test: is it ordinary, necessary, and primarily for business? Don't "burn dollars to save cents." Strategic spending and clean documentation are how you legally reduce your tax bill and sleep well at night.

5. Professional Help Is an Investment, Not an Expense

Trying to DIY your taxes can cost you in mistakes, missed opportunities, and time. Hiring a bookkeeper or CPA who asks the right questions, understands your industry, and helps you build a long-term tax strategy is often the smartest financial move you can make.

Chapter 8:
Bookkeeping, Accounting, and the Profit Strategist: Building the Backbone of Business Clarity

Section 1: The Truth About Financial Clarity

Let me share with you a time I planned one of the boldest solo trips I've ever taken with Zeus, my incredibly badass motorcycle.

I had been dreaming about this trip for months—a solo ride on Zeus, my motorcycle, through the Badlands, ending with the legendary Needles Highway in South Dakota.

If you're not familiar, Needles Highway is one of the most iconic rides in the country. It winds through jagged granite spires, sharp switchbacks, and tunnels literally blasted through the rock. It's technical. It's stunning. And it demands your full attention.

I was so excited! I tuned my bike, checked the tires, and began to plan what to pack in my saddlebags.

But as I looked at the map to plan the finer details of my route, something hit me: This wasn't just a joyride. There was a reason they called it the Badlands and Needles Highway (think threading a needle). This ride required strategy.

I needed to know:

- When I'd hit the curviest terrain.
- Where the gas stations were (because there aren't many out there).
- How to navigate single-lane tunnels, angled roads, wildlife, and blind turns safely.
- How to prepare for the scorchingly hot weather and keep myself and my bike from overheating.
- And what to do if the weather turned, the fog rolled in, or the road conditions changed.
- And, of course, who to notify in case of an emergency.

A bike, no matter how powerful, is only as good as the rider's awareness, the route, and the ability to respond in real-time.

And that's when it clicked:

Running a business without financial clarity is like riding Needles Highway with no map, no mirrors, and no fuel gauge.

I may get by for a while, but I needed to prepare in order to be successful. The same is true in business.

I realized that when the turns get tight and the road gets long—and they always do—I would regret not having planned ahead. So I did. I planned the trip down to the last detail.

And although it wasn't without its expected challenges (this wasn't supposed to be easy, after all), my trip was one for my record books!

The Trifecta That Keeps You Upright

Every rider knows you don't go into a ride like that without the necessary tools. In business, those tools necessary tools are:

1. **Bookkeeping**—This is your fuel gauge. Your day-to-day tracking system. An accountant tells you how much gas is in the tank, what you've spent, and how far you can go. Without it, you run out of gas on the side of the road. (*Side note:* this actually happened to me once while I was on my bike and ended up paying $20 to a nearby farmer who gave me a very small and dirty-looking gas can with a small amount of very old gasoline. I apologized to Zeus as I poured it into his tank, but that little amount of old and very, very expensive fuel did get us to the next gas station. Don't let that story be you with not having a bookkeeper on board as fuel in the tank.)

2. **Accounting**—This is your dashboard and rear view mirror. An accountant gives you visibility, speed, direction, and performance metrics. It helps you respond to what's happening now and assess what just happened behind you.

3. **Profit Strategist**—This is your route plan, your weather check, and your GPS all in one. A profit strategist guides your choices and answers questions like, Is *now the right time to accelerate? Do I need to stop and refuel? What's the smartest path forward?*

Bookkeeping keeps you fueled.

Accounting keeps you from getting pulled over by the police.

Strategy keeps you safe and on course.

It's not about perfection. It's about preparedness.

And just like that ride, **running your business isn't about going fast—it's about riding smart.**

The Truth About Financial Clarity

Most business owners never hear this part: Financial clarity isn't waiting for you at the top of some revenue mountain. It's not a reward for success. It's something you build right now. It begins with habits, with systems, and with the small, consistent decisions you make every day.

Clarity isn't a byproduct of growth—it's a product of intentional systems.

Bookkeeping provides the *raw data* with every invoice, every expense, and every transaction.

Accounting steps in to *organize that data into meaningful insights,* helping you understand where your money went and what it's trying to tell you.

And financial strategy takes those insights and turns them into action so you can *make smarter decisions,* avoid costly detours, and steer your business toward sustainable growth.

Together, these three roles form the backbone of any strong business. Without even one of them, the whole system starts to wobble.

In the pages ahead, we're not just going to talk about spreadsheets and systems.

We're going to talk about:
- Who belongs on your financial support team,
- What you really need to track (and what you can let go),
- And how to stop riding blind and start leading with clarity.

You don't need a finance degree or a complicated accounting setup to run a successful business, but you do need clarity, structure, and the right support systems working together.

In the next section, we're not just going to introduce your financial team, we're going to break down their individual roles and show you how they work together to form the trifecta of business financials: bookkeeping, accounting, and financial strategy.

When aligned, these three create the stability and clarity every business needs to move forward with confidence.

Section 2: Who's Who in Your Financial World— Bookkeeper, Accountant, and Profit Strategist

You don't need titles. You need the right support.

If you're like most business owners, you didn't start your business to become a finance expert. But whether you're building a brand, selling a service, or scaling a team, your business lives and dies by your ability to make good financial decisions.

That's why clarity doesn't come from doing it all yourself. It comes from assembling the right team of people who understand your numbers, help you interpret them, and support you in using them well.

This section is about introducing your financial dream team: the bookkeeper, the accountant, and the profit strategist. Each one plays a distinct role. Together, they form the trifecta that keeps your business legally compliant, financially stable, and strategically positioned for growth.

Let's break them down and help you recognize who's already in place and who you might want to add.

The Bookkeeper: Your Daily Discipline

Bookkeeping is the backbone of your financial operations. It's the daily or weekly practice of tracking income, recording expenses, and keeping your financial systems organized. It's not glamorous, but it is essential.

Without accurate bookkeeping, you can't trust your reports, file your taxes correctly, or make informed decisions. It's like trying to drive a car without knowing how much gas is in the tank; you might make it to your destination, but it's going to be stressful.

What a Bookkeeper Does:
- Tracks every transaction
- Categorizes income and expenses
- Reconciles accounts regularly
- Maintains clean, current records

Why It Matters:
- You pay less in taxes by tracking deductible expenses
- Tax season becomes painless instead of panic-inducing

- You can actually *see* what's working in your business

Enter the Brigitte the Bookkeeper Archetype

Brigitte is the kind of bookkeeper every business owner dreams of hiring. She's steady, trustworthy, and just detailed enough to make magic happen behind the scenes. She doesn't just "do your books", she brings calm to the chaos.

Brigitte reconciles your accounts before you even remember it's month-end. She spots errors, tracks down receipts, and keeps everything buttoned up so you can focus on running your business. She doesn't give financial advice, but she makes sure your data is clean and your records are reliable and ready for you to use and understand so you can make business decisions from a solid financial viewpoint..

Brigitte doesn't make your decisions—she makes your decisions possible.

Do You Have a Brigitte?
- Are your books up to date every month?
- Can you pull a clean Profit & Loss report on demand?
- Are your business expenses consistently categorized?
- Is someone regularly reconciling your bank and credit card accounts?
- Are your personal and business finances completely separated?

If you answered "no" to most of these, it's time to find your Brigitte. Financial clarity starts here.

Good and timely bookkeeping is the foundation of financial wealth

as a business owner. If you want long-term success, you can't skip this step. Clean books create clear decisions, and that's where financial growth begins. — *Doreen M. Letofsky*

The Accountant: Your Compliance Partner

An accountant makes sure your business plays by the rules. Their primary role is filing taxes, ensuring compliance, and helping you avoid penalties or costly mistakes.

While some accountants offer basic advice, most are focused on what has already happened. Their job isn't to help you grow; it's to make sure you report everything properly and legally.

What an Accountant Does:
- Files your business and personal taxes
- Helps with estimated tax payments
- Prepares tax documents and responds to IRS inquiries
- Ensures your business is compliant with current tax laws

Enter the Frank the Accountant Archetype

Frank is dependable, detail-focused, and maybe a little dry, but that's what you want when dealing with the IRS. He knows how to get the numbers right. He doesn't do fluff. He doesn't do futurecasting. But when it's time to file, Frank has your back.

He's the one who knows if your LLC should be taxed as an S-Corp. He reminds you when your quarterly taxes are due. He keeps you out of trouble.

Just don't ask Frank for pricing strategy or financial forecasting. He'll politely tell you, "That's not my role."

Frank keeps you legal—not visionary. And that's okay. You need both.

Do You Have a Frank?
- Do you have an accountant or tax professional who files your business taxes?
- Do you know what you owe in quarterly taxes, and are you paying it?
- Do you feel confident that your business is compliant with federal and state requirements?
- Do you have someone to call if you get a tax notice or audit letter?

If not, don't wait until April. Now's the time to get your Frank in place.

The Profit Strategist: Your Forward-Facing Guide

This is the person most small businesses don't realize they need until they're overwhelmed or stuck.

A Profit Strategist bridges the gap between your numbers and your next move. They help you make decisions about hiring, investing, pricing, and scaling. They analyze trends, interpret your reports, and help you understand the bigger picture.

They're not your bookkeeper. They're not your tax preparer. They're your thought partner—the one who helps you plan, prioritize, and grow with intention.

What a Profit Strategist Does:
- Reviews your numbers for patterns and insight
- Creates forecasts and cash flow plans
- Evaluates your pricing and profit margins
- Guides financial decision-making based on goals
- Aligns your financial structure with your growth strategy

Enter the Vanessa the Profit Strategist Archetype

Vanessa is curious, thoughtful, and strategic. She's not afraid to challenge your thinking or to ask, "Why are you still offering that service that barely makes a profit?"

Vanessa helps you prepare for your future by using your past and present data wisely. She turns overwhelming reports into simple, smart decisions. She gives you confidence, not just in your numbers, but in your leadership.

Vanessa helps you stop guessing and start leading with clarity.

Do You Have a Vanessa?

- Do you review your numbers regularly with someone who helps you make decisions?
- Do you have a financial forecast or plan for the next quarter or year?
- Do you understand your margins, cash flow, and best-performing offers?
- Is someone helping you align your financial structure with your goals?

- Are you making financial decisions proactively — not just reactively?

If not, it may be time to bring Vanessa in. She doesn't just make sense of your numbers—she helps you use them to move forward.

Why You Need All Three: Brigitte, Frank, and Vanessa

These roles are not interchangeable, but when they work together, they create the financial clarity, structure, and insight your business needs to grow.

Here's a helpful summary of all three roles:

Table 8.1: Bookkeeper, Accountant, and Profit Strategist Comparison Chart

Role	What They Do	Example of What They Do	What They Don't Do
Bookkeeper: Records	Tracks income and expenses, reconciles accounts, and categorizes transactions	Records a $3,000 expense.	They don't offer financial strategy or file taxes
Accountant: Interprets	Files taxes, ensures compliance, handles documentation	Classifies the expense, helps with tax deduction.	They don't provide business growth advice
Profit Strategist: Strategic Planning	Interprets numbers, forecasts, and advises on growth	Asks: Should you have made that expense? What ROI did it generate? Can we shift that money for better outcomes next time?	They don't do daily bookkeeping or tax filing

Brigitte grounds you. Frank protects you. Vanessa helps you grow.

Together, your bookkeeper, your accountant, and your profit strategist provide you with clarity, confidence, and control.

Section 3: The Bookkeeper—Your Daily Discipline

If you don't track it, you can't change it.

You cannot lead your business with confidence if you don't know your numbers. And you cannot know your numbers if you don't have consistent, accurate bookkeeping. Bookkeeping is not just a task to check off your list or something you delegate at tax time. It's a daily, weekly, and monthly discipline that keeps your business upright. Without it, you're not steering, you're only guessing. And guessing is not a growth strategy.

Bookkeeping is the ongoing, detailed process of recording a business's financial activity. That includes every invoice sent, every dollar received, every expense paid, and every bank transaction cleared. It may sound tedious, and sometimes it is. But it's the foundation of everything else—your strategy, your profitability, and your ability to sleep at night all begin with this discipline.

When bookkeeping is neglected, the consequences ripple across your business. You miss deductions. You get surprised by tax bills. You make decisions based on faulty assumptions or outdated data. And worst of all, you carry the constant weight of financial anxiety, wondering what you've missed or whether you're really okay.

You've probably heard business owners celebrate revenue milestones: "We hit six figures!" "We made half a million this year!" But here's the truth that no one tells you: none of that matters if the bottom line is negative. I've seen business owners pull in incredible revenue on paper, yet they can't pay themselves. Their cash flow is a mess. Their expenses are out of control. Financial chaos doesn't go away when revenue increases. It usually grows with it.

That's because financial success isn't about how much money you make. It's about what you keep. **It's about what you control.**

And the only way to know what you're truly keeping is to track everything. If you don't track it, you can't change it.

5 Common Bookkeeping Mistakes to Avoid

Respecting your numbers means paying attention, staying organized, and avoiding costly mistakes that can derail your progress. Here are five of the most common bookkeeping missteps, and how to fix them before they become major problems.

1. Mixing Business and Personal Finances

This is one of the most damaging habits out there. Swiping your business card at the grocery store or paying for dinner with your personal account "just this once" might seem harmless, but over time, it creates a tangled mess that's hard to unravel.

When you mix personal and business finances, you:
- Complicate your tax deductions
- Risk triggering an audit
- Lose sight of your actual profitability
- Undermine your business's legitimacy

Fix it: Open separate business checking and savings accounts. Get a business credit card (even if it's just a low-limit starter). Keep every transaction aligned with its proper account. Your future self—and your accountant—will thank you.

2. Waiting Until Tax Season to Catch Up

If you've ever found yourself in a spreadsheet panic in late March, you're not alone. Many business owners treat bookkeeping like something they'll "get to later." But the longer you wait, the messier it gets.

Rushed bookkeeping means:
- Missed write-offs
- Incorrect data
- Higher tax bills
- Elevated stress levels

Fix it: Bookkeeping should be a habit, not a seasonal scramble. Schedule a weekly "money date" with yourself to reconcile transactions, review expenses, and update your records. It doesn't have to take hours, but it does have to happen regularly.

3. Ignoring Expense Categories

Categorization matters more than most people realize. When your expenses aren't properly sorted, you can't generate accurate reports, track spending trends, or maximize deductions.

For example, lumping software, advertising, and office supplies all under "miscellaneous" gives you no insight into how your money is actually being used.

Fix it: Use consistent, meaningful categories that align with your financial reports and tax strategy. Most accounting software will let you customize these, but consistency is key. If you're not sure how to categorize something, ask your bookkeeper or accountant early on.

4. Skipping Account Reconciliation

If you've never reconciled your bank statements, you're likely working with incomplete or incorrect data. Reconciliation is the process of comparing your bookkeeping records to your actual bank and credit card statements to catch discrepancies, missed entries, or duplicate transactions.

Skipping this step can lead to:
- Misreported income or expenses
- Overstated revenue
- Undetected fraud or errors
- Mismatched tax filings

Fix it: Reconcile every account monthly. It's not glamorous, but it ensures your numbers reflect reality, not wishful thinking. Think of it as the quality control step in your financial process.

5. DIY-ing Too Long

There's nothing wrong with doing your own books in the beginning. It can save money and help you stay connected to your finances. But at some point, DIY becomes a bottleneck.

If you're:
- Spending hours on tasks that take a pro minutes
- Falling behind every month
- Second-guessing your numbers
- Avoiding your finances altogether

...it might be time to pass the baton.

Fix it: Hire a bookkeeper before your systems fall apart. A good bookkeeper will not only keep your records up to date but will also help you spot trends, catch issues early, and reduce your tax burden. You don't have to go it alone...and you shouldn't.

Tip: Most business owners think they need an accountant, but what they actually need first is a great bookkeeper. If your books are a mess, your accountant can't help you. They work with the information you provide, and if that information is incomplete or incorrect, their advice is worthless.

> **66**
>
> ### *You Can Delegate Tasks, But Not Responsibility*
>
> *Hiring a bookkeeper doesn't mean a business owner can relinquish financial knowledge.* You still need a high-level understanding of what you own, what you owe, what's coming in, and what's going out. You don't need to know every detail but you do need to stay engaged. Because informed leadership is what keeps a business strong. — Jennifer *"JJ" Jank*
>
> **99**

Respect First, Mastery Second

You don't need to become a bookkeeping expert. However, you must respect your numbers enough to build effective systems, avoid costly mistakes, and bring in the right help at the right time. Financial clarity doesn't start with spreadsheets. It starts with intention. And this is one of the smartest places to start.

Bookkeeping isn't a chore. It's a commitment.

But bookkeeping is only powerful when it becomes a habit. Too many business owners treat it like a quarterly or annual task and avoid it until they absolutely have to deal with it. But good bookkeeping is more like brushing your teeth. It's not glamorous, but it prevents bigger problems. You don't wait until you have a cavity to start brushing. You do it regularly because it keeps everything healthy.

Here's a rhythm to aim for:

- **Daily** - Record new sales or payments, upload receipts, and review any recent charges.
- **Weekly** - reconcile your bank accounts, review outstanding invoices, and categorize new transactions.

- **Monthly** - run and review your Profit & Loss report and Balance Sheet, look for spending trends, and flag anything that seems off.

These steps take minutes, not hours and they save you from weeks of stress later.

You owe it to yourself, to your business, and to your vision for the future.

Three Reasons Why Bookkeeping is Essential

As is now (hopefully) crystal clear, bookkeeping is the quiet powerhouse behind every financially sound business. While it may not be glamorous, it is essential, and when done right, it keeps your entire financial system upright. Below are three primary reasons bookkeeping should never be ignored.

1. You Will Pay Less in Taxes

The biggest reason entrepreneurs overpay in taxes isn't a lack of revenue. It's poor bookkeeping. If you don't properly track your business expenses, you're missing out on legal deductions. And if you're mixing personal and business finances, you're setting off red flags with the IRS. Clean, categorized records help you minimize your tax burden without fear or guesswork. Good bookkeeping protects your wallet and your peace of mind.

2. They Will Make Filing Taxes Less Painful

If you dread tax season, chances are your books are out of date. Scrambling to pull together numbers in March is a symptom of bad financial habits for the rest of the year. But when your records are current and organized, tax time becomes straightforward. You hand your accountant a clean file, they take it from there, and you move on—no stress, no surprises.

3. You Will Understand Your Business and Make Better Decisions

Here's a truth most entrepreneurs miss: the real purpose of bookkeeping isn't just for taxes—it's for decision-making. Your books exist so you can see what's happening in your business financially. When you have that insight, you can make better choices. Without it, you're making decisions in the dark. And even good instincts can't replace solid financial data.

The Bottom Line Tells the Story

Want to know whether your business is really working?

Look at the bottom line.

Instead of focusing on revenue or top-line sales, you should focus on your net income.

It's easy to brag about making $500,000 a year, but if your expenses are $520,000, you're in the red. *That's why it's not about what you earn. It's about what you keep.*

Bookkeeping gives you the truth behind the numbers, not just what's sitting in your bank account today, but what's really happening in the bigger picture. That clarity helps you make confident moves instead of costly assumptions.

Section 4: The Accountant—A Strategic Advantage

What Is Accounting?

Accounting is more than just tax prep and spreadsheets. It's the process that helps you understand how your business is performing, where your profits are coming from, and what's costing you more than it should. While bookkeeping captures the data, accounting is about turning that data into meaningful insights. It involves analyzing, interpreting, and reporting financial information in a way that supports smarter business decisions.

With accurate accounting, you get visibility into your financial health. You understand how much you're really earning, what it costs to operate, and how to evaluate financial decisions with logic instead of gut instinct.

The Difference Between Bookkeeping and Accounting

It's easy to confuse the two, but bookkeeping and accounting serve distinct functions. Bookkeeping is the act of recording transactions—tracking income, expenses, and maintaining orderly records. It's about precision and process.

Accounting takes that information and translates it into something useful. Think of it like this: bookkeeping is gathering the ingredients; accounting is cooking the meal. Without good bookkeeping, accounting can't function. Without accounting, bookkeeping has no context.

When combined, these two disciplines give you a comprehensive financial picture and prepare you to make sound business decisions.

What Does a Good Accountant Actually Do?

Many business owners think of an accountant as someone who swoops in at tax time. But the truth is, a skilled accountant is a partner throughout the year, not just in April.

Here's what a good accountant actually does:
- Produces essential financial reports (Profit & Loss, Balance Sheet, Cash Flow).
- Analyzes spending and revenue trends to help you plan ahead.
- Identifies tax-saving opportunities throughout the year
- Offers insight into the financial viability of decisions like expanding services or making new hires.
- Ensures compliance with local, state, and federal tax laws and reporting deadlines.

Most importantly, they interpret your financial records in a way that empowers you to act with clarity, not confusion. They don't just give you numbers; they explain what those numbers mean in real terms.

The Strategic Role of Accounting

The strategic role of accounting goes far beyond filing taxes. When used intentionally, accounting becomes a powerful tool for preparing your business to grow and thrive. It shifts you out of guesswork and into informed, confident decision-making.

Strategic accounting gives you visibility into where your money is truly going. It uncovers your actual profit margins and helps you identify which areas of your business are producing strong returns and which ones are quietly draining your resources. It also helps you understand the right timing for big decisions like making investments, hiring new team members, or expanding your services.

Without solid accounting practices, it's easy to fall into the trap of celebrating top-line revenue while ignoring bottom-line realities. But when your accounting is clear and well-maintained, you gain the insight to improve profitability, reduce waste, and build a stronger financial foundation. It becomes the difference between reacting to problems and proactively steering your business toward long-term success.

When to Bring in an Accountant

It's tempting to think you can DIY your accounting forever, especially in the early stages. But as your business grows, complexity increases. Multiple revenue streams, payroll, contractors, or changing tax laws are all reasons to call in professional support.

You should consider hiring an accountant when:
- Your revenue nears or exceeds $100K annually.
- You manage inventory, employees, or subcontractors.
- You're preparing for funding, investment, or business loans.
- You feel lost or overwhelmed interpreting financial reports.
- You want to optimize taxes year-round, not just in March.

Bringing in an accountant doesn't mean you're not smart. It means **you're smart enough t**o focus on what you do best and delegate the rest to experts.

How to Find a Great Accountant

A great accountant is more than a tax preparer—they're an interpreter, an advisor, and a steady presence during both growth and tough seasons.

Look for:
- Experience with small businesses or your specific industry.
- Someone who communicates clearly and without jargon.
- A partner who values ongoing support, not just annual filings.
- An actual accountant, if possible, but practical experience matters more than letters.
- Solid referrals or reviews from other entrepreneurs.

Ask potential accountants, "How will you help me make better decisions?" The right one will talk about collaboration, not just compliance.

Accounting Is a Business Growth Tool

Accounting isn't just about keeping your books clean or staying out of IRS trouble. It's how you understand your business, identify opportunities, and prepare to grow.

The business owners who succeed long term aren't just lucky, they're informed. And that begins with treating accounting as a strategic tool, not a necessary evil.

Section 5: The Profit Strategist–Turning Numbers Into Decisions

What Is a Profit Strategist?

A Profit Strategist is not a bookkeeper, and they're not your accountant. They're your guide—the person who helps you take all the data from your books and reports and turn it into clear, aligned decisions. If bookkeeping is about tracking and accounting is about interpreting, financial strategy is about applying.

This is where you ask, "What should I do next?" and get an answer that fits your goals, your business model, and your unique stage of growth.

A strategist sees the big picture. They know the numbers, yes — but more importantly, they understand *you*. Your ambitions, your risk tolerance, your values. They help you align your financial decisions with the life and business you're building.

What a Profit Strategist Actually Does

While titles may vary—consultant, advisor, strategist—the core function remains the same: a Profit Strategist is there to guide you from where you are to where you want to be, using data-backed decisions to pave the way.

They don't just look at what has happened; they help you chart a confident path forward. A strategist can help you clarify your business model by asking questions like, Are you priced for profit? Do your offers align with your income goals?

They support revenue forecasting—mapped out how much you need to sell to hit your targets and when that income will actually hit your account. They help with expense planning, showing you when it's smart to hire or where you can trim costs without stalling growth.

A strategist also helps design a reliable owner pay strategy, ensuring you can pay yourself consistently even when revenue ebbs and flows. And perhaps most importantly, they offer guidance for turning short-term business income into long-term personal wealth.

A Profit Strategist's work isn't just about spreadsheets—it's about clarity, alignment, and building a business that actually supports the life you want.

Why Most Business Owners Need a Profit Strategist

Here's the honest truth: most business owners are making decisions based on gut feelings, bank account balances, or whatever feels urgent. That might work when you're just getting started, but it quickly leads to burnout, blind spots, and bad decisions as your business grows.

A Profit Strategist helps you:
- **Plan ahead** instead of reacting in the moment.
- **Forecast growth**, rather than just chasing revenue.
- **Align money decisions** with long-term goals.
- **Navigate complexity** such as hiring, pricing, or major investments.
- **Build wealth**, not just income.

They're the missing piece for most small business owners, especially those in the messy middle who are earning decent money, but unsure how to make it work for them.

The strategist helps you zoom out. They assess your goals, resources, and trajectory to help you determine the best course of action. They don't just look at the last quarter; they plan for the year ahead.

When to Bring in a Profit Strategist

While every business is different, here are some strong signs you need strategic support:

- You're making more money but feeling less in control.
- You aren't sure how much to pay yourself or when.
- You've hit a revenue plateau and don't know how to grow next.
- You're making a good income, but can't explain your cash flow.
- You're tired of feast-and-famine cycles.
- You need help prioritizing investments (team, software, marketing).
- You're ready to build wealth, not just chase income.
- If you've outgrown gut-based decision-making, you're ready for strategy.

How to Find the Right Profit Strategist

Unlike accountants, there's no one-size-fits-all certification for strategists, so choosing the right one requires discernment.

Here's what to look for:

- Experience working with entrepreneurs or service-based businesses.
- Someone who asks about your goals and vision, not just your QuickBooks file.
- A person who can talk about money without judgment.
- Someone who understands both numbers and mindset.
- They should offer clear frameworks and strategic thinking, not just tactics.

Ask, "How do you help business owners make decisions?" Their answer will reveal whether they're truly strategic or just posing.

Referrals are gold. So are testimonials that mention clarity, partnership, and financial confidence.

Tying All Three Together to Give You (and Your Business) the Ride of Your Life

Bookkeeping, accounting, and financial strategy aren't just financial functions; they're the foundation of a healthy, scalable business. Each plays a distinct and essential role.

Bookkeeping is your daily discipline. It's where clarity begins. When you consistently track every transaction, categorize your expenses, and maintain clean records, you give your business structure and stability. You stop flying blind and start understanding what's happening in real time.

Accounting is the next level—it turns your raw data into meaning. A good accountant helps you interpret the numbers, understand patterns, and prepare for the road ahead. Accounting transforms chaos into clarity by showing you what's working, what isn't, and where your money is really going. It empowers you to make informed decisions, reduce risk, and strengthen profitability.

But it's **financial strategy** that truly puts you in the driver's seat. A strategist helps you forecast your revenue, align your pricing with your goals, and plan your growth intentionally. They connect the dots between your numbers and your next move. When you have a Profit Strategist on your team, you stop reacting and start leading. You no longer chase numbers blindly—you chart your path with purpose.

This is where real CEO confidence lives. Not in how much you make, but in how well you manage what you've built. Financial strategy helps you understand what you need to earn, what it costs to run your business, and how to get from here to there, without burning out. And no, you don't need a finance degree to do it. You just need the right support system—a bookkeeper, an accountant, and a strategist—to give you visibility, clarity, and control.

Financial Reports That Matter

When these three roles work together, they produce the most valuable tools in your business: financial reports. These aren't just documents to hand off at tax time—they're critical decision-making tools that every entrepreneur should understand.

- **Profit & Loss Statement (P&L):** This report tracks your income and expenses over a specific period and tells you whether your

business is operating at a profit or a loss. It offers a snapshot of
your operational health.

- **Balance Sheet:** A moment-in-time snapshot of what your business owns (assets), what it owes (liabilities), and what's left over (owner's equity). It's a clear picture of your financial position.
- **Cash Flow Statement:** This report shows how cash moves in and out of your business. It reveals if and when you'll have the funds you need to cover obligations, regardless of what your revenue says.

Understanding these reports isn't optional. It's essential. Together, they provide you with the financial clarity to make informed, timely decisions.

When you combine day-to-day organization (bookkeeping), strategic insight (accounting), and forward-thinking decision-making (financial strategy), you stop running your business by guesswork and start leading with intention. This trifecta forms the financial backbone of any successful, sustainable business.

That's not just control—its power. And it's yours to claim.

——————

Section 6: The 5 Financial Success Principles

Financial success isn't about guesswork—it's about systems. Each layer of your financial backbone plays a role: bookkeeping tracks the facts, accounting makes sense of the data, and your Profit Strategist turns it all into decisions.

These five principles work across each step, giving you the structure and mindset to lead with clarity.

Your mindset + your systems = financial leadership.

So, how do our five Financial Success Principles apply to financial success and systems?

1. Know What You Want

Vision translated into financial clarity.

Your future always begins with a vision, but vision alone isn't enough. That vision needs numbers behind it. Financial clarity is about defining what success looks like for your business and backing it with data you can trust.

What does financial clarity look like to you as a business owner? Is it being able to confidently check your numbers and pull reports at any time? Is it having a 90-day forecast so you can plan ahead instead of reacting to emergencies? Is it being able to sleep at night knowing where you stand?

When you define what clarity looks like, you know what to track. And when you know what to track, you know what to change.

Bookkeeping gives you the data. Accounting gives you the meaning. And strategy gives you the power to act. This is the first step to taking financial control—deciding where you're going and measuring every decision against that vision.

2. Know How Much It Costs

Every dollar matters—track each one.

Financial clarity isn't just about knowing how much you're earning. It's about knowing how much you're spending. Whether it's a $2 toll or a $20,000 investment in new equipment, every dollar that flows through your business should be accounted for. Small leaks sink big ships. Plug them early.

This is where bookkeeping shines. It's your first line of defense against waste and confusion. When your books are accurate and current, you gain a real-time view of what it actually costs to run your business day-to-day. Every tracked transaction contributes to a more complete and trustworthy financial picture. Without it, you're simply guessing.

But as we've learned throughout this chapter, tracking alone isn't enough. That's where accounting steps in—to make meaning from the data. Accounting takes your categorized transactions and uncovers the story they're telling. It highlights trends, flags inefficiencies, and helps you evaluate where your money is going and whether it's helping you grow.

You start asking bigger questions: Are you overspending on subscriptions? Is your cost of goods sold eating into your profit margin? Are your operational expenses aligned with your income?

Bookkeeping tracks the numbers. Accounting interprets them. And together, they reveal what your business truly costs to operate—and whether the return is worth the investment. Knowing your costs allows you to adjust, optimize, make smarter financial decisions, and stop leaving money on the table.

3. Know Your Numbers

Categorization is the bridge between chaos and clarity.

Tracking transactions is just the beginning—categorizing them accurately is what helps you truly understand and make meaning of your numbers. Using consistent and meaningful categories allows your accountant to produce essential financial reports like your Profit and Loss Statement, Balance Sheet, and Statement of Cash Flows.

These aren't just documents generated by your software—they're windows into the financial health of your business. They help you see where your money is going, what's profitable, and what's draining your resources. They help you get up close and personal with your numbers. They help you make meaning.

And what does meaning create? The ability to take action. When your numbers are clear, your decisions become smart, timely, and aligned with your goals. Because if you don't know your numbers, you don't truly know your business.

4. Act As If

Approach bookkeeping, accounting, and strategizing as non-negotiable habits.

If you want a business that runs like a high-performing machine, you have to operate like the kind of business owner who builds one. That means doing the unglamorous things consistently, like showing up for your finances.

This starts with creating routines: entering transactions, reviewing reports, and staying current. Maintaining the financial health of your business isn't something to catch up on quarterly or hand off once a year during tax season. It's a daily act of leadership. When you act like the CEO, you prioritize your financial operations with consistency and integrity.

Acting "as if" doesn't mean faking it—it means showing up today like the business owner you're becoming. When you make financial stewardship a core part of your operations, you put yourself in a position to seize opportunities, avoid costly surprises, and make bold, confident decisions that move your business forward.

5. Take Inspired Action

Pull in financial professionals to gain deeper insights.

There are no trophies for doing things the hard way. You don't earn bonus points for struggling through spreadsheets at midnight or trying to DIY your business finances out of sheer will. In fact, the longer you wait to get support, the more likely you are to miss key opportunities or, worse, make costly mistakes. Inspired action isn't about doing more; it's about doing what matters most and knowing when to hand off the rest.

As a business owner, your time is one of your most valuable resources. Your energy is best spent in your zone of genius: creating, leading, and growing your vision. Delegating your bookkeeping and accounting isn't a sign of weakness. It's a strategic move that clears your path forward. It frees up mental space while providing expert insights that you simply can't get from DIY tools and guesswork.

Inspired action means bringing in professionals not because you're incapable, but because it's not the best use of your brilliance. You built this business with purpose. Now it's time to build a support system around that purpose. Let a trusted financial pro take the numbers and turn them into strategy so you can lead with confidence, make informed decisions, and create the kind of business that not only grows but thrives.

Together, these 5 Financial Success Principles help you move from chaos to clarity by aligning your vision with actionable strategy, systems, and expert support.

Section 7: CEO Thought Leadership—How to Build a Financial Backbone

Any successful CEO will tell you the same thing: your business isn't scalable without structure. And that structure starts with your numbers.

Every high-performing business has a spine or a financial backbone that supports growth, absorbs impact, and stands tall through uncertainty. Without it, you're not running a business. You're running on adrenaline.

Your financial system is not a side project. It is your business infrastructure.

A backbone isn't decorative. It's functional. It protects, supports, and stabilizes. In business, your financial backbone is the system that connects profit, cash flow, forecasting, and decision-making into one aligned structure. When it's strong, everything else performs better.

Here's what building a financial backbone looks like in real terms:

1. Foundational Clarity: Clean, Consistent Bookkeeping

It doesn't matter how big your vision is if your books are a mess. Start with financial hygiene:
- Set up a proper chart of accounts
- Separate business and personal expenses
- Track income and expenses weekly, not when taxes are due

This isn't administration. It's strategy. Accurate books aren't just for the IRS—they're how you measure momentum.

2. Strategic Oversight: Monthly P&L and Cash Flow Reviews

The most successful CEOs don't ask, "How much is in the bank?" They ask:
- Are we operating inside our margins?
- Is revenue growing in the right areas?
- Are expenses aligned with strategy?

Set a monthly rhythm to review Profit & Loss statements, cash flow forecasts, and burn rate. Your numbers are feedback. Use them.

3. Forecasting: Don't Budget—Predict

Budgets limit. Forecasts expand. Build financial models that help you predict what's coming, not just record what happened. Start asking:
- What does it take to hit our next profit goal?
- How will this hiring decision affect our cash runway?
- Where is growth hiding in our service mix?

This mindset moves you from reactive to responsive. From guesswork to leadership.

4. Capital Discipline: Profit is a Requirement, Not a Reward

If profit is something you hope to see "after everything's paid," you're not leading it—it's leading you.

Treat profit like payroll. Build it into your pricing. Allocate it first. Let it fund:

- Owner's compensation
- Growth reinvestment
- Team bonuses
- Strategic reserves

Profit isn't greed. It's gravity. It keeps your business grounded when everything else is in motion.

5. Team Integration: Financial Fluency Across the Org

Your financial backbone isn't just your job. It's a cultural standard. Build financial literacy into your leadership team. Share targets. Contextualize goals. Make metrics part of how the team wins together.

When your COO, your marketing lead, and even your customer success manager all understand how profit works, they start optimizing their decisions for outcomes, not just effort.

And when your team realizes that you don't just have a compelling vision, but you also have a strong operating plan with numbers to support that vision, they'll be even more motivated to help you bring that vision to reality.

Ultimately, a CEO without a financial backbone is like a body without a spine—floppy, reactive, and prone to collapse.

But when your systems are strong, you move with power. You can pivot, scale, delegate, and reinvest with clarity and confidence. You stop guessing and start leading.

The takeaway is simple: Structure doesn't slow you down. It stabilizes you to scale.

Build the backbone. Then build whatever business you want on top of it.

Section 8: Your Call to Action—Moving From Chaos to Clarity

Before I send you off to set up or re-evaluate your own financial systems, I want to introduce you to someone.

Meet Jen.

A talented service-based entrepreneur, Jen had built her business from the ground up. She was passionate about her clients, excellent at her craft, and proud of the six-figure revenue she had sustained for nearly three years. On the outside, everything looked successful. But behind the scenes, something was missing.

She hadn't looked at her numbers—really looked—since she launched.

There was no bookkeeping system. No reports. No real understanding of her cash flow or margins. She paid bills as they came in, and as long as her bank balance didn't dip too low, she assumed she was doing fine.

But something didn't add up. She felt stressed about money all the time. She hesitated before taking on new projects. And even though the revenue looked strong, she could never quite explain where the money actually went.

The Wake-Up Call

When tax season rolled around and her accountant asked for financial reports, she froze.

What reports?

That moment led to a hard truth: she had no idea whether her business was truly profitable.

With a lump in her throat and a mountain of receipts on her kitchen table, Jen decided it was time for a change. She reached out for help and hired a bookkeeper and a Profit Strategist.

What happened next changed everything.

The Turnaround: Three Months to Clarity

In the first 30 days, her new bookkeeper caught up on the last 12 months of transactions. They categorized every dollar and reconciled every account. What they found wasn't catastrophic, but it was eye-opening.

She had been leaking over $3,000 a month in forgotten subscriptions, mismanaged ad spend, and underpriced services.

The moment she saw the numbers in black and white, she had two emotions: fear... and relief.

Fear, because she finally saw how close she was to burning out her business.

Relief, because for the first time, she had a path forward.

Once her books were clean, her Profit Strategist stepped in. Together, they built a 90-day financial plan. They forecasted her cash flow, restructured her pricing to ensure a 40% margin, and created an owner pay schedule so she could finally pay herself regularly and with confidence.

Jen started making data-backed decisions. She paused one of her offerings that was consistently losing money and leaned into the one that was wildly profitable. She trimmed expenses by 17% and raised her rates by 20%—without losing a single client.

But more than that, she slept better.

She finally stopped guessing and started leading.

The Emotional Transformation

The big takeaway here?

It wasn't just the numbers that changed. It was Jen.

She went from avoiding her finances to leading them.

She showed up to her strategy calls with questions, ideas, and curiosity instead of dread. She reviewed her monthly reports with the same energy she used to reserve for marketing. She stopped cringing when her accountant emailed. She stopped guessing and started leading.

And it didn't stop there. One of my favorite moments came toward the end of our time working together. Jen turned to me, eyes wide with pride, and exclaimed, *"I can't wait for my husband to see this!"*

There was confidence in her voice. Even joy.

Because for the first time, she *got it*. She felt like the CEO of her business, not just the operator. She realized she was doing better than she ever gave herself credit for.

Why Clarity Feels Like Relief

Here's what most people don't talk about: numbers come with emotion.

Guilt. Fear. Pressure. Pride.

Couples rarely talk about money at the depth they do with me because I'm not just looking at spreadsheets. I'm listening to the stories behind them. That's why bookkeeping isn't just gold—it becomes *platinum* when you have someone you trust to talk through the financial truths of your business, good or bad.

There's one report I especially love to share with business owners, particularly those who have been in business for three years or more and have consistently maintained accurate books. It's my favorite report to share and its a simple one: a year-over-year Profit and Loss statement.

We lay out the last three years side by side. And then?

Magic.

Patterns emerge. Progress reveals itself. That $12K profit in year one? It increased to $ 48,000 in year three. That offering that used to lose money? It's now your biggest driver. That dip you thought was the end of everything? You survived it — and came out stronger.

More than once, I've heard, *"I learned more in the last 30 seconds than I have in five years working with my accountant."*

Why? Because that report doesn't just show you the numbers. It shows you the **story**—your growth, your grit, and the power of staying the course.

From Guesswork to CEO Thinking

Jen's story isn't rare.

Many entrepreneurs spend years building a business, but never build the financial clarity that lets them lead with confidence. They focus on doing great work and serving others, but without the financial infrastructure, that growth feels fragile.

Here's the truth: your talent can take you far. But clarity? Clarity takes you to the next level.

Running a business without bookkeeping is like trying to drive cross-country without a map. You might eventually arrive somewhere, but not without stress, detours, and wasted time.

Bookkeeping gives you the map.

Accounting gives you the dashboard.

Strategy gives you the GPS.

And you? You get to drive with control, clarity, and confidence.

From chaos to clarity. That's not just a nice phrase. It's the path forward for every entrepreneur who's ready to stop guessing and start leading.

Make your money work for you by rewiring your money brain.

If you want to make more—and keep more—stop trying to do it all alone. Get help. Without support, most people just keep making the same mistakes on repeat. Change your mindset, change your habits, and your financial results will follow. — *Jeannie Dougherty*

Part 3:
Growing Success

This section focuses on scaling your business and achieving lasting impact. You'll prioritize profit with purpose, ensuring your business fuels both personal and professional goals. Through strategic investing, you'll shift from earning to building long-term wealth, and by mastering delegation, you'll create the freedom to focus on your highest-value contributions. This is the stage where vision culminates in impact—your entrepreneurial success becomes a vehicle for financial independence, growth, and meaningful change.

Chapter 9:
Profit with Purpose and Why Profit isn't Optional

66

If people don't have exposure to what they believe their purpose to be, they don't even know where to begin.

Purpose isn't always intuitive—it's discovered. And sometimes the first step is simply being shown what's possible.
— *Yahweh Khao Sok*

99

Section 1: Profit with Purpose

Most new business owners start with a vision: freedom, impact, and purpose. But somewhere along the way, profit starts to feel like an afterthought or worse, a pipe dream. The truth is, profit isn't selfish or greedy. It's essential.

Profit isn't what's left over. It's what leads. It gives your business oxygen, your vision structure, and your dreams traction.

In this chapter, you'll learn why profit is the foundation of sustainable success, not just for your business, but for your life. You'll meet entrepreneurs who've made powerful mindset shifts, and you'll walk away with the tools to do the same.

We'll unpack:
- Why paying yourself first is non-negotiable
- How to stop comparing your pricing to others
- The five financial principles of purposeful profit
- Tools and strategies to align money with meaning
- And how to fuel your business with values, not just effort

If you're ready to lead with profit and live with purpose, this chapter is your roadmap.

———————————

Section 2: Know Your Terms & Pay Yourself First—Be the Hero of Your Business

Be Your Own Hero

When I first started my business, I was filled with hope, drive, and a fierce belief that I could build something meaningful. So many people cheered me on—friends, colleagues, even strangers who saw the spark in my eyes. But not everyone believed in the dream. And not all of the voices that doubted me were distant or irrelevant. Some of the people I wanted most to support me didn't. Their silence or skepticism hurt, but it didn't stop me.

Because at the end of the day, this journey? It's mine.

As a business owner, no one is coming to save you. The vision belongs to you. The weight of the decisions, the cost of the risks, the lessons from the failures—all of it rests on your shoulders. And that's not a bad thing. In fact, it's the most empowering truth you can embrace.

When I realized the buck truly stops with me, everything changed. I stopped waiting for approval. I stopped assuming someone else would tell me when I was "ready." I stopped thinking I needed to prove my worth through constant hustle.

I decided to be the hero of my own story.

Not the martyr. Not the sidekick.

The hero.

That meant putting boundaries in place. That meant deciding that I was not only worth investing in but that I *must* invest in myself. I couldn't keep giving my energy away without ever filling my own cup. I had to stop bleeding out in service to everyone else while starving my own vision.

This is your permission slip. But more than that: it's your call to rise. Because no one else is responsible for your success. No one else is accountable for your fulfillment.

You are the leader. And heroes lead from the front.

If profit is the reward, then leadership is the journey, and you are the one holding the pen. It's time to stop waiting for someone else to validate your success. Too many business owners hustle without ever pausing to take in what they have. They give their time, their talent, and their energy until there's nothing left.

But real success? It requires boundaries. It requires bravery. It requires you to step into the role of the hero, not just for your clients or your team, but for yourself.

I once worked with an attorney, Rick, who had done everything "right." He became a partner at his firm in just eight months. On paper, he was wildly successful. But when I asked him if he felt successful, he hesitated.

"No," he said. "I don't feel like I've made it."

Why? Because he hadn't taken the time to acknowledge what he'd already built. He was stuck on the hamster wheel of doing, chasing the next big client, the next promotion, the next win. Purpose had taken a back seat to performance.

We broke the cycle by anchoring his next steps in meaning. Instead of another vague day full of Zoom meetings and networking calls, I asked him to list five meaningful actions that would move him forward with intention.

Here was the list he came up with:
- Make one meaningful connection call
- Send three personalized follow-up emails
- Post one purposeful message to his audience
- Make five strategic follow-ups
- Attend two events aligned with his deeper mission

He shifted overnight. From reactive to intentional. From scattered to aligned. He stepped into his power, and profit followed. Most importantly, he became the hero of his own journey by choosing to lead with purpose instead of pressure and to validate his success from within. That story isn't just about him. It's about all of us.

You don't need permission to thrive. You need a plan. You don't need to keep giving everything away. You need to receive what your work is worth.

You don't need to prove yourself. You need to pay yourself.

How to Pay Yourself First

Let's address one of the most persistent myths in business ownership: the idea that you should pour every dollar back into your business and "take care of yourself later."

Later rarely comes.

Paying yourself first is not greedy. It's responsible. It's not about taking from your business. It's about giving it a leader who is stable, secure, and empowered.

When you pay yourself, you are modeling sustainability. You are reinforcing the belief that your business exists to serve your life, not the other way around. Even if the amount feels small at first, it builds a habit of financial health.

It's also a signal to your nervous system: I matter. I'm safe. I'm not just surviving—I'm building something sustainable.

By integrating profit into your payment plan from day one, you set the tone for every decision you'll make. You start acting like the CEO you are, not a burned-out employee of your own company.

Whether it's $50 or $5,000, start now. Start small if you must, but start with intention.

Know Your Terms

Financial empowerment starts with literacy. If you don't know what your numbers mean, it's easy to stay stuck. Let's break down the essential terms every entrepreneur should understand:

- **Profit:** The money left after all business expenses are paid. Not what's left by accident—what's built in by design.
- **Reinvestment:** Putting money back into the business strategically to fuel growth or stabilize operations.
- **Profit Margin:** The percentage of revenue that remains as profit after expenses. A key indicator of business health.
- **Breakeven Point:** The exact point where income covers expenses but nothing more. Knowing this helps you set minimum targets.
- **Profit Threshold:** The amount of revenue needed to meet your ideal profitability goals.
- **Sustainability:** The ability to operate your business over time without depleting your energy, finances, or health.

Understanding these terms transforms your relationship with money. It provides you with language for your goals, data for informed decisions, and clarity in your growth.

You can't lead what you don't understand. And you can't scale what you don't measure.

But you? You're not just here to survive. You're here to thrive.

So pay yourself. Learn the terms. Build your system.

Because when you own your profit, you own your power.

Section 3: Beth's Story: Stop Comparing, Start Valuing

Beth was one of those entrepreneurs who did everything with heart. She cared deeply about her clients, poured hours into perfecting her services, and always over-delivered. But when it came to pricing, she hesitated. There was a business down the street—a competitor—who charged significantly less. Beth couldn't shake the thought: "If I raise my rates, they'll just go to her."

Fear, not strategy, was guiding her pricing. She was shrinking her value to match someone else's numbers. And worse, she was under-cutting her own sustainability in the process.

We had a heart-to-heart. I asked her one question: "Do you honestly believe what you offer is the same as what Sally down the street offers?"

She paused. "No. I know I go deeper. I know my clients get better outcomes. I know they trust me more."

"Then why are you letting her price set your worth?"

Beth realized she had been pricing based on fear, not value. On assumptions, not results. And most dangerously, on comparison, not confidence. She took a leap. She raised her rates to reflect her expertise, her energy, and the outcomes she consistently delivered.

And what happened? She didn't lose clients. She gained better ones. The kind who respected her boundaries, trusted her process, and referred more people just like them. Her confidence rose. Her revenue increased. And her burnout started to heal.

But something deeper shifted, too. Beth began to trust herself. She stopped looking outside of herself for permission. She stopped letting others define her worth. She stopped apologizing for her excellence. She began to lead from within. She became the hero of her business. She showed up with clarity. With confidence. With courage.

She understood that the minute she stopped comparing herself to others, she could finally start building a business that reflected her values, not someone else's race to the bottom.

Beth's story is a poignant reminder that:

- **Confidence is built, not borrowed.** You won't find it in someone else's pricing. It grows when you align your rates with the value you deliver.
- **Comparison is a thief.** It steals your creativity, your clarity, and your courage. When you stop comparing and start owning your lane, your power multiplies.
- **Your worth is not up for debate.** You've worked hard, you've built trust, and you get results. Price like it.
- **You are allowed to charge in alignment with your outcomes, not just your industry average.** Set a standard based on what you bring to the table, not what someone else settled for.
- **Being the hero means choosing to value yourself, even when others don't.** It's easy to wait for the world to recognize your worth, but leadership begins when you recognize it yourself.

Beth stopped shrinking. She started leading. And in doing so, she built a business rooted in value, not just visibility.

Don't charge based on what others are doing. Don't assume lower prices make you more appealing. Don't let fear dictate your value.

Price with clarity. Price with purpose. Price with courage.

Because you are not Sally down the street. You're you. And what you offer is worth every penny.

Section 4: Fuel Your Gas Tank First

If your business is a car, what fuels your gas tank?

Too often, entrepreneurs engage in tasks that drain them rather than energize them. We say yes to obligations that don't align with our mission. We take on projects out of fear instead of purpose. We keep spinning the wheels, not realizing we're running on empty. But burnout isn't a badge of honor. It's a warning sign.

Start paying attention to how tasks feel. Are they lighting you up or wearing you down? Do you find yourself constantly saying, "I have to..."? If so, pause. Ask yourself, Is this truly necessary? Or is it based on an old belief, fear of scarcity, or people-pleasing?

When you fuel your gas tank first, by pouring energy into what fills you up, you move from obligation to intention and from burnout to purpose. You transition from a state of fatigue to one of flow.

Try this simple shift: Replace "I have to" with "I choose to."

For example, "I have to meet with this client" becomes "I choose to serve people who value my time."

"I have to finish this proposal" becomes "I choose to pursue aligned opportunities."

Let purpose, not panic, drive your decisions. Fuel your purpose first, and profits will follow with clarity and confidence. This approach is about energetic alignment. When your energy, effort, and execution are in sync, you create sustainable success, not just busy success.

And this is where profit becomes more than a financial concept. It becomes fuel. When your business is aligned with what energizes you, your profit becomes a reflection of your clarity, not just your hustle. Profit becomes a measure of purpose in motion. It becomes evidence that you're not just surviving the grind but thriving in your genius.

Thought leadership in business starts with this alignment. You cannot influence, lead, or scale with burnout dragging behind you. But when you're fueled by work that energizes you, you become magnetic. Your message sharpens. Your impact deepens.

And your profit?

It grows in proportion to the alignment you've created.

Because when you're full, you lead better. You think more clearly. You create stronger. And you attract clients, partners, and opportunities that match your highest contribution.

Fuel yourself. Then fuel your mission. Let profit become the engine, not the exhaust. And watch everything else accelerate.

Section 5: The 5 Financial Success Principles

By now, you know the drill: these five financial principles aren't just business best practices; they're also your roadmap to profit with purpose. They'll help you lead with intention, make confident financial decisions, and ensure your business is built on a foundation that supports your life, not just your workload.

Each principle can be viewed as a building block for profit. They serve as intentional fuel for freedom and growth, not as accidental leftovers.

❝

Don't disconnect from your purpose. Ever.

If you do what you love, you'll be the richest person in the world— and that's not just a cliché. When you chase money, it always feels like something's missing. There's no such thing as *enough* if your worth is tied to numbers. The minute you stop obsessing over money, you actually open yourself up to receive more. Because money is just a tool. It offers stability, yes—but it's not your identity. If you rely on it for validation or self-worth, it creates a false sense of security that will never satisfy you. So chase alignment. Chase purpose. That's where real wealth lives. — *Lana Kinberg*

❞

1. Know What You Want

Profit grows where clarity lives. When you define what success looks like, you can make informed, profit-driven decisions that help you achieve it. And remember: vague goals like "make more money" don't build sustainable businesses. You need concrete targets.

Ask yourself:

- What percentage of revenue do I want to convert into profit?
- How much do I want to reinvest?
- What do I want to set aside for future dreams?
- When you factor in business needs and personal income, what does a financially successful year look like for you?

The moral of the story?

Profit goals need to be as concrete and visible as any other business goals.

2. Know How Much It Costs

Take the time to calculate the expenses required to generate consistent profits.

Why?

Because profit doesn't exist in isolation, and it doesn't happen by accident. It is the result of carefully managing both your revenue and expenses. If you want to generate repeatable and predictable profits in the long term, understanding the costs of maintaining your operations and their growth is the most important thing you can do.

I once worked with a wellness studio owner named Jenna who thought she had a profit problem. Her classes were full, and clients loved her offerings. But she never seemed to have money left over at the end of the month. She kept cutting expenses in hopes of "fixing" the issue, but the profit never came. When we finally sat down and went through her numbers, we discovered the real problem: she didn't know what it truly cost to run her business.

She was undercharging for her most popular service and overpaying for software she didn't use. Her rent had quietly increased, and she hadn't updated her pricing to reflect that shift. And worse, she had been making emotional purchases—new décor, unnecessary merch—that felt good in the moment but didn't contribute to her bottom line.

We walked through her fixed costs like rent and payroll, her variable costs like instructors' hours and cleaning supplies, and her hidden expenses — the things she didn't realize were draining her profits. Then we found her breakeven point, and, more importantly, her profit threshold.

Once she saw what she needed to earn to not just survive but thrive, everything clicked. She adjusted her pricing, eliminated unnecessary spending, and created a simple budget. Within three months, she wasn't just covering her expenses — she was putting money into savings and finally paying herself consistently.

In order to do this, you must know all of your operating costs. This includes:

- Fixed costs like rent, payroll, and software subscriptions
- Variable costs such as materials, advertising, and subcontracted work

- Emotional spending—those "nice-to-haves" that drain your budget but don't drive results

When you know what it really costs to be profitable in your business, you hold the key to sustainable success. With this clarity, you can price your services intelligently, manage spending proactively, and scale with intention and confidence.

3. Know Your Numbers

We've said it before, but it deserves to be said again: What gets measured gets managed. And this is just as true for your profits as it is for any other aspect of your business. Knowing your numbers ensures your profit doesn't get lost in the noise.

So, when should you be deep-diving into your business profits?

Ideally, tax time and year-end reviews are not the only times you should be thinking about your profit. Regular and consistent financial check-ins should be part of your leadership rhythm. Whether it's weekly, biweekly, or monthly, schedule time to review your Profit and Loss (P&L) statements and other key financial reports. Doing so will give you a clear picture of your profits and help you uncover strategic moves that can increase profits over time. It's a win-win.

Case Study

I once worked with a creative agency founder named Marcus. He was brilliant at branding and client delivery, but completely avoided his numbers. "I'm just not a numbers guy," he told me. Yet month after month, he couldn't figure out why he wasn't making more money. His business was growing on the outside, but not on the inside. When we sat down and reviewed his P&L, the issue became obvious. One of his biggest clients was actually one of his least profitable due to constant scope creep and undercharging. Meanwhile, his smallest retainer clients brought in higher margins.

Once Marcus started tracking profit margins by service line and client, he made strategic decisions: he raised rates on low-margin accounts, eliminated unnecessary tools and subscriptions, and focused on services with the highest return. Reviewing his numbers changed everything. He went from being confused and reactionary to confident and proactive.

Your P&L doesn't just tell you what happened. It shows you what to fix, where to focus, and how to grow.

When you review yours, get curious:
- Which projects are most profitable?
- Which clients drain your resources?
- Are your costs creeping up without return?

These patterns conceal profit, but you can only uncover them if you actively search for it.

4. Act as If

Waiting to feel "ready" to draw a profit from your business won't grow your bottom line. When you act like the profitable CEO you are, your business rises to meet you. Profit should not be thought of as something you might receive from your business someday. It should not be treated as a reward for good behavior or as an outcome that just might happen.

Being profitable must be a priority from day one. That means building it directly into your pricing, your planning, your hiring decisions, and your spending habits. Design your business model around the belief that profit is non-negotiable. Set your revenue targets with margins built in.

Be intentional about what you say yes to—and just as strategic about what you say no to. There are endless opportunities in business, but not every opportunity is profitable or aligned with your mission.

Sometimes, discipline is more powerful than ambition.

I worked with a leadership consultant named Rachel who always undercharged because she wanted to be "accessible." But the truth was, she was bleeding money. When she finally shifted her mindset and priced her programs with built-in profit, she not only started thriving financially, she became a better coach. She showed up with more energy, confidence, and impact. She stopped taking projects just to stay afloat and started choosing clients aligned with her bigger vision.

Profit isn't a happy accident. It's the result of consistent, courageous decisions. When you operate your business as if profit is a core outcome, you bring a level of clarity and commitment that transforms everything else.

Act like a CEO who expects a return. Lead like a founder whose vision deserves funding. Profit without purpose is empty. Use your earnings to fund the future you believe in because your numbers should reflect your values.

5. Take Inspired Action

Taking inspired action means using your profit in ways that build the life you envisioned. It doesn't happen overnight. But when you use your profit wisely instead of letting it sit idly, you're leveraging your greatest asset in pursuit of your greatest dreams.

So what might this look like?

One way to take inspired action with your profit is to use it to build up or expand your business in ways that move you closer to your goals. Things like investing in a new product line, opening a second location, upgrading your technology, or even just hiring someone to handle some work that will free up your time are all excellent uses of profit that can drive you toward your goals.

You can also use your profit to "pay yourself first," giving yourself the opportunity to make transformative moves—like buying your first home, funding your children's education, traveling more, donating to causes you love, or retiring earlier than you originally thought you could. The options are endless.

Running a profitable business not only provides multiple options to build your dreams, but it also grants you freedom. It allows you to say yes to opportunities that you may not have had previously and prevents you from having to compromise in areas where you want to hold a strong bottom line or see a particular vision through.

Ultimately, you are the owner of your business, and you get to decide how you do business, including how you use profits to further your business goals and your life. A profitable business is not just a business that survives but a business that thrives, serves, and creates a lasting change.

Inspired action is about truly using that financial success as fuel to create even bigger dreams. This is what it means to build a life and business that reflects your values.

Using My Profit for Purpose

I needed $15,000 for IVF treatment. And for a while, I almost gave up. The cost felt overwhelming—completely out of reach. But then I realized something: profit isn't just about money in the bank. It's about possibility.

I made a decision to prioritize profit with purpose. I stopped treating income as just survival and started seeing it as a tool to fund the life I wanted. That shift—using my profit to pursue the dream of becoming a mother—changed everything.

The profit I made through my business didn't just pay bills. It gave me a future. One filled with hope, family, and purpose. And I believe that same power is available to anyone willing to use their profit with intention.

Section 6: Purpose Checkpoints & Other Rituals— Aligning Profit with What Matters Most

Profit is a powerful tool, but only if you use it with intention.

It's easy to get caught in the day-to-day grind of business ownership: closing the next deal, putting out the next fire, hitting the next milestone. But without regular reflection, your business can drift off course, even while it looks successful on paper.

This is why it's critical that you take time regularly to check in on the purpose and profit behind your business. We call these "purpose checkpoints," and they matter mightily for the future of your business. They bring you back to your vision. They force you to pause and ask the question that every business owner must revisit over and over again:

"Is this profitable, and is it purposeful?"

It's not one or the other. Your best decisions align with both.

A teacher once told me she made $30,000 a year but still managed to save $250 a month into an investment account. Meanwhile,

I worked with a lawyer who made nearly $1 million annually and claimed she didn't have a dime to invest.

The difference?

Not income. Not intelligence. But **intention.**

The teacher had a clear sense of purpose, and every dollar was aligned with it. Profit isn't about the size of your income. It's about what you *do* with what you earn.

Start using profit as a way to create momentum around what matters most to you, and realize that profit doesn't happen *after* you achieve your goals.

Profit *is* what helps you reach them.

Here's how to build that alignment into your weekly rhythm:

Weekly Purpose Checkpoints

1. Review your Profit & Loss Statement (P&L)

Look beyond the top-line revenue and dig into:

- Gross vs. net profit
- Profit margins by service line or product

- Which clients, offerings, or projects are yielding the best returns

Ask yourself:
- Am I building the business I truly want?
- Is this current level of profit aligned with the life I want to live?
- What's draining time, money, or energy that no longer serves my goals?

Don't just track the metrics. Interpret the story they tell.

Team Integration: Profit Is a Shared Vision

If you have a team, bring them into the conversation. Profit isn't just a financial outcome. It's a shared result of everyone's work.

Make your profit goals part of your team culture. Let them know what you're working toward. When your team understands the vision, they make better decisions, innovate more effectively, and feel part of something bigger than themselves.

This doesn't mean sharing every dollar and detail. But it does mean building a culture where people understand how their efforts drive not just activity, but *results.*

Profit Rituals: Celebrate, Allocate, Elevate

Profit isn't only meant to be saved or reinvested. It's also meant to be enjoyed. Build rituals that reward progress and reinforce purpose.

- **Celebrate small wins**—every profit milestone matters.
- **Allocate a portion of profit** toward something joyful: a retreat, a bonus, a charitable gift, or a personal dream.
- **Create meaning behind the metrics.** Make profit feel human, not just numeric.

These rituals fuel the belief that your work matters and that your business is a tool for something greater.

Purpose Checkpoint Summary
- **Ask Weekly:** Is this profitable *and* purposeful?
- **Track What Matters:** Review your P&L like it's your business journal, because it is.
- **Bring Your Team In:** Make profit part of your collective mission.
- **Celebrate Strategically:** Let your profit fuel not just strategy but also joy.
- **Build with Belief:** Treat profit as essential, not aspirational.

Because when you build profit with purpose, your business becomes more than a paycheck. It becomes a legacy.

Section 7: CEO Thought Leadership: You Have the Ability to Build Your Profit System

Profit is not an accident. It's a systematized outcome.

And yet, far too many business owners treat profit like a fluke—something that shows up at the end of a good month if they're lucky. But sustainable profit isn't created by chance. It's engineered through systems designed to make profit inevitable.

This is where real leadership steps in.

Hope is not a strategy. Hustle without structure is just burnout waiting to happen. If you want profit to be predictable, not sporadic

— scalable, not seasonal — you need to architect your business around systems that build profit from the start.

How?

Though systems.

Systems are the language of sustainability. They replace reactive decisions with intentional rhythms. They create consistency in how you earn, spend, save, and grow. A true profit system is what transforms chaotic cash flow into financial clarity. It turns the unknown into the actionable. Every dollar, whether earned or spent, has a job, a destination, and a purpose.

So what does a system for profit actually look like?

1. Revenue Tracking with Intention

Know not just how much you're earning, but where and why. Break down revenue by service, product, or offer. Track patterns. Identify what's performing and what's draining. Strategic leaders don't guess where the money is — they follow the data and double down on what works.

2. Expense Categorization with Precision

Lumping expenses together is like driving blind. Separate fixed costs (like rent and payroll), variable costs (like contractors and supplies), and discretionary spending. This level of clarity empowers proactive decisions instead of reactive cuts when margins get tight.

3. Profit Allocation on Purpose

Profit needs a plan. Decide in advance where every earned dollar should go:
• Owner's pay
• Tax reserves
• Business savings
• Strategic reinvestment
• Joy (yes, joy is a legitimate line item)

These allocations create stability, resilience, and intentional growth. Profit without a plan becomes cash without direction.

4. Weekly (or Biweekly) Financial Rituals

We've said it before, and it merits a repeat here: set aside time each week to review your P&L, check your margins, and ask critical leadership questions like:

- Is this working?
- What's changing?
- Where am I leaking money?

Regular check-ins build financial fluency, and fluency breeds foresight.

5. Quarterly Profit Planning Sessions

Step back every 90 days and reassess. Compare your projected profit with your actuals.

- Did you overspend?
- Undercharge?
- Miss your targets or blow past them?

Adjust your pricing, offers, and goals based on data, not instinct. This is where momentum is either created or lost.

6. Team Integration and Financial Transparency

Your team isn't just executing tasks. They're powering the engine of your business. Let them in on the numbers. Share profit goals and the rationale behind pricing, scope, and strategy. When your people understand the "why," they show up with greater ownership, and outcomes follow.

Case Study: Unpredictable Income Cycles

I once worked with a solopreneur who felt trapped in a cycle of unpredictable income. Some months, she was flush. Others, she barely covered expenses. The stress was constant, and profit felt impossible.

Together, we built a simple but effective system: tracked revenue by source, created a fixed monthly profit transfer, and implemented weekly money dates.

Three months later, she had clarity. Six months later, reserves. One year in, she had hired her first employee, and her profit margin was growing every quarter.

That transformation didn't come from working harder. It came from working smarter **with systems that supported the outcome she wanted most: profit.**

Here's the truth: profit isn't the reward for surviving your business. It's the result of building it with discipline and intention.

When you build systems that expect profit—not just hope for it—you stop riding the rollercoaster. You stop reacting to your numbers and start leading with them. That's when real freedom begins.

Bottom line? Profit shouldn't be a surprise. It should be the default. Be your own CEO and build your system like you mean it, because you do and you can.

Section 8 Call to Action: Lead With Profit, Live With Purpose

Oxygen is what a thriving business needs to survive and profit is that oxygen. Without it, you're not building a business; you're simply keeping yourself employed.

Profit powers growth, innovation, resilience, and generosity. It gives you the flexibility to weather uncertainty, seize new opportunities, reward your team, and pursue your personal dreams. Everything about how you operate will shift when you stop treating profit as a bonus and start treating it as essential.

You're not just building a business. You're building a life. And profit is what gives that life structure, stability, and room to grow. It's not about greed; it's about freedom. It gives you the ability to choose wisely, lead boldly, and anchor every decision in purpose.

When you chase money, it always feels like something's missing.

Chase alignment. Chase purpose. That's where real wealth lives.
— *Lana Kinberg*

So here's your call to action: Don't wait until your business is "bigger" or you feel more ready.

Start now.

Build systems. Set targets. Track your numbers. Lead with purpose. Expect profit—not as a reward, but as a requirement. Because a purpose-driven business deserves profit. And so do you.

The Top 5 Takeaways from Chapter 9: Profit With Purpose

1. Profit is Not Optional—It's Foundational

Profit isn't a leftover or a reward for hard work. It's the oxygen your business needs to thrive. When you treat profit as essential, you build a business with structure, stability, and long-term sustainability.

2. The Five Financial Principles Guide Purpose-Driven Profit

Knowing what you want, understanding your costs, tracking your numbers, acting with intention, and taking inspired action are not just financial habits. They are profit strategies. These principles align your business model with values and vision.

3. Your Numbers Tell a Story—Listen to It Regularly

Monitoring P&L statements, reviewing profit margins, and tracking performance by client or service are critical for making informed decisions. You can't grow what you don't measure.

4. Profit Enables Impact, Not Just Income

Profit allows you to invest in your team, pursue personal goals, weather business fluctuations, and say no to misaligned opportunities. It's what transforms your business into a vehicle for freedom and fulfillment.

5. Lead With Profit, Don't Chase It

Waiting to "feel ready" keeps you in survival mode. Designing your business for profit from the start—through systems, pricing, and boundaries—positions you to lead with clarity, confidence, and purpose.

Chapter 10:
Investing—Making Your Money Work for You

"

Strategy Secures the Dream.

Your greatest assets aren't your products or services—it's the financial health and resilience of your business.

Protect your income streams. Plan for growth. Build a safety net for the unexpected. Align your vision with your financial strategy, because clarity and preparation today create freedom and success tomorrow.

Invest in guidance. Don't let the urgent drown out the important. You've built this dream—now secure it for the future.
— Yahweh Khao Sok

"

Introduction:

I once went to Vegas with a friend who had a very specific strategy for gambling: turn all his money into the smallest chips possible so it felt like he had more to play with. Meanwhile, I did the opposite—I exchanged my cash for higher-value chips. We both started with about the same amount of money, but our approaches couldn't have been more different.

Because his stack looked massive, he tossed chips around like candy, betting here and there, throwing money at whatever table seemed fun at the moment. I, on the other hand, had fewer chips. So every time I placed one down, it made me think. I paused. I made more intentional decisions, not because I was cautious, but because each chip meant something.

He had the "Vegas, whoo-hoo!" approach—and lost most of it. I walked out into the bright morning sunlight with enough in my pocket to cover my trip and pay for Christmas presents that year.

Most people treat investing like Vegas: roll the dice, cross your fingers, hope for a lucky break. But real wealth? It's less poker table, more chessboard. It's not about chance—it's about positioning, patience, and knowing your next move before the game begins.

That's the heart of investing. It's not about having more—it's about using what you have with clarity, strategy, and intention.

Let's dive in.

Section 1: Shift the Script—From Earning to Building Wealth

Let's start by addressing a common mindset: the idea that the only way to build wealth is to work harder and earn more.

That's not entirely wrong—but it's incomplete. If working harder was all it took to build wealth, most business owners would be financially set. The reality is, income alone doesn't create wealth. What you do with your income is what makes the difference.

At some point, you have to stop thinking like an income earner and start thinking like a wealth builder. That means shifting from asking, "How can I make more?" to "How can I make what I already have work for me?"

Every dollar you bring in has a job to do. You can spend it, save it, or put it to work through investing.

Think of your money like an employee. Don't let it sit idle—assign it a task.

This isn't about micromanaging every expense or cutting out every small joy. It's about being more intentional with how your money moves. Building wealth doesn't happen overnight, and it doesn't require perfection. It requires consistency and a clear plan.

When you treat investing as a regular part of how you handle your money—not a someday task—you start creating momentum. You don't need a six-figure income to begin. You need a strategy.

Wealth isn't about how much you earn—it's about how you manage what you earn.

Say it out loud if you need the reminder: *"I am building wealth. I don't wait—I create."*

Now let's get into how that actually works.

I work with many clients who come to me saving nothing and investing nothing. So we start small—**one dollar a week.** Then we move to **two dollars a week.** It's about building the muscle.

I have them **skip just one cup of coffee a week** and redirect that money. Why? So they can confidently say, *"I am a saver."* Once that habit sticks, we take the next step: I have them put that same "coffee money" into an investing app like **Acorns** or **Robinhood.** Now they can proudly say, *"I AM AN INVESTOR."*

It may sound simple, but here's why it works: **when you operate out of the energy and frequency of "I am an investor," you naturally invest more.** Identity shifts behavior.

Traditional banks often require a $500 minimum to open a savings account, and most financial advisors require a significant upfront deposit. But with **Acorns** or **Robinhood, you can start investing with as little as $1 a day.**

Try this simple exercise—it changes not only your money habits, but the way you see yourself.

Section 2: The Hero Returns—Turning Profit Into Power

There's a time in every business owner's journey when you finally come up for air.

The chaos slows. The sales stabilize. The checks clear. You've got a working business model, a little rhythm, maybe even a growing sense of confidence. The hustle that once defined your day-to-day starts to give way to systems and strategy.

It's a quiet but powerful turning point. And most people don't talk about it. Because this part of the journey feels... uncertain. You've fought hard to build profit. You've learned how to sell, lead, and deliver.

But once you've made money, what do you do with it?

This is the moment that separates the income earners from the wealth builders.

Profit Is the Beginning—Not the Finish Line

Let's be clear: profit is essential. Without profit, you're running a passion project, not a business. It's the fuel that powers your decisions. It proves your model is viable and your effort is valuable. But profit alone won't give you freedom.

If your profit only exists to be spent on overhead, on convenience, or on an upgraded lifestyle, it isn't building anything. It's cycling.

Profit becomes powerful the moment it starts working for you. And the way to make that happen? You invest it.

Why Investing Is the Hero's Power Tool

In the Hero's Journey, there's always a return. The protagonist doesn't just survive the challenges. They come back changed. And they come back with something. A lesson, a tool, a new sense of responsibility. That's what this moment is.

You've survived the early-stage chaos. You've earned the right to lead differently.

And now you return to your business, your life, your finances, with a new role: the builder of systems.

Investing is your next power move. It's the practical expression of everything you've worked so hard to create.

You're not just working for money anymore. You're designing a system where your money begins working for you. This isn't about luck, timing, or insider knowledge. It's about structure and consistency. And it's about making choices that create momentum over time.

Investing is how profit becomes infrastructure.

It's how you turn income into:

- **Passive revenue streams** that support your life beyond business hours
- **Long-term assets** that grow over time, even when you're resting
- **Financial freedom** that gives you leverage, not just security

And it's how you stop being the only one holding everything up.

Power That Feels Different

Let's redefine power in this stage of your journey.

Power is no longer just the ability to create revenue—it's the ability to create space.

- Space to choose which clients you take on
- Space to say no without fear
- Space to rest, travel, care for your family, or think bigger

Power looks like a growing investment account, a healthy emergency fund, and a retirement plan that doesn't depend on selling your business someday.

Power is not about working more. It's about owning what you've already earned and using it with intention.

You Are the Hero—and the CFO

Here's the truth: no one else is coming to organize this for you. Not your accountant. Not your assistant. Not your financial advisor.

You are the hero of your own story. And now, you're also the CFO of your own future.

That means the decisions about how your money works, grows, and multiplies start with you. That's not overwhelming—it's empowering. Because you already have the most important resource: profit. Now, you just need to give that profit a job.

This is where the journey gets strategic. You're not chasing every dollar anymore. You're leading them. You're not just running a business, you're building a foundation.

You're not just surviving, you're scaling. And investing is the tool that makes that possible.

Let's move into the how.

Section 3: Busting the Myths—Why You Can Be an Investor

Let's talk about one of the biggest mindset blocks many entrepreneurs face once they start earning: the belief that investing is something only other people do.

Have you ever thought to yourself:
- *"I'm too late."*
- *"I don't make enough."*
- *"I have no idea where to even begin."*

If any of that sounds familiar, you're not alone. Most of us weren't handed a roadmap for building long-term wealth. We were told to work hard, save what we could, and hope for the best.

The result?

A lot of high-performing people make good money but never learn how to make their money work for them.

That's where investing comes in. And that's exactly why it can feel so intimidating. Because it represents a new identity: one where you're not just the earner—you're the builder. The owner. The strategist.

But first, we need to confront the mental roadblocks that stop so many business owners from taking this step.

Let's bust the most common myths that keep people out of the investing game.

The Top 5 Myths About Investing (And Why They're Flat-Out Wrong)

Myth #1: "Investing is risky."

Yes, there's risk involved. But there is also a risk in starting a business (and you did that already!). So is keeping all your money in a savings account while inflation eats away at its value. The truth is, not investing carries risk, too, especially when your entire financial future depends on your ability to keep working. Smart investing is about managing risk, not avoiding it.

Myth #2: "I'm not good with money."

This one is personal for many. Maybe you've made mistakes. Maybe money was a source of shame growing up. But that doesn't mean you're not capable. If you can run a business, manage cash flow, or make payroll, you already have the brain for money. What you need is confidence, support, and a few practical tools.

Myth #3: "I'll start when I make more."

Waiting until you have "enough" to invest is like waiting to go to the gym until you're in shape. It defeats the purpose. The earlier you start, even with small amounts, the more time your money has to grow. *Time in the market* matters more than timing the market.

Starting small now beats starting big later.

Myth #4: "It's too complicated."

We've all seen the charts, the acronyms, and the talking heads on TV. But investing doesn't have to be complicated. In fact, some of the most successful investors use the simplest strategies: automate monthly contributions, invest in low-fee index funds, and leave it alone. You don't need to become a stock analyst, you just need to get in the game.

Myth #5: "That's for rich people."

This one is perhaps the most dangerous. It suggests that building wealth is only for those who already have it. But investing is how people become wealthy. It's not the result, it's the process. The tools are accessible. Platforms have made investing affordable and user-friendly. You don't need $10,000 to get started. Sometimes, you just need $10 and a plan.

Where the Fear Comes From

Most of us didn't grow up talking about asset classes or compound interest around the dinner table. If anything, money was whispered about, argued over, or avoided altogether. Combine that with a school system that prioritized geometry over personal finance, and it makes sense that we enter adulthood feeling underprepared.

But not knowing something isn't a character flaw. It's just a gap in education. And unlike most subjects, learning to invest is highly forgiving. You don't need to do it perfectly. You just need to start.

The Reframe: Inaction Is the Real Risk

Here's what no one tells you: the longer you wait, the harder it gets to catch up. Time is the one thing you can't manufacture later. But starting now, even with tiny steps, creates momentum. A $100 investment today is worth more than a $1,000 investment a decade from now. The compounding effect of consistent investing is what builds wealth, not luck, timing, or complexity.

Every month you delay is a month your money could have been working.

You Don't Have to Be Perfect—You Just Have to Begin

You're already doing things that once felt impossible—running a business, managing deadlines, and solving problems. You don't need to be a financial expert to invest. You need a system you trust and the discipline to follow it.

Start with a decision:
- Open an account.
- Automate a small monthly deposit.
- Read one book.
- Follow one voice you trust.

Because you can be an investor. In fact, you already are. Every intentional money move you make is a vote for your future. So let's drop the myths and step into the mindset of someone who builds, not just income, but lasting wealth.

Section 4: The Three Buckets—A Simple System for Serious Wealth

If investing still feels overwhelming, this section is for you.

You don't need a dozen accounts or a wall of financial spreadsheets to build wealth. What you need is a simple framework and a way to think about where your money goes, why it goes there, and how it serves your bigger goals.

That's where the **Three-Bucket System** comes in. It's an easy and powerful model to organize your financial world and ensure you're not just saving or spending—you're building.

Think of your financial life as a garden. Not every seed grows at the same pace. Some things need fast access. Others take years to mature. The key is knowing what belongs where and nurturing each one consistently.

Bucket 1: The Security Fund (Your Safety Net)

This is your financial foundation. It's what keeps you steady when life throws a curveball, like a slow business season, unexpected medical bills, or the water heater giving out the same week your biggest client is late on payment.

Your **Security Fund** should cover 3–6 months of essential living expenses—ideally kept in a high-yield savings account or money market fund where it's easily accessible. This is not an investment account. It's a cushion.

But security doesn't stop at a bank account. It also includes basic protections that safeguard your income and health, like:

- Health insurance
- Disability insurance
- Life insurance
- Long-term care coverage

Think of this bucket as your business continuity plan. You hope you never need it—but when you do, it's the difference between survival and scrambling.

Bucket 2: The Freedom Fund (Your Wealth Builder)

This is where your long-term goals take root.

The **Freedom Fund** is designed for retirement, lifestyle freedom, and financial independence. These are your slow burn investments; the ones that grow quietly in the background while you live your life.

This bucket might include:

- Roth or Traditional IRAs
- SEP IRAs (for business owners)
- Employer-sponsored 401(k)s
- Index funds or ETFs
- Brokerage accounts for long-term gains

You don't need to check these every day. In fact, the less you tinker, the better. The magic of this bucket comes from **time + consistency + compound growth**.

This fund buys you time later. It gives you options. It means someday you can choose to work because you want to, not because you have to.

Bucket 3: The Growth Fund (Your Strategic Risk)

This is your innovation engine.

Your **Growth Fund** is where you make strategic moves that come with higher potential and higher risk. These are the investments that could accelerate your timeline or create new streams of income.

It might include:
- Real estate (rental properties, flips)
- Business reinvestment
- Individual stocks or sector funds
- Venture capital or startups
- Skill-building or certifications that expand your earning power

This bucket isn't about reckless gambling. It's about **calculated risks** with money you can afford to see fluctuate. Think of it as the fund that lets you say yes to opportunities when they knock *without jeopardizing your financial stability.*

Why Buckets Work

Each of these buckets fills at a different pace and serves a different purpose. But together, they create balance, momentum, and clarity. They allow you to:
- Cover the basics without fear (Security Fund)
- Build a life of freedom and options (Freedom Fund)
- Take smart risks that open doors (Growth Fund)

You don't have to start with all three at once. Begin where you are. Fill the first. Start adding to the second. Allocate what you can to the third.

Wealth isn't built in one bucket—it's built by using all three wisely.

The **Three-Bucket System** gives you a simple visual, a solid plan, and a strategy that grows with you. It turns investing into something you can manage, track, and trust.

And most importantly?

It's not just a system. *It's a shift in how you see your money.*

Section 5: The 5 Financial Success Principles

These five principles give you a repeatable, values-aligned framework to build wealth intentionally, and they apply just as well to investing as they do to every other principle we've covered in this book.

Whether you're just starting or scaling up, this system shows you how to think, plan, and act like an investor—no guesswork, no overwhelm.

1. **Know What You Want** — Set clear, personal investing goals.
2. **Know How Much It Costs** — Reverse-engineer your vision
3. **Know Your Numbers** —Track your net worth, investments, and allocations
4. **Act as If** — Behave like the investor you're becoming
5. **Take Inspired Action** — Invest with alignment

1. Know What You Want

"Clarity is the beginning of confidence."

Long-term wealth doesn't happen by accident. It starts with vision and not just any vision, but one that's deeply personal, specific, and emotionally connected to the life you actually want to live. As business owners, we're used to goal setting in our business: revenue targets, client numbers, and marketing funnels. But when it comes to our personal wealth, too many of us stay vague. We say things like, "I want to retire someday" or "I want to be financially free," but we never define what that actually looks like.

Here's the problem with that: vague goals create vague results.

If you don't know where you're headed, it's easy to lose motivation, make reactive financial choices, or delay investing because there's no sense of urgency or meaning behind it. Specific goals, on the other hand, create momentum. They help you focus your energy and make aligned decisions. And they remind you why it's worth doing the hard work now.

So instead of saying, *"I want to retire someday,"* say, *"I want to have $1 million invested by 2045, generating $40,000 a year in passive income, enough to travel, donate to causes I care about, and enjoy a life that's not ruled by a to-do list."*

That one clear sentence can shift your entire financial posture. It transforms investing from a confusing obligation into a purposeful, empowering action. That kind of clarity fuels commitment.

One of the best tools you can use to get there is creating a **personal investing vision**. Just like businesses create mission statements to guide their growth, you can write a mission statement for your money. It doesn't have to be formal, and you don't have to get it "right" the first time. The point is to create something that aligns your financial goals with the life you actually want to live.

Start by reflecting on a few key questions:

- *What does financial freedom look like for me, not the version I've seen online, but my version?*
- *How much income would I need each month to feel peaceful, not pressured?*
- *What kind of work/life rhythm do I want in 10, 20, or 30 years?*
- *Who else is impacted by my financial decisions—family, community, future generations?*

You might discover that your goal isn't about retiring early but about creating flexibility now. Maybe you want the option to walk away from clients who no longer align with your values. Maybe you dream of taking a year off to travel or care for aging parents. Maybe it's about building generational wealth or setting your kids up with financial literacy and opportunity.

Whatever your "why" is, get it on paper. When you can picture it, you can plan for it. When you can plan for it, you can take action.

It's also important to use benchmarks that are meaningful to you, not just large, round numbers like "$1 million."

A number means nothing if you don't know what it buys.

For example, if your ideal lifestyle would cost $60,000 a year and you're aiming to replace that income passively, you may only need a $1.2 million investment portfolio (based on the 5% annual withdrawal rule). But if you already have some passive income or plan to keep working part-time, your number may be much lower.

Here's where the power of specificity shows up again. Let's say you determine you want to generate $2,500 a month in passive income within 10 years. That's a clear, measurable target. It lets you reverse-engineer how much you'll need to invest each month and what kind of return to aim for. It also helps you stay motivated, because every time you contribute to your investment account, you know exactly what future you're building toward.

Here are a few examples of goal statements that have worked well for others:

- *"I will build a $500,000 investment portfolio by age 50 that gives me the option to downshift my business hours and focus on mentoring."*
- *"I want to earn $30,000 a year in passive income through a combination of index funds and real estate so I can fund mission work without relying on donations."*
- *"I'm building a legacy fund that provides each of my children with $25,000 by the time they graduate college—and teaches them how to manage it."*

Your money should be working for *your* version of success. That's the mindset shift. Not success as the world defines it, but success as you define it. The clearer you are about what you want, the more you will be able to plan and the more powerfully your investments can support it.

66

Plan for the Unseen.

Have a strong financial plan that includes protecting your loved ones in case you're not here tomorrow. And don't stop there. Make sure you have a strong succession plan in place, too. One that offers a stable off-ramp when the time comes to retire. Financial success isn't just about growth. It's about preparing for the transitions you can see and the ones you can't. — Kevin Peterson

99

2. Know How Much It Costs

"If you can define it, you can design it."

Once you've clarified your vision, the next step is to figure out the price tag. This is where a lot of people freeze. They get overwhelmed by the math, scared by the size of the numbers, or discouraged by how far they feel from their goals. But here's the truth: calculating how much your dream costs isn't meant to intimidate you — it's meant to empower you.

Clarity gives you control. When you break down what your goals cost, they stop being distant hopes and start becoming targets with timelines.

It's no longer, *"Maybe I'll get there."*

Instead, it's, *"I know what I need to do to get there and I've already started."*

Let's walk through a simple example. Suppose your goal is to have $50,000 a year in passive income by age 60. Using a conservative 5% annual return, that means you'll need about $1 million invested. That may sound like a lot, and it is, but the number isn't meant to scare you. It's meant to help you reverse-engineer a plan.

Here's the math: If you invest $1,000 a month for 25 years, and you earn an average return of 8% annually, you'll reach that $1 million target. Can't do $1,000 a month yet? Start with $250. Start with $100. Start with anything. What matters most is building the habit and increasing your investment over time.

This isn't about perfection. It's about consistency. And consistency always beats intensity over the long haul.

Use Tools to Map the Journey

You don't need to be a spreadsheet wizard or financial advisor to calculate these numbers. There are plenty of free tools that make it easy:
- NerdWallet's Retirement Calculator
- Vanguard's Investment Goal Planner
  FIRE (Financial Independence, Retire Early) Calculators
- Fidelity's Planning & Guidance Center

These tools allow you to plug in your age, contribution amount, and estimated rate of return to see how your investments will grow over time. They're not perfect, but they give you a roadmap. And roadmaps build confidence.

Here's a tip: Run two scenarios—one based on your current investment amount and one based on your ideal future contributions. The comparison will give you a sense of urgency without guilt. You're not "behind", you're just planning forward with new information.

Think in Layers, Not Just a Lump Sum

When people think about investing, they often imagine a giant mountain they have to climb. But most wealth is built in layers. There's no single finish line. It's a series of stepping stones:

- Maybe your first goal is a $10,000 emergency fund.
- Then $100,000 in retirement accounts.
- Next, you might consider investing in a rental property, opening a brokerage account, or creating a legacy fund for your children.

Each layer is progress. Each dollar invested is a step forward. And the earlier you start, even with small amounts, the more powerful compound growth becomes.

As Albert Einstein allegedly said, "Compound *interest is the eighth wonder of the world. He who understands it earns it... he who doesn't pays it.*"

Visualize What Your Money Can Do

Let's bring this back to something tangible. Imagine this: you put away $500 a month starting at age 35. You stick with it for 30 years. At an 8% average return, you'll end up with over $680,000. That's nearly seven hundred thousand dollars from regular, manageable contributions—no windfalls, no luck, no timing the market.

Now, imagine you wait 10 years to get started. Same $500/month, but now you've only got 20 years left. Your total? Just $295,000. That 10-year delay cost you $385,000 in lost growth. That's the cost of waiting.

The best time to start was yesterday. The second-best time is today.

Let the Numbers Motivate, Not Paralyze

Don't let the size of your dream scare you off the starting line. You're not expected to leap the whole mountain. You just need to take the next step — and then the one after that.

You can't hit a target you can't see. When you know what you want and how much it costs, you move out of wishful thinking and into strategic action. That's when investing stops being intimidating and starts being exhilarating. You're not just hoping things work out. You're building a future with intention and precision.

And you're doing it one smart, consistent move at a time.

3. Know Your Numbers

"You can't scale what you don't measure."

As a business owner, you wouldn't run your business without checking your metrics. You track revenue, expenses, client retention, and conversion rates because those numbers tell you what's working and what needs your attention. So why do so many of us try to build personal wealth without tracking the numbers that matter?

Your financial life deserves the same level of visibility as your business. In fact, it needs it. Unlike business KPIs, your personal wealth doesn't have quarterly review meetings or investor reports forcing accountability. That's up to you.

Knowing your numbers isn't just about spreadsheets or apps. It's a mindset. It's the shift from "I'm bad with money" to "I'm the CFO of my own wealth." It's about reclaiming agency over your finances— and realizing that confidence comes from clarity, not perfection.

Start with a Personal Dashboard

You don't need to become a financial analyst to know your numbers. You just need a system that works for you. The simplest place to begin? A personal financial dashboard. Whether it's a spreadsheet, an app, or a whiteboard on your office wall, your dashboard should show:

- **Net Worth:** Assets minus liabilities. This is your 30,000-foot view.
- **Monthly Contributions:** What are you consistently investing or saving?
- **Account Allocation:** Are you diversified, or too concentrated in one area?
- **Investment Performance:** How have your accounts grown over time?
- **Cash Reserves:** How much is in your emergency or security fund?

Update this monthly. Yes—monthly.

It doesn't need to be complex. You're not doing a deep audit. You're simply checking in, the same way you'd check sales metrics or web traffic in your business.

Develop the Habit of Financial Visibility

Your numbers shouldn't just be something you check at tax time or when your accountant calls. They should be part of your rhythm. Set a monthly financial check-in on your investments, just like you'd schedule a team meeting or a client review. This is your CEO moment (and at this stage in the book, you are probably already doing this in other areas of your business, too).

During your investment check-in, ask:
- *Are my investments growing?*
- *Am I staying on track with contributions?*
- *Are there any red flags—unusual dips, missed deposits, or out-of-control spending?*

This doesn't need to take hours. Even a 15-minute monthly review builds familiarity and ownership.

Bookkeeping Isn't Just for Business

One of the most underrated wealth-building strategies is keeping your personal finances as clean and organized as your business books. This starts with having separate accounts for personal and business expenses so your records stay clear and easy to manage. Make it a habit to review your bank statements at least once a month, not just for oversight but to stay actively engaged with where your money is going. Label and categorize your transactions—especially your investments—so you can track patterns, performance, and spending categories with ease. Store important documents like IRA statements, insurance policies, and tax returns in one easily accessible place.

Clean books don't just help you at tax time. They make everything easier, from applying for loans to planning for retirement. More importantly, they lower your stress. When you know where everything is and how it's doing, you don't panic; you lead.

Reading Your Investment Statements Without Panic

Many people avoid logging into their investment accounts because they're afraid of what they'll see. But ignoring your accounts doesn't protect you. It just blinds you. Markets fluctuate. That's normal. You don't need to obsess over daily changes, but you *do need to understand the big picture:*

- *What's your total balance?*
- *What percentage is invested in stocks vs. bonds?*
- *How much have you contributed this year?*
- *How are your investments performing compared to your goals?*
- *And in today's world, we have to ask ourselves what world events are happening that will impact our investment strategy.*

If your portfolio is down for a month or two, don't freak out. Zoom out. Look at the five-year trend. Remind yourself that volatility is part of the process and that long-term investors ride out short-term storms. Think of it like checking your weight once a month instead of every day. You're not reacting to fluctuations—you're watching for patterns and progress.

4. Act As If

Behave like the investor you're becoming. Start now, build consistency, and let the habit create the results.

"Wealthy people don't wait until they feel ready—they act like they're ready."

Start Where You Are: Open an Investment Account

One of the most important truths about building wealth is this: the habit comes first, then the outcome. Most people think they'll start investing once they "feel ready" or once they've hit some magical income milestone. But the people who succeed financially aren't waiting. They're acting, not perfectly, not with massive resources, but consistently.

The simplest, most tangible way to act as if you're an investor is to become one. That starts with opening an account. For most business owners or self-employed professionals, a Roth IRA or SEP IRA is a solid starting point. These accounts are widely available through platforms like Vanguard, Fidelity, Schwab, or even user-friendly apps like Betterment or Wealthfront.

You don't need to understand everything about investing to take this first step. You just need to get started. Choose a low-fee index fund, pick your contribution frequency, and hit confirm. Just like that, you've crossed the line from intention to action. And no, you don't have to max out your contributions in year one. If all you can do is $50 or $100 a month, that's still building the habit. You've put a stake in the ground. That's what matters most.

Automate to Stay in the Game

Automation is where consistency is born. Once you've opened your account, set up a recurring transfer—weekly, biweekly, or monthly. You don't want to leave your financial future to memory or will-power. You want it on autopilot. This is especially critical for business owners who often deal with fluctuating income. Automation brings stability. During lower-revenue months, it keeps you connected to your long-term goals. During big months, you can always increase your contribution, but you won't have to start from scratch.

The secret of wealth-building isn't in a windfall. It's in the habit. Consistency beats intensity every time. A modest but regular contribution is more powerful and sustainable than sporadic bursts of large deposits followed by long gaps. Automation keeps you in the game.

Rewriting Your Financial Identity

Every time you make a contribution, review your account, or read a financial article, you're reinforcing a new identity. You're no longer just a spender, a saver, or a business owner with cash flow. You're becoming a wealth builder. And that shift is powerful. Because money isn't just about dollars. It's about confidence.

When you act as if you're the kind of person who builds wealth, you start making decisions from that place. You start seeing options where you used to see obstacles. That belief system starts to shape your behavior, which in turn shapes your outcomes.

You're not just playing defense with your money. You're building a strong offense.

Real Power is Found in Repetition

This isn't about perfection. It's about showing up. Making the choice. Building the muscle. You won't feel like a pro investor after your first $100 transfer. That's okay. You didn't feel like a CEO the first time you launched your business either. But you kept going. You learned. You adapted. And now, look where you are.

Treat your finances with the same respect. The real power of acting "as if" is that it shifts you from reaction mode to leadership. You're not just earning. You're allocating. You're planning. You're creating a system that supports your future, one small decision at a time.

Open the account. Automate the transfer. Trust the process.

You're not pretending—you're becoming. You're not waiting to be wealthy—you're stepping into it, right now.

5. Take Inspired Action

"Money is more than math—it's meaning and a language all its own."

You've opened the account. You've automated the contributions. You're tracking your progress. Now comes the heart of it all: putting your money where your mission is. Inspired action is more than just movement. It's aligned movement. It's what happens when your financial strategy reflects your values, your goals, and the change you want to create in the world. This is where wealth becomes leadership.

Investing as a Form of Leadership

We often think of investing as a personal, private endeavor, something you do quietly, behind a screen, on your own time. But here's a reframe: investing is leadership. It's a way of exercising influence. Every dollar you invest supports a company, a system, or a vision for the future. And you get to choose which future that is.

For example, ESG (Environmental, Social, Governance) funds allow you to invest in companies that are committed to sustainable practices, fair labor, and strong corporate ethics. Impact investing takes it a step further by funding ventures that produce measurable social or environmental benefits — such as clean water initiatives, affordable housing, and access to healthcare. When you choose these routes, your money becomes more than a growth engine—it becomes a statement.

And maybe more importantly?

When your investments reflect what matters to you, they don't feel disconnected or abstract. You're not just accumulating dollars. You're funding a future that's meaningful. That emotional connection can help you stay the course when markets dip or when life gets noisy.

It turns investing into a values-driven decision rather than just a financial one.

Your portfolio, like your business, can be an extension of your values. Wealth gives you options, and those options become actions that ripple far beyond your bank account. Whether you realize it or not, you are leading with your money.

Empowering Your Circle Through Financial Education

The more you learn about investing, the more equipped you are to teach and inspire others. That ripple effect is real, especially for business owners. Your habits and mindset around money set the tone for your team, your clients, and even your family.

Consider this: Have you ever hosted a financial Q&A for your team? Shared a book or video that helped you shift your mindset? Helped a family member open their first investment account? These small moments can create a culture of financial empowerment.

You don't need to have all the answers—you just need to be willing to talk about money in a way that's honest, accessible, and encouraging. Every conversation that normalizes financial literacy becomes an act of service and a legacy move. You're not just growing your wealth—you're raising the tide for everyone around you.

See It Before You Build It: Visualize Your Legacy

Money is a tool. And the best tools are used with intention. One of the most powerful exercises you can do is to visualize your ideal future and ask, What kind of investor do I need to be to get there?

Close your eyes and imagine the life you're building with your investments. Not just the balance sheet, but the lifestyle. The freedom. The legacy. Maybe it's early retirement and travel. Maybe it's paying for your grandchildren's college. Maybe it's buying land, funding a nonprofit, or finally having the power to say "no" to projects that don't align with your values.

Now write it down. Be specific. This vision is more than a motivational tool. It's a guidepost for every financial decision you make. When you connect your money to your mission, your investment habits gain meaning. You're no longer saving just to save. You're building something real, something lasting, something uniquely yours.

Section 6: From Scarcity to Strategy—Real Stories, Real Wins

Most of us weren't born with a roadmap to financial independence. We learned through trial, error, and the stories passed down to us—stories often rooted in scarcity, fear, or silence. Maybe your family didn't talk about money. Maybe your early financial lessons came from mistakes. But at some point, every wealth-builder has to choose a new narrative: one rooted in strategy, not scarcity.

This section brings that transformation to life. These real stories show how mindset shifts, small steps, and intentional decisions helped everyday people build momentum and wealth. Some started with apps, some with spreadsheets, and some with wake-up calls. All of them show that the journey to financial power begins with one brave decision.

Greta: From Stress to Structure

Greta was a successful business consultant who made great money but carried constant financial anxiety. Despite the income, she felt behind. Investing felt intimidating, and she assumed she had to understand everything before she could begin. But one book—*The Simple Path to Wealth*—flipped that script.

She began by opening a Roth IRA and automating a modest $200 monthly contribution. She also began routing a percentage of her consulting checks into a low-cost brokerage account. Nothing flashy, just small, steady steps.

Within a year, Greta wasn't just building wealth. She was building confidence. The fear she used to feel every time she thought about retirement? Gone. Not because she had it all figured out but because she had a system. She moved from surviving to planning, and that shift created peace she couldn't buy.

Sarah: Changing Her Identity, $5 at a Time

Sarah always thought investing was for "other people"—the "ones who grew up with money or had six-figure jobs. She didn't think she had enough to get started, so she didn't start at all. Until one day, she downloaded Acorns, an app that rounds up your purchases and invests the change.

Watching those small amounts grow into something tangible changed everything. Suddenly, she saw herself not as someone who was "too broke" to invest but as someone who was building. This small mindset shift paved the way for more significant actions, such as opening her first Roth IRA, setting a goal, and learning about index funds.

Her identity changed first. The wealth followed.

Mike: Learning the Hard Way

Mike poured every penny back into his fast-growing creative agency. For years, it worked until life threw him a curveball. A family health crisis hit, and Mike realized he had no emergency fund, no personal savings, and no investments. All of his money was tied up in his business.

That crisis forced him to face a hard truth: he had built something great, but he hadn't built anything for himself. He began diverting 10% of his income into a SEP IRA and created a separate personal "Freedom Fund" that existed outside his business bank account.

Mike still reinvests in his company but now, he invests in himself first.

As he puts it, *"The business is valuable, but I'm the one who built it. I had to start protecting the builder."*

Joseph Lombardi's Family: A Cautionary Tale

Joseph grew up in a family business worth millions. But when his father died unexpectedly, the lack of a will, life insurance, or succession plan unraveled everything. Legal battles drained resources. Assets were sold under pressure. Generational wealth was lost, not because the business failed, but because the planning never happened.

Now, Joseph teaches other business owners how to protect what they're building. His message is clear: if you want to leave a legacy, you can't afford to avoid the uncomfortable conversations. Wealth without a strategy is a house without a foundation.

Each of these stories has a different starting point, but they all reach the same conclusion: Strategy is stronger than scarcity. Hope is not a financial strategy. You don't need perfection. You need intention, action, and a willingness to see yourself differently.

That's how real people build real wealth and so can you.

Section 7: Your Call to Action—Your 15-Minute Wealth Builder

Let's keep it simple: building wealth doesn't have to start with a windfall or a 10-year plan. It can start today—in the next 15 minutes. You don't need a financial degree, a six-figure salary, or a perfect portfolio. You need a willingness to act. Small, consistent steps create the foundation of long-term wealth, and this section is your quick-start guide.

Think of this as your personal launchpad. Whether you've never invested a dollar or you're restarting after a long break, this checklist will walk you through exactly how to begin. Pick one action and do it today.

Not next month.

Not when the market "feels better."

Today.

Your Action Steps:

✔ Choose a Platform

Your first step is selecting a platform where you'll open your investment account. Pick one that matches your comfort level and get familiar with the layout. You'll be surprised how much easier it feels once you log in and look around.

✔ Choose an Account Type

Next, decide which type of account you want to open. This will depend on your goals, income, and whether you're self-employed. Here are three common options: You can't go wrong starting with a Roth IRA if you qualify. If you're a business owner, consider both a Roth IRA and a SEP for different goals.

✔ Set Up Auto-Transfers

This is where the magic happens. Choose an amount you won't miss—$10, $25, $100 — and set up a recurring transfer from your checking account to your investment account. Weekly, biweekly, monthly — it doesn't matter. What matters is automation. Automation removes the emotional rollercoaster and eliminates the decision fatigue. You're building wealth while you sleep.

✔ Track Progress. Celebrate Consistency.

Don't obsess over daily numbers — but do keep tabs on your growing wealth. Use a free tracker, such as a simple spreadsheet, to monitor your contributions and account value over time. More importantly, celebrate your consistency, not your balance. Every auto-transfer is a deposit into your future freedom. Every check-in reinforces your identity as an investor.

✔ Pick One New Source of Education Every Month

Choose one investing book, podcast, or YouTube channel to follow every month and develop your curiosity for lifelong learning. Education builds confidence, and confidence builds action. You don't have to become an expert overnight, but committing to learning a little each week will pay off in clarity and motivation.

You don't have to do everything. You just have to do something. Wealth doesn't grow from perfection. It grows from motion.

So take 15 minutes today. Choose a platform. Open an account. Set a transfer.

That small action?

It's not just an investment in your future. It's a declaration: *I am someone who builds wealth.*

Section 8: CEO Thought Leadership—Lead Wealth-First and Build Like a CEO

For most entrepreneurs, investing gets pushed to the bottom of the list. It's treated like a personal finance task—something you'll "get to later" once the business grows, expenses settle, or life slows down. But that mindset is a liability.

The truth is, smart CEOs don't wait until things are perfect to make strategic decisions. They invest early. They prioritize long-term infrastructure. And they build systems that give them leverage, not just income.

Wealth is one of those systems. When you treat investing like a leadership function—not a side project—you shift the way you operate. It stops being about saving a few dollars and starts being about buying back your time, securing your future, and creating options. That's what margin is. And margin is what fuels growth.

Think of it this way: CEOs invest in R&D, in talent, in new markets. Not because they're already ahead, but because they *want* to stay ahead. They make decisions that serve both the present and the future. Investing does the same thing for your personal life. It builds a buffer. It buys freedom. It allows you to weather seasons of uncertainty without panic.

Investing should be part of your regular CEO checklist. Not just revenue targets and client acquisition, but contributions to your Roth IRA, reviewing your asset allocation, checking your emergency fund, and setting new investment goals.

You don't need to be an expert. You don't need to have it all figured out. But you do need to act like the leader of your financial life.

Think less about when you'll be ready and more about what actions reflect the business owner you want to become. Lead with systems, not just hustle. Build wealth the same way you build your business: with purpose, consistency, and a long-term strategy.

Treat investing as part of your leadership role.

Because if you're serious about sustainability, freedom, and legacy? Wealth isn't optional. It's foundational.

———————

Top 5 Takeaways for Chapter 10: Making Your Money Work for You

1. Investing Is a CEO-Level Strategy, Not a Luxury

Entrepreneurs must treat investing as a business decision, not a someday task. It builds leverage, freedom, and long-term security.

2. Profit Is the Beginning, Not the End

Earning money is step one. The real power comes when you give that profit a job through intentional, consistent investing.

3. Small, Consistent Actions Build Wealth

You don't need to start big. You just need to start. Automating even $20 a week can shift your mindset and build momentum.

4. Mindset Is the First Investment

Reframing limiting beliefs—like "investing is risky" or "I'm bad with money"—is essential. Wealth-building starts in your thoughts before it shows up in your bank account.

5. Structure Beats Strategy

Tools like the **Three-Bucket System,** automation, and wealth dashboards are what turn good intentions into actual outcomes. Investing is about systematizing, not gambling.

Chapter 11:
It's Okay (and Maybe Even Good) to Ask for Help: Outsourcing vs. Delegating

66

Focus on what you do best — and delegate the rest.

Financial success doesn't come from doing everything yourself. It's built through consistency and adaptability. You must track and understand your cash flow, your profit margins, and your break-even point—because those numbers don't lie. They reveal the true health and heartbeat of your business. — *Daniel Kochka*

99

Section 1: Why Doing it All Yourself Doesn't Work

When I first started my business, it was just a side hustle. By day, I went to my main job and was focused, responsible, and committed. But when 6:00 hit, I'd shift gears. I'd head home, eat dinner, spend a short amount of time with my family, and then I'd crack open my laptop.

Nights, weekends, early mornings—I poured myself into building something more. And slowly but surely, it started to work. I began to make consistent money. I could see the potential. But instead of stepping into a new rhythm, I found myself teetering between two worlds—my job and my growing business—still trying to do everything myself. It was exhausting. And worse, I was stuck in a loop of almost scaling and almost burning out.

It reminded me of something from childhood: trying to ride a teeter-totter by myself. Have you ever done that? I remember sitting on one end and quickly realizing that it didn't work unless someone else was on the other end.

So I'd run and find a friend to climb on the other side. And then came the next challenge—balance and rhythm. If my friend weighed more than I did, I'd be stuck in the air, legs dangling, calling out, "Farmer Brown, Farmer Brown, let me down!" If I weighed more, they'd be the one stranded up in the air. But when we were evenly matched and when the weight was distributed just right...that's when the fun began. Up and down, back and forth—we could finally teeter-totter like we were supposed to. We'd sing songs, count, laugh, and play games on that cherished childhood playground game.

Growing a business by yourself is like trying to ride a teeter-totter alone—you push with everything you've got, but you don't get very far. When you refuse to ask for help, you end up expending all your energy with little movement. That was exactly where I found myself until I started outsourcing the tasks that drained me and delegating the work I didn't need to own. That's when the balance finally shifted. I stopped trying to play every role and started focusing on what only I could do.

Delegation wasn't about giving up control. It was about creating the momentum I needed to grow. It was the key that changed everything.

Section 2: Delegation Is Growth, Not Weakness

So if doing it all yourself doesn't work, why do so many of us insist on operating solo?

Many business owners struggle with delegation, not because they don't understand its value, but because they're holding onto beliefs that feel practical in the moment.

You've probably said or thought at least one of the following:

- *"It's just easier if I do it myself."*
- *"I'll hire help when I'm making more money."*
- *"No one can do it the way I do it."*
- *"I don't have time to train anyone."*
- *"It'll take longer to explain it than to just get it done myself."*

These statements sound reasonable, especially in the early stages of business. But left unchallenged, they create a cycle that leads to exhaustion and prevents growth. They keep you stuck doing low-value work that eats your time and mental bandwidth—without actually moving the business forward.

The reality is this: if you want to scale your business, you can't do everything yourself. Delegation isn't a sign of giving up or losing control. It's a strategic decision to focus your time and energy where it delivers the greatest return.

Most business owners wait too long to ask for help. There's this unspoken belief that needing help somehow means you're not capable or not ready. But learning to delegate is actually the sign of a leader. It's the difference between working *in* your business and working *on* your business. Delegation creates space for vision, leadership, and growth.

Letting go is scary. You may worry that no one will do it like you—or that everything will fall apart if you're not in every detail. But if you stay stuck in that mindset, you become the bottleneck.

Here's something that you must understand in order to move forward. As the business owner, your highest-value tasks are the ones that require your experience, expertise, or leadership. These include things like setting the company vision, making key financial decisions, deepening relationships with clients or strategic partners, and developing offers that drive revenue. These are tasks that should stay on your plate. But everything else—especially operational, administrative, and repetitive tasks—can be handed off with the right systems in place.

Start with an honest assessment of your time. Track everything you do for one week. Categorize your tasks based on how valuable they are to the business and whether or not they require *you*.

Use Three Buckets:

1. Only I Can Do This
2. Someone Else Could Do This With Training
3. Why Am I Still Doing This?

You'll quickly start to see which tasks are draining your time and attention. Examples might include managing your calendar, posting on social media, responding to general inquiries, or sending invoices. These are important—but they don't require your brainpower.

Now, let's talk about cost. One of the most common objections to delegation is, "I can't afford to hire someone." But that's not always true. You may be looking at the expense without factoring in the opportunity cost.

Let's say your time is worth $100/hour based on the value you bring to your business through high-level work. If you're spending five hours a week on $20/hour tasks, you're effectively losing $400 in potential value every week. That's $1,600 a month. Meanwhile, a virtual assistant or contractor could take that workload off your hands for a fraction of the cost—and free you up to bring in more revenue.

Additionally, there's a non-financial ROI that matters just as much: your focus, your energy, and your ability to make clear decisions. Delegation reduces decision fatigue and creates space for better strategy. When you're not constantly in reactive mode, your thinking becomes sharper, and your leadership improves.

Once you've identified a task to delegate, your next step is to create a system. Don't just hand it off without structure. Take 30 minutes to document how the task is currently done. You can use a checklist, write out step-by-step instructions, or record a quick Loom video walking through the process. This becomes your standard operating procedure (SOP)—something that ensures consistency even when the person doing the task changes.

Start small. Choose one task you do every week that takes time but doesn't require your unique skill set. Create a process, delegate it, and then observe. Did the work get done on time? Were the results satisfactory? Did it free up time on your calendar? Use that feedback to improve the process, and then move on to the next task.

You don't need a full team to start delegating. You can begin with a freelance contractor, a part-time assistant, or even an automation tool. The point is to begin *removing yourself* from tasks that limit your ability to grow.

As your systems improve and your trust in the process increases, delegation will become more natural. It's not just about handing things off—it's about building operational resilience. Eventually, your business becomes less dependent on your direct involvement, which gives you the flexibility to focus on scaling — or even step away when needed without everything falling apart.

Also important: build in time to review how delegation is working. Are your team members clear on expectations? Are you providing the support and feedback they need to succeed? Delegation is not a set-it-and-forget-it process. It requires communication, refinement, and mutual trust. But once the rhythm is in place, it creates exponential leverage.

This isn't about being inspirational. It's about being strategic. If your goal is to build a business that scales without burning out, delegation isn't optional—it's operationally necessary.

———————

Section 3: Outsourcing vs. Delegating

As your business grows, you'll quickly realize that doing everything yourself is neither sustainable nor strategic. But getting support isn't one-size-fits-all. There are two main ways to lighten your load: outsourcing and delegating.

While both involve handing off tasks, they serve different purposes and require different approaches. Understanding the difference will help you make smart, intentional decisions about what to keep on your plate—and what to confidently pass to someone else.

Let's take a look at some of the differences between outsourcing and delegating.

Table 11.1: Outsourcing vs. Delegating

Category	Outsourcing	Delegating
Who You Assign It To	External professionals (contractors, freelancers, agencies)	Internal team (employees, VA, interns)
Typical Work Type	Specialized services or expert-level tasks	Routine or recurring operational tasks
Examples	Bookkeeping, copywriting, graphic design, paid ads, tech support	Scheduling, inbox management, client follow-ups, administration tasks
Scope	Often project-based or task-specific	Ongoing responsibilities integrated into daily workflow
Goal	Tap into external expertise without hiring full-time	Free up internal time and improve operational efficiency
Cost Structure	Usually a flat rate or an hourly contractor rate	Salary, hourly wage, or retainer (if VA)
Best For	When you need expertise you don't have in-house	When you're doing too much that doesn't require your expertise
Ownership of Process	Usually handled externally with minimal oversight	Typically managed and refined internally over time

The key takeaway here?

Both outsourcing and delegating are essential. The goal isn't to offload everything—it's to offload the *right* things to the *right* people.

Case Study: My Story from Burnout to Breakthrough

For a long time, I believed that being busy meant I was doing it right. I was proud of how much I could juggle—client calls, writing, editing, invoicing, emails, scheduling, social media, content creation, and everything in between. I was building my business after hours while still holding down a full-time job, squeezing in work wherever I could. I wasn't afraid of hard work—but eventually, the hustle started to feel like quicksand.

On paper, my business looked solid. I was charging $150 an hour for my work and staying consistently booked. But something felt off. I was always tired. Always behind. So I decided to track my time — honestly and completely — for one full week. I wrote down every task, every time block, every interruption. And when I sat down to run the numbers, the truth was humbling.

Although I was billing $150 per hour, once I factored in all the other tasks I was doing—emails, admin, tech issues, formatting, designing, managing my calendar, creating slide decks—I was actually making closer to $30 an hour!

That was a wake-up call.

I realized that I had become the bottleneck in my own business. I was holding onto tasks that didn't require my brain, my voice, or my leadership. And until I let go, nothing would change.

So I started small. The first step was **outsourcing**. I hired a freelance bookkeeper to take invoicing and financial tracking off my plate. Then I brought in a graphic designer who could build out brand visuals, presentation decks, and social media templates far faster—and better—than I ever could.

Next, I leaned into **delegating**. I hired a part-time virtual assistant and trained her to manage my inbox, schedule calls, prep newsletters, and post content from my templates. I recorded quick training videos, wrote simple checklists, and created a system she could step into without needing me every five minutes.

Within just a few weeks, the results were clear. I had more breathing room, more focus, and more energy. I wasn't buried in busywork anymore—I was back to doing the work that actually moved the needle.

Within a year:

- My workweek dropped from 70+ hours to a focused, manageable 40.
- My income increased because I was finally spending time on high-value, revenue-generating work.
- I reclaimed my weekends—and didn't feel guilty about it.

My biggest regret? **Not doing this sooner.**

So, what impact did my choices to outsource and delegate tangibly have on me and my business? The table below captures the very real benefits of these decisions.

Table 11.2: Outsourcing vs Delegating: Solutions & Impact

Type	Task	Support Solution	Impact
Outsourcing	Bookkeeping + invoicing	Freelance bookkeeper	Saved hours, reduced stress, cleaner reports
Outsourcing	Graphic design	Contract designer	Stronger brand visuals, less time in Canva
Delegating	Inbox + scheduling	VA with clear SOPs	Reclaimed focus and response time improved
Delegating	Blog uploads, content formatting	VA following templates	More consistency, no more late-night tech work
Refocused time	Strategy, consulting, creative work	Blocked calendar time	Higher income, better results, more fulfillment

Delegation and outsourcing didn't just make my business more efficient — they made it more sustainable. And profitable. And enjoyable. It wasn't about giving up control. It was about getting clear on what only I could do — and then building support systems for everything else.

If you're feeling stuck or spread too thin, start by tracking your time. Get honest about where your hours are going and how much those tasks are actually costing you. You might discover, like I did, that the key to earning more is doing *less* — but doing it better.

Section 4: How To Get Started: Simple Steps to Begin Delegating

If the thought of delegation makes you nervous, you're not alone. Most business owners wait too long to start because they assume it has to be perfect — or that they need a big team or big revenue first. The truth is, delegation is a skill you build, not a single switch you flip. And the sooner you start developing that skill, the faster your business will grow.

The first place to begin is with your time. Track it. For one full week, document what you're doing throughout each day. You can track it with an app or the old fashioned way with pen and paper — your choice. Don't just track the big things: include everything. Writing emails, scheduling calls, formatting documents, updating your website, answering DMs, sending invoices, editing graphics—if it takes up time, it goes on the list. Be honest and detailed. You're not doing this to impress anyone—you're doing it to diagnose what's keeping you stuck.

After the week is up, sit down and look at your time log. Highlight anything that:

- Drains your energy
- Doesn't generate revenue
- Could easily be done by someone else with basic instructions
- Repeats weekly or monthly

These are your **low-leverage tasks**. They are important, but they don't require *you*. This is where most business owners spend the majority of their time — handling operational clutter that could be delegated with the right support.

Next, calculate the **opportunity cost**. Let's say your work is worth $150 an hour when you're doing high-level consulting, coaching, or sales calls. If you're spending 10 hours a week on $25/hour tasks like scheduling, emails, or formatting, you're losing over $1,000 in potential value. Delegation isn't an expense — it's a way to recapture that lost value and reinvest it into growth activities.

Once you know what to delegate, don't rush to hand it off without preparation. Build a system around the task. This can be as simple as:

- A step-by-step checklist

- A screen recording showing how you complete the task
- A template or document to use repeatedly

Remember: people don't just need instructions — they need clarity. The better your process, the smoother the handoff. This also helps ensure consistent results, even if your support person changes over time.

Now it's time to start small. Pick one task. Just one. Maybe it's sending your weekly newsletter or managing your calendar. Train your VA, contractor, or team member on that task using the system you created. Set clear expectations: What does "done" look like? When is it due? What tools or access do they need? Be available to answer questions, but resist the urge to micromanage. You're training yourself to lead as much as you're training them to support.

After a few weeks, evaluate:
- How much time did this free up?
- Did the task get done consistently and well?
- What would make the process even smoother?
- What's the next task I can hand off?

And then? Keep going.

Delegation is iterative. Each small success builds confidence and capacity. Over time, you'll create a rhythm where your role becomes more strategic and less reactive.

Also, be aware of common traps. Don't delegate in a panic, without a plan. Don't assume people will "just figure it out." And don't expect someone to do something perfectly the first time without context or feedback. Delegation takes communication and adjustment — but the payoff is worth it.

Here's the entire process in summary:
- **Track your time** for one week.
- **Identify low-leverage tasks** that drain energy or don't require your expertise.
- **Calculate the opportunity cost** of keeping those tasks on your plate.
- **Create a simple system** (checklist, video, template) for one task.
- **Delegate one task** with clear expectations and support.
- **Evaluate and adjust**, then delegate the next task.

And remember, the goal isn't to remove yourself from your business overnight. The goal is to build a structure that allows your business to grow *with* you, not just *because* of you.

Section 5: The 5 Financial Success Principles

You know the drill. It's time to dig into how the 5 Financial Success Principles can support your delegation strategy.

The 5 Financial Success Principles of Delegation

1. **Know What You Want**
   Focus on your highest-value tasks only you can do.

2. **Know How Much It Costs**
   Calculate ROI — delegation costs less than burnout.

3. **Know Your Numbers**
   Measure time saved, revenue growth, and productivity impact.

4. **Act As If**
   Lead like a CEO by building a culture of empowerment and clarity.

5. **Take Inspired Action**
   Start small, systematize, and scale with intention.

1. Know What You Want

Before you can delegate effectively, you need to know what's worth keeping on your plate. Delegation begins with clarity — and that starts by identifying the tasks that truly require *you*. These are your high-value activities, the ones that drive revenue, set the vision, and shape the future of your business. They include:

- Strategic planning and business development
- Building and nurturing key client relationships
- Making high-level financial decisions
- Leading your brand, voice, and creative direction

These tasks are not easily replaceable. They require your judgment, leadership, and expertise. This is your *zone of genius*—where your time creates the most impact.

Once you've identified what only *you* can do, everything else becomes a candidate for delegation. This includes routine admin tasks like responding to emails, scheduling meetings, formatting documents, managing your calendar, handling tech setup, or maintaining your CRM. These may be necessary to run your business, but they don't require your brain to be the one doing them.

You might be capable of doing them—and you may even be good at them—but that doesn't mean you should do them. This can be a tough pill to swallow for some business owners, but just because something falls within your skillset doesn't mean it's always the best use of your time.

Your role as a business owner is to protect your time like it's your most valuable asset—because it is.

If you're unsure where to draw the line, ask yourself:
- Does this task require my voice, creativity, or leadership?
- Would doing this move the business forward in a meaningful way?
- Could someone else do this task with the right system or training?
- Is this task worth my hourly rate—or could I delegate it at a lower cost?

The clearer you are about your true role, the easier it becomes to let go of the rest—without guilt. And when your team or support structure is aligned around the right tasks, you don't just save time—you multiply your capacity.

Clarity creates freedom. When you know your worth, it becomes easier to release what's not yours to carry. This is the foundation of smart delegation. Get clear on what matters most, and protect it. Your growth depends on it.

2. Know How Much It Costs

Delegation costs less than burnout, especially when you factor in your energy.

We've already talked about the financial side of delegation: how doing $25/hour tasks when your time is worth $200/hour is actually costing you money. But there's another layer that's just as important—if not more so—and that's the emotional and energy return on investment (ROI).

Because here's the truth: not all costs show up on your bank statement. Some show up in your body, your mindset, your ability to think clearly, and your capacity to lead.

What does it cost you when your brain is constantly in reactive mode? When you're bouncing between client work, tech issues, and inbox overload?

When your entire day is filled with micro-decisions that have nothing to do with your core expertise?

That's **decision fatigue,** and it's real. It drains your focus, makes even simple tasks feel heavy, and eventually impacts the quality of your thinking. You might find yourself second-guessing things you used to do confidently. Or worse, you stop making decisions at all and just keep reacting.

There's also the cost of **creative block**. When your mind is cluttered with low-level to-dos, there's no room for strategy, vision, or fresh ideas. You're too busy keeping the machine running to step back and optimize it. Delegation doesn't just clear your calendar. It clears your head. And for most business owners, that's where the real breakthroughs happen.

And let's not forget about **missed opportunities,** such as that podcast interview you declined because you were behind on admin work or the proposal you didn't send because you were formatting a newsletter. How about the speaking gig you didn't pursue because your brain was fried? These things add up not just in lost income, but in lost momentum.

The **emotional ROI of delegation** can look like this:
- Clearer thinking
- A renewed sense of leadership
- Better sleep
- More consistent creativity
- The ability to be fully present with clients, your team, and your family

It's hard to measure peace of mind, but you know when you have it and when you don't. Delegation, done intentionally, isn't just a business strategy. It's a way to protect your mental clarity and preserve the energy that makes your business run.

You also get the **gift of relief,** not just in your calendar, but in your nervous system. Business owners often normalize stress until they forget what calm feels like. Delegation reintroduces ease. You get to walk into your day with a plan, not just a pile of tasks. You have breathing room between meetings. You're not constantly toggling between roles.

And don't underestimate how your energy sets the tone for your business. If you're frazzled, distracted, and rushing, your team feels it. Your clients feel it. Delegation gives you back the ability to show up with intention, not just get through the day.

So yes, delegation might cost you money on paper. But the real question is:

What is it costing you to stay overwhelmed, overbooked, and overstretched?

Because burnout has a price tag, too, and it's much higher than you think.

Delegation pays dividends — in clarity, creativity, and capacity. It's not just a cost. It's an investment in how you lead and live.

66

Most people want a quick fix.

But transformation doesn't happen in an instant—it happens in the cocoon. The cocoon stage is sacred. It's where growth, struggle, and evolution occur. If you cut it open too soon, the butterfly may never fly. And the same goes for people: they must go through the process. You can offer advice, encouragement, and support, but you cannot do it for them.

When the butterfly finally emerges, flight depends on balance. To soar, all four wings must work in harmony. For me, those wings are money, love, health, and time. If one wing is weak or neglected, you cannot fly. — Monique Gagné

99

3. Know Your Numbers

Measure the financial and time impact of delegation.

Delegation isn't a one-and-done decision. It's a system. And like any system, it only improves when you track what matters.

One of the biggest mistakes business owners make is handing off tasks without measuring the results. They either assume it's helping or they panic when the invoice arrives. But when you begin to track the true impact in time, money, and performance, you give yourself the data you need to delegate with confidence.

I'll never forget the first time I hired a virtual assistant. (I had waited too long, remember??) By the time I brought her on, I was underwater. Everything felt urgent. So I did what most business owners do in a state of panic: I started throwing tasks at her without a plan. Branding, client follow-ups, social media posts and engagements, and random to-dos that felt important in the moment but had no priority order.

At the end of that month, her invoice landed in my inbox, and I froze. The number was higher than I expected, and I had no system in place to understand what those hours went toward. My first instinct was to retreat. Maybe I'd made a mistake. Maybe I couldn't afford help after all.

But then I paused. I knew I had to treat this like a business owner, not a burned-out freelancer. So I got intentional. I created a task tracker. I assigned work based on specific goals. I monitored how long those tasks took and how much time I had reclaimed. That's when everything changed.

Turns out, my VA was faster than I was. She wasn't wasting time—she was saving it. She was getting through tasks in half the time, organizing files I hadn't touched in weeks, and freeing up my calendar so I could actually think again. Once I looked at the numbers clearly, I realized she wasn't an expense—she was an asset. Delegation, done right, wasn't draining money. It was creating capacity.

That's why knowing your numbers is essential.

Start with time tracking.

- *How many hours per week have you regained since you began delegating?*
- *How many of those hours are now being spent on higher-leverage activities—like client calls, strategic planning, or content creation?*

Then track your revenue trends.

- *Are you landing more business?*
- *Are proposals going out faster?*
- *Are your offers more polished because your energy is no longer diluted?*

You can even measure non-financial metrics:

- *Are tasks being completed faster or more accurately?*

- *Are your client response times improving?*
- *Are your conversion rates increasing?*
- *Are you finally consistent with content or outreach?*

Even things like sleep, stress levels, or how often you feel "caught up" are signs of ROI. They all count. They all matter.

You can't improve what you don't measure.

Delegation without data is just hopeful outsourcing. Delegation *with* numbers becomes a growth strategy.

5 Metrics to Track After You Delegate

Want to know if delegation is really working for you?

Don't guess—track it.

These five simple but powerful metrics can give you a clear picture of the return on your investment:

1. **Hours Reclaimed Per Week**
   Track how many hours you've regained since handing off specific tasks. This is your most immediate ROI — more time equals more opportunity for focus, strategy, and revenue-generating work.

2. **Revenue Growth**
   Compare your monthly or quarterly revenue before and after delegating. Are you closing more deals, onboarding more clients, or increasing your average sale? Often, freeing up your schedule directly impacts your bottom line.

3. **Task Efficiency**
   Are delegated tasks getting done faster or more accurately than when you handled them yourself? Track turnaround times, error rates, or backlog reduction. If your support is more efficient, you're already winning.

4. **Lead Response Time**
   Track how quickly you're now able to respond to new leads or customer inquiries. A faster response time often leads to higher conversion rates and better client satisfaction.

5. **Stress or Burnout Rating**
   Each week, rate your stress or burnout level on a simple 1–10 scale. Are you feeling more in control? More creative? Calmer? While not

a financial metric, this qualitative data can be just as powerful in showing how delegation is improving your life and leadership.

Pro Tip: Track these in a shared spreadsheet, task management tool, or weekly journal. Over time, you'll have tangible proof that delegation isn't just a cost—it's a smart business strategy.

And remember: this isn't about micromanaging your team — it's about managing your energy and optimizing your business. When you know what's working, you can do more of it. When you see inefficiencies, you can course-correct.

The more clearly you understand the impact of your support system, the more confidently you'll invest in it. Because the real win isn't just saving time — it's getting your business, your focus, and your peace of mind back.

4. Act As If

Embrace your role as a leader who empowers others.

If you want to run a successful business, you need to act like a CEO now—not someday when you're "big enough" or making a certain amount of money. That mindset is exactly what holds people back.

Here's the truth: CEOs don't do everything. They don't micromanage every task or get stuck in the weeds. Instead, they make high-level decisions, set the vision, and surround themselves with capable people they trust to get the job done. They don't just hire help—they **empower it**.

This doesn't mean you need a massive team or a corporate org chart to get started. Even if you're working with one part-time contractor, you can still act like a leader. Treat that contractor like your future COO. Set expectations. Create systems. Communicate clearly and respectfully. Honor their time and talents the way you'd want them to honor yours.

When you operate from this mindset, everything begins to shift. You stop running your business like a one-person show and start building something that can grow beyond you. You stop hoarding control out of fear and start building trust that frees you up to lead. You stop waiting for things to feel less chaotic before creating structure — and you create the structure that calms the chaos.

295

This is what leadership actually looks like. It's not about doing more. It's about **leading better**.

When I started working with CEOs, CFOs, COOs, and other high-level leaders from successful companies, I noticed something right away: there's a distinct difference between business owners who say, *"I want to be..."* and those who say, *"I am here."* The ones who had truly stepped into leadership didn't wait for a certain milestone, title, or bank balance. They acted as if they had already arrived—because in their minds, they had.

That observation changed everything for me. I rewrote both my internal and external soundtracks and started acting as if I was already the business owner I wanted to become. The rest followed. Clients, growth, clarity—it all aligned once I aligned.

Because here's the truth: success isn't defined by your bank account, the stage you're standing on, how many books you've written, or even the clients you serve. Success is something you feel first. And "acting as if" is the bridge that takes you from doubting your identity as a business owner to showing up as the boss you truly are.

Mindset Shift: *If you act like a solopreneur, you'll stay stuck. If you act like a CEO, you'll build something that lasts.*

Act as if. Lead as if. Build the business your future self will be proud of. Because leadership isn't just what you do — it's how you show up. So step fully into your role as a visionary and build the business—and life—you actually want. Act as if...and it will follow.

5. Take Inspired Action

Start small and build systems for scaling.

Throughout this chapter, we've touched on several key ideas: knowing your value, identifying tasks to delegate, calculating ROI, and beginning to build support systems. We've covered a lot, but now, it's time to tie those ideas together and anchor them in this final Financial Success Principle: Take Inspired Action.

This is where everything shifts from thinking to doing. Taking inspired action doesn't mean hiring a full team overnight or restructuring your whole business. It means choosing one small, intentional step to get your time back and build momentum.

The truth is, you won't always feel "ready." But that's not the point. Growth doesn't come from perfection—it comes from movement. When you act before you feel fully prepared, you give yourself the chance to learn, adapt, and lead. That's how true CEOs are built—not by waiting, but by deciding.

Start by asking yourself:
- *What drains me the most?*
- *What keeps falling through the cracks?*
- *What task could someone else do better, faster, or with more consistency?*

Then choose one of those tasks. Maybe it's invoicing, email management, client onboarding, or social media. Don't overthink it—just start.

Here are a few small but powerful steps you can take:
- **Hire a VA** for 2 hours a week to handle calendar management or inbox sorting.
- **Use automation tools** for scheduling, reminders, or repetitive client touchpoints.
- **Create a screen recording** showing how you complete a task and delegate it.
- **Outsource** design work, bookkeeping, or content editing to free up your creativity.

Document one system this week so that when you're ready to delegate it, the instructions are clear.

These actions might feel small, but they add up fast. Every system you build, every task you delegate, gives you more time, energy, and clarity to focus on what only you can do.

And here's a powerful reminder: delegation is not a one-time event—it's an ongoing business practice. If you want it to work, it has to have space in your schedule.

Pro Tip:

Put delegation and outsourcing on your calendar. Set a recurring block of time—weekly or even daily—to focus specifically on these tasks. This is your CEO hour. Use it to track time, evaluate priorities, assign or refine tasks, and build the infrastructure that will support your future growth. These areas don't improve on their own; they need your attention.

By taking inspired action, you're not just getting things off your plate—you're reclaiming your energy, creativity, and leadership capacity. You're shifting from reactive to intentional. From over-whelmed to empowered. From stuck to scalable.

Start today. Delegate one task. Build one system. Reclaim one hour.

That's the difference between hustle and flow. And that's the beginning of real growth.

Section 6: Personal Stories: How Letting Go Changed Everything

I used to believe that hustle was the only way to grow a business. That, unless I was constantly working and doing tasks such as answering emails, filling my calendar, and pushing projects forward, things would fall apart. I carried that belief like armor. It felt like responsibility. But in reality, it was fear disguised as diligence. And that fear was slowly burning me out.

I remember a specific week when life forced me to let go. My daughter had a series of medical appointments at the Mayo Clinic in Rochester, Minnesota, a five-hour drive from home. It was a heavy week, emotionally and logistically. I made the conscious decision to step back completely from work. No emails. No Zoom calls. No "just checking in" messages. I simply focused on being present with her.

And then something surprising happened.

When I got back, I logged into my email, expecting a backlog of problems. Instead, I saw a message from a potential client. They had been referred by someone I barely knew, had already looked at my work, and were ready to book. No chase. No pitch. No perfect fun-nel. The business came to me. And not because I worked harder, but because I created space.

That wasn't the only time life offered a reality check.

One snowy morning, we woke up to a full-on blizzard. School was canceled, and my to-do list was bursting at the seams. Normally, I would have tried to juggle everything—working from my laptop while the kids played around me, feeling guilty no matter where my attention was. But that day, I made a different choice. I closed the laptop and chose snowmen over sales calls.

We played outside until our faces were red and our gloves were soaked. We drank hot chocolate and watched a movie in our pajamas. And later that evening, when I finally opened my laptop, there it was: a client payment notification. No pitch. No follow-up email. Just a reminder that maybe, just maybe, I didn't need to hustle to be worthy of income.

Another moment that stays with me happened after a routine doctor's appointment with my son CJ. On our way home, I thought of my friend Lisa and asked her if she wanted to grab lunch. We met in the city, talked about life, and caught up like old friends do. On our way out, CJ spotted a Dollar Tree and asked if we could stop. My gut reaction was, "No, we've got to get home—I have work to do." But then I paused. What if I just said yes?

So I unbuckled him from his car seat, and we wandered the aisles of Dollar Tree together. We picked out a coloring book and a pack of glow sticks. We didn't hurry. And when we got home, I sat down to check my emails and saw a $500 payment come through from a client I hadn't even followed up with that week.

That's when I realized something deep and true:

"Letting go doesn't mean you lose control—it means you stop gripping so tightly that nothing else can grow."

Delegation, rest, and white space on the calendar—these are not signs of weakness. *They are signals of trust.* They say, "I trust my systems. I trust my value. I trust that what I've built can carry on, even if I step away."

And trust is a muscle. You don't just wake up one day feeling confident in your ability to let go. You build that confidence one decision at a time. You practice letting go in small ways—a few hours offline, a task delegated, an email answered by someone else—and slowly, your business begins to shift from hustle to flow.

This shift didn't just make me more rested. It made me *better*. My creativity came back. My decision-making got sharper. I stopped spinning my wheels and started thinking strategically again. I had room to dream, to plan, to breathe.

Letting go changed everything. It created space for the right people, the right clients, and the right opportunities to show up. It reminded me that my business doesn't need me to be perfect. It just needs me to be present and protected from burnout.

Let go.

Outsource.

Delegate.

Trust what you've built.

The business will still be there—and so will the joy.

"

You need a life outside the job you love—

for your mental, physical, and emotional health. Taking time with loved ones or engaging in activities that bring you joy recharges your brain. It gives you more in the tank for the next day at the office. Work-life harmony isn't a distraction from success—it's fuel for it. — Jennifer *"JJ" Jank*

"

Section 7: CEO Thought Leadership—You Are Worthy of Support

When I was a kid, I hated anything that restricted me—tight clothing, rules, and especially seatbelts. My parents were always telling me to buckle up, and in my young and overly confident mind, I couldn't see what the big deal was. I thought if we were going to crash, I'd just put my seatbelt on "super duper fast." I had all the confidence in the world that I could beat the system with speed and timing.

But we all know the flaw in that logic.

You don't get the luxury of buckling up during a crash. By the time you realize you need the protection, it's already too late. And it's the same with outsourcing and delegation.

Most business owners wait way too long to ask for help. We tell ourselves we'll buckle up later — when things calm down, when the next launch is done, when we finally catch our breath. But if you're waiting for the crash to start delegating, you're already behind. CEOs don't wait for things to break before putting systems in place. They build support structures early. They're already buckled in for the ride.

When I started working alongside high-level leaders—CEOs, CFOs, COOs, CMOs,—I began to notice a pattern. The ones who had built thriving, sustainable companies didn't just dream about success, they operated from it. They didn't wait to "feel ready." They made decisions, built systems, and delegated with the belief that their business was already worthy of support. They didn't just act like leaders — they led, with clarity and conviction.

That energy? It's magnetic. And it's a big part of what separates those who stay stuck from those who scale.

That realization changed everything for me. I stopped approaching delegation like a desperate backup plan and started treating it like the growth strategy it is. I began outsourcing before I felt ready. I stopped clinging to every task and started asking, "Who can help me do this better?" That shift—from scrambling to supported—wasn't just a mindset upgrade. It was the moment I truly started running my business like a CEO.

Because here's the hard truth: if you don't let go, you become the bottleneck.

And your business? It will suffocate under the weight of your to-do list.

Outsourcing and delegation aren't luxuries. They are the seatbelt, the safety structure, and the strategic tools that allow your business to scale. They restore your energy. They protect your mental bandwidth. They unlock your ability to lead at the level your vision requires.

Here's what I've learned:
- Successful people don't do everything. They build systems and teams that support growth.
- Successful people let go sooner. They trust more. They prepare early. And as a result, they move faster and further.

You started this business to create freedom, impact, and success.

That only happens when you stop reacting and start leading.

You don't need to prove anything by doing it all yourself.

The time for change is now.

Section 8: Your Call to Action—Building Your Delegation Plan

So buckle up, CEO. It's time to make a commitment to growth, let go of fear, and trust in yourself and your business.

It's time to build your plan for delegation.

In order to do this well, go back to the templates and reflection questions in section five of this chapter and take the time to complete them (or schedule time in your calendar to do this if you can't do it now.) The Five Principles of Financial Success hold the power to truly transform your ability to delegate wisely, if only you take the time to dive into them with bravery.

And then?

Lean into that last principle — *take inspired action*. Find a tangible way to take one step forward toward releasing control and allowing for growth through delegation or outsourcing.

As a reminder, that might look like:

- **Hiring a VA** for 2 hours a week to handle calendar management or inbox sorting.
- **Using automation tools** for scheduling, reminders, or repetitive client touchpoints.
- **Creating a screen recording** showing how you complete a task and delegate it.
- **Outsourcing** design work, bookkeeping, or content editing to free up your creativity.
- **Documenting one system** this week so that when you're ready to delegate it, the instructions are clear.

Whatever inspired action you choose to take, know that your movement matters.

And if you're standing at the edge, afraid to ask for help, afraid to take your foot off the gas?

Hear this: You don't have to hustle to be worthy. You don't have to do it all to be successful. And you don't have to sacrifice your life to build your business. Growth and abundance are found in letting go.

I promise—it will be worth the jump.

Top 5 Takeaways for Chapter 11: The Delegation Mindset Shift

1. Delegation Is a Strategic Move, Not a Sign of Weakness

Letting go of tasks doesn't mean you're incapable — it means you're stepping into your role as a visionary leader. True CEOs focus on what only they can do and empower others to do the rest.

2. Outsourcing and Delegating Are How You Scale

You won't build a thriving business by doing everything yourself. Offloading tasks frees up your time, energy, and mental space so you can focus on high-impact decisions that move the business forward.

3. Track the ROI of Delegation

Knowing your numbers is essential. Track time saved, revenue shifts, response times, and conversion rates. Delegation without measurement is just guesswork — data helps you optimize and refine.

4. Start Small, but Start Now

You don't need a full team to begin. Choose one draining task, document the process, delegate it, and build from there. Done is better than perfect, and progress is better than paralysis.

5. The CEO Mindset Requires Preparation, Not Panic

Waiting until you're overwhelmed to delegate is like trying to buckle your seatbelt mid-crash. Build systems early. Don't wait for chaos — prepare for growth by acting now like the leader you're becoming.

Chapter 12:
Ready, Fire, Aim

Don't take two years to make a one-second decision.

People say money is the reason they can't move forward—but that's rarely true. The real barrier is mindset. Procrastination is the assassination of dreams. We wait, we doubt, we get in our own heads—and most of the time, it's not our critics holding us back. It's us.

I've seen it over and over: people delay their dreams, not because they're unrealistic, but because they're afraid. And yet—I believe this with everything in me—*God doesn't put a thought, a vision, or a dream in your head that isn't achievable.* If more people understood that, their lives would completely change.

You have to trust your gut, your gifts, and the goals placed on your heart. Then take action—even when it's uncomfortable. That's how success is built. — *DJ Barton*

Section 1: Don't Wait—Launch Imperfectly

Skis, Sled Dogs, and Showing Up Anyway

Once upon a time, I used to race sled dogs.

Sometimes I'd be behind a full team—lead dogs (my "gee-haw" dogs), team dogs, and wheel dogs—pulling a traditional sled across snowy trails. The kind of team you picture when you think of the Iditarod. Other times, though, I competed in something a little more chaotic: skijoring.

Skijoring is a wild sport where you hook up one or two sled dogs to a cross-country skier (yes, you read that right) and see who can tear through the course the fastest. It's fast, unpredictable, and the only real job of the skier is to stay upright while the dogs pull like their lives depend on it.

On one particular race day, I was almost ready to go. My racing suit was on. My bib was secured. My skis were strapped in. I was just about to put on my poles.

My two race dogs, Boots and Muck, were already in their harnesses. They knew what was coming. These dogs *loved* to run. Their job was to pull and respond to my commands. My job? Stay standing.

Mort, my dog handler, was holding the dogs steady while I got myself set. But these dogs weren't about to wait patiently. They were lunging in their harnesses, vibrating with anticipation.

Then—it happened.

Mort lost control of the dogs for just a second. That was all it took. Boots and Muck launched forward with full force, and the jolt yanked me clean off my feet. I hadn't even strapped in my poles yet. I slammed to the ground, hip and outer thigh landing hard on something buried in the snow. It hurt. Not broken, but bruised deep.

Mort managed to rein the dogs back in, but the damage was done. I was rattled and sore. Still, I could move. And the dogs were ready. So we made our way to the starting line.

The countdown began.

Three... Two... One... GO!

Mort let go, and we were off like a shot.

Almost immediately, I had to snowplow to try and slow us down. But here's what every dog musher knows: if sled dogs feel any pull behind them, they don't slow down. They pull harder. Boots and Muck were doing exactly what they were born to do—run flat-out. And me? I was just trying to stay upright on a body that was already hurting.

I remember wiping out on one of the sharper turns. The dogs didn't stop. They just kept pulling, dragging me across the snow until I could scramble to my feet and get my skis under me again. With a sled, at least you have a brake. You've got a snowhook to drop and stop the team. But on skis? There's no such thing. We were going too fast to grab a tree. Too far in to stop. I just had to keep going.

By some miracle, we made it through. I crossed the finish line battered, bruised, exhausted, and...victorious! We won our division.

I still have the bib and the medal, and I'll keep them forever. Not because it was my cleanest race. But because it was my grittiest. My most determined. And probably my most meaningful.

Lesson From the Trail

You don't need to be perfectly ready. You don't need a flawless start.

You need to get to the line. You need to listen for the buzzer. And when it rings, you go.

Stay upright as long as you can. Get back up when you can't. Finish what you started.

Even if you fall. Even if it hurts. Even if you have no brakes and the course is wild.

Because sometimes the best wins happen when you've got no business winning at all—except for the fact that you didn't quit.

Ready, Fire... Then Aim

Here's what most people get wrong: they think the sequence of success is *Ready, Aim, Fire*. They spend months, sometimes years, trying to aim before they ever take the shot. They over-plan, over-perfect, and overthink in the name of feeling "ready." And in doing so, they miss the starting line entirely.

But life and business rarely work that way. The truth is, you don't fully know what works until you fire. You don't truly understand your ideal client until you've served a few. You don't know what your market wants until you've put something out there and watched the response. You don't know how it feels to sell until you've had an awkward sales call, learned from it, and tried again. You don't aim your way into clarity—you move your way into it.

That's why the real order for success is this: Ready. *Fire.* Aim.*

Preparation still matters. You do need enough structure to start. Enough clarity to step forward. Enough purpose to keep going when things get messy. But don't confuse getting ready with waiting for perfection.

Remember the sled dog race? My dogs were ready. The course was set. I had everything I needed to get to the line, even if I wasn't feeling 100%. And once the countdown began, I didn't have the luxury of checking my aim. It was go-time.

And sometimes, that's how it is with business. You launch while your heart's still racing. You move forward even when your hip still

---

*The phrase "Ready, Fire, Aim" encourages action over perfection, and was popularized by Jack Canfield in his book *The Success Principles*™ *How to Get from Where You Are to Where You Want to Be* (© 2005,2010, 2020).

hurts. You hit "publish" before your website feels 100%. You offer the service while you're still finding your voice. You fire.

You will fall. You will wipe out. You might crash on a sharp turn with no trees to grab. But when you fire before you feel fully ready, you get something far more valuable than more planning could ever give you. You get real-world feedback. You get data. You get traction. You get momentum. And momentum matters more than a perfect plan.

Don't let the fear of doing it wrong keep you from doing it at all. Don't wait until every piece is perfectly aligned. That day might never come. You can adjust your aim along the way.

And that brings us to the next step: *aim better.*

Once you're in motion, *that's* when it's time to refine. You begin to notice what resonates. You look at what's working. You listen to your audience. You track your numbers. You learn. And with every step, you get better.

But here's something most people miss: you're not aiming for a bullseye on your first try. That kind of precision doesn't come from your first attempt —it comes after experience, feedback, and iteration. Most people don't hit the center of the target on their first shot—or even their tenth. Your goal isn't to be perfect. Your goal is to hit the board. To get in the game. To put something out there that you can learn from and improve. *You can't refine what doesn't exist.*

Progress comes from motion. Precision comes from practice. You're not expected to know the entire course in advance. You just need to know the next turn — and have the guts to take it.

So if you're standing at the edge of your next big thing—your launch, your pivot, your reinvention—this is your countdown: 3... 2... 1... GO.

You don't need a flawless start. You need a faithful one. You can always aim more precisely once you're moving, but if you never fire, you'll never know what could have happened.

So tighten your harness. Take the step. Fall if you have to. Then get back up and finish strong. The medal doesn't go to the one who planned the cleanest race. It goes to the one who showed up, stayed in motion, and crossed the line.

Ready. Fire. Aim.

———————

Section 2: From Vision to Impact—Critical Mindset Shifts for Taking Action

Perfection is procrastination in disguise. Action builds clarity and momentum.

Yet so many business owners stay stuck in the "almost ready" zone. One more course. One more spreadsheet. One more late-night brainstorm session. It's easy to get caught in the loop of preparing and polishing, waiting to feel fully ready. But here's the truth:

Clarity doesn't come before action. *It follows it.*

You don't need to have it all figured out before you begin. You simply need enough direction to take the first step. Because the most valuable feedback you'll ever get won't come from your imagination. It'll come from the real world. From your audience. From the market. From trying, adjusting, and trying again.

Most successful business owners? They launch, then learn. They don't wait for certainty—they build it through movement. They move through the messy middle, collect real data, and evolve in response.

That's the heartbeat of progress—not polish, not perfection, but *motion*.

And that's where these five principles of taking action come in. These aren't just mindset mantras or abstract theories. They're actionable, grounded truths that will guide you as you stop overthinking and start building. Use them as a compass to keep moving forward—one imperfect, intentional step at a time.

1. Move Towards Clarity, Don't Wait For It

You don't need perfect clarity, but you do need a starting point. Think of it like setting a GPS: you need a destination, but you don't need every turn M.A.P.ed out in advance. You'll reroute. You'll make U-turns. But the important part is that you're heading somewhere.

The real insight? **Action is what sharpens your focus.** Don't wait for clarity—move toward it.

Know that clarity doesn't usually strike boldly and strongly like lightning. It's more like little "aha" moments and carving a trail through a winding forest trail. Each step you take reveals more of what's ahead. Waiting until you see the whole path is like refusing to leave the driveway until every light in the city turns green. Start moving—and the lights turn on as you go.

In fact, some of the best turns I've taken in business weren't part of the original route. If I had clung too tightly to the first map I made, I would've missed out on scenic detours—unexpected opportunities that not only changed my course but improved it.

Business ownership isn't about blindly following a rigid plan. It's about knowing where you want to go and being open to shifts that better serve the people you're here to help. Aim on purpose—but stay flexible. Because growth often lives just beyond the plan.

2. Purpose Fuels Discipline

When your *WHY* is strong, you stay steady — even when things feel uncertain or messy. If you don't have a clear purpose, burnout will catch you quickly. But if you have vision without action, you'll end up with something even more painful: regret.

Your purpose needs to run deeper than profit. Whether it's freedom, family, impact, faith, integrity, or legacy—*that's* the fuel that helps you push through the hard parts with grit and resilience. Motivation fades, but purpose sticks. When you're tempted to quit, your "why" becomes the anchor that reminds you: *this matters.*

A clear purpose also acts as your filter. It keeps you from chasing every shiny tactic or trend. If it doesn't serve your mission, it doesn't belong in your business. Your "why" doesn't just keep you moving— it keeps you moving in the right direction.

3. Success Is Felt, Not Just Measured

You don't have to hit six figures to feel successful. Celebrate the fact that you're in motion. That you showed up. Success doesn't live in a spreadsheet—it lives in momentum. It's felt the moment you take a risk, send the email, ask for the sale, and show up again the next day.

Progress is the new currency. Every brave step counts. Don't discount the small wins: a client testimonial, a courageous pitch, or a tough conversation you didn't avoid. These are proof that you're in the game. That you're growing. That you're choosing courage over comfort.

When you only measure success by results, you rob yourself of joy in the journey. Let yourself *feel* successful *while* you're building. Because what you're doing already matters—even before it's "done."

And if you need permission to let go of perfection? Let me borrow a line from someone who gave it to me straight.

Remember my coach, Barbara?

Yep, *that* Barbara— I had just one 1:1 call with her, and I soaked up every second. She has this uncanny ability to see straight through people—and she reads me like a book. In minutes, she cut through the noise and called out the mindset that was keeping me stuck.

"You don't need to be perfect," she told me. **"You need to be good enough. And good enough is 80%. So get started."**

That hit hard. And it stuck. I realized I was waiting to feel "ready," chasing this illusion of polish and perfection—when what I actually needed was to show up, do the work, and learn in motion.

So if you're hesitating because it's not quite right, not quite ready, not quite "there" yet—take it from Barbara:

Good enough is enough. Get it out there. Let it breathe. Let it teach you.

Progress beats perfection. Every. Single. Time.

4. Reverse Engineer the Dream

No plan survives first contact with reality perfectly—and that's okay. Knowing your end goal gives you a compass, even if the terrain changes. It helps you adjust faster and pivot with purpose. You don't have to know how everything will unfold—you just need a clear sense of where you're going.

Don't let the pursuit of perfection keep you from progress. *Done* is better than perfect—especially when it gets you one step closer to what you truly want. Focus on alignment over elegance.

Ask yourself: *Is this moving me closer to the life and business I want?*

Reverse engineering doesn't mean rigid planning. It means intentional execution with a flexible mindset.

5. Redefine As You Grow

Every launch is a lesson. Every offer, every post, every pitch is a test that teaches you something. Your audience is your co-author. They'll show you what works, where there's resonance, and what needs to shift—*if* you're willing to listen.

Be flexible. Be curious. And most of all, be willing to evolve. The business owners who succeed aren't the ones who never change—they're the ones who **adjust in real time.** What worked in the beginning may not serve your next season.

Let go of what no longer fits and upgrade what does.

Growth isn't about rigid systems. It's about adaptive leadership. Let the journey refine your process. Trust that every step forward—especially the imperfect ones—is shaping you into the kind of leader who can handle what comes next.

Section 3: M.A.P.ing Out Your Vision for Impact: Formulas for Success

The Road of Trials

Welcome to the messy middle—the part of the journey Joseph Campbell calls "The Road of Trials." This is the place where you stop dreaming and start building. Where clarity is earned, not granted. This stage isn't clean, linear, or easy. It's hard. It's real. But it's where everything changes.

So let me ask you:

- *Do you have an idea?*
- *A business you want to start?*
- *Dreams that keep tapping you on the shoulder at night?*

You don't need more time. You need to begin. Because the truth is—you already have everything you need. You're not lacking tools. You're not waiting on permission. The first step doesn't require perfection. It just requires courage.

You eat an elephant one bite at a time. You build a business the same way—one intentional step, one imperfect decision, one brave move forward.

And the framework that gets you there?

MAP: Mindset + Action + Purpose = Profit. When you have the right mindset, take clear action, and allow purpose to drive you, you go from dreaming about a vision to actually *living* it. You make real progress.

Of course, taking the action required to make this formula work can feel risky. That's because the moment you start, that little voice in your head fires up with a vengeance. It's the one we know all too well that that whispers:

- *"You're not good enough."*
- *"You're not ready."*
- *"You don't have what it takes."*

But that voice? It is just fear masquerading as logic. It's your subconscious mind trying to protect you from discomfort. But here's the good news: you can rewrite that script.

Daily affirmations rewire your internal dialogue. Try:

- *"I am a business owner."*
- *"I work with 10 clients a month."*
- *"I am open to receiving money for my knowledge and purpose."*

Speak it until you believe it. Because you get to decide what story you live out.

But belief alone isn't enough. Intention is only powerful when paired with attention. Your dream needs energy. It needs consistent focus. It needs your presence. You can have all the vision boards and journaling prompts in the world, but without movement, you stay stuck.

Action builds momentum, even in the face of challenges.

The M.A.P. formula teaches us that with the right mindset and a clear purpose as the foundation, action can truly drive momentum. And when you take inspired action—*that gut-led, goosebump-giving, a little-bit-scary kind*—you move faster, with more clarity and conviction.

That's not to say there won't be challenges. And I can prove it. Trust me, I've faced plenty:

- I was once fired after a work comp injury.

- Then I was fired again after a government budget cut, right after I'd survived a shutdown.
- I've dealt with infertility.
- Raised kids with special needs.
- Got fired the same day I found out my daughter needed emergency surgery.

And to be honest? I used to fear adversity. Run from it. Avoid it at all costs.

Now? I honor resilience. Every setback carved out strength. Every hard thing gave me insight. And every step led me here.

One of the most powerful tools I ever learned when it comes to resilience comes from Jack Canfield, author of *The Success Principles™: How to Get from Where You Are to Where You Want to Be*. It is a simple but transformative formula:

E + R = O
Event + Response = Outcome

You can't always control the event, but you can always control your response. And that changes everything.

Your response determines your outcome. You can't change the "E," but you have total power over the "R" and that's where your success lives. This isn't just theory. I've lived it. And so have people like Brigitte, whom we met earlier in the book. You may remember that she faced heartbreak and roadblocks but *chose* to respond with clarity, courage, and consistency over fear.

Her outcome? Impact. Fulfillment. Legacy.

Now it's your turn. You have the mindset. You have the map. You have the tools. You have the story.

Ask yourself:
- *What event am I letting define my outcome instead of shifting my response?*
- *Where am I over-aiming instead of firing?*
- *What's one brave step I can take today?*

You don't need to be perfect. You need progress. Let this be the moment you go from dreaming about your future to building it—one bold, imperfect step at a time.

Section 4: Changing Your Internal and External Soundtracks

Your mindset isn't just shaped by what you know—it's shaped by what you say. The stories we repeat become the beliefs we hold. And in business, those internal and external soundtracks play on repeat unless we intentionally change the tune.

When your mental loop is filled with fear, doubt, and limitation, it's like running a race with the brakes on. You're trying to move forward, but you're dragging old narratives behind you. It's time to rewrite those loops and replace them with language that aligns with the future you're building.

Start by identifying the soundtracks that hold you back. Write them down on paper if you have to in order to really confront them. Then, replace them with better soundtracks—soundtracks for success. Statements that move you forward, not keep you stuck.

Here's a simple but powerful chart to help you shift:

Table 12.1: Rewriting Your Ready, Fire, Aim! Soundtracks

Disempowering Soundtracks	Ready, Fire, Aim! Rewrites
"I'm not ready yet."	"I'm ready enough to begin."
"What if I fail?"	"What if I grow?"
"I'm not good at this."	"I'm still learning—and I get better every time."
"I'm too late."	"There's no deadline on my dreams."
"I can't afford to make a mistake."	"Every mistake makes me smarter and stronger."
"I have to do it all myself."	"I can ask for help and still be a strong leader."
"No one is paying attention to my work."	"The right people will see the value in what I create."
"I'm not making enough progress."	"Every step forward counts—even the small ones."
"I don't know where to start."	"Clarity comes from action. Let's take the first step."
"I have to be perfect."	"Progress beats perfection every time."
"I'm just winging it."	"I'm experimenting—and that's how innovation starts."
"I'm terrible at marketing."	"Marketing is a skill I can learn and get better at."
"I should be further along by now."	"I'm right where I need to be to learn what's next."
"I don't have enough time."	"I can make time for what matters most."
"There's too much competition."	"There's more than enough room for my unique voice."

Disempowering Soundtracks	Ready, Fire, Aim! Rewrites
"I don't know what I'm doing."	"I figure things out as I go—and that's how growth works."
"What if they say no?"	"Every 'no' gets me closer to the right 'yes.'"
"I'm not qualified enough."	"My experience, heart, and drive make me uniquely qualified."
"I'm overwhelmed."	"One thing at a time. I've got this."
"I can't charge that much."	"I deliver real value—and I'm worth it."

The words you choose—internally and externally— set the tone for what you'll believe, build, and bring to the world.

Every time you replace a disempowering thought with an empowering one, you're realigning with the future you're working to create. This isn't fluff. It's neuroscience. It's psychology. It's a strategy. And it works.

So go ahead: choose your soundtracks. Curate your inner playlist. Tune your mindset to match your mission. And then turn it up—because the world needs to hear what you're really made of.

Section 5: The 5 Financial Success Principles

This chapter is about moving forward before you feel ready. It's about starting where you are and refining as you go. You don't need perfect clarity to begin—you just need enough to take the first step. Each of the 5 Financial Success Principles can help guide you through messy, real-world momentum, where clarity is earned through action.

Here's what it looks like:

1. **Know What You Want**
   Define your version of success so your money has a mission.

2. **Know the Cost**
   Understand what it actually takes—financially and energetically—to fund your vision.

3. **Know Your Numbers**
   Get clear on your income, expenses, and profit so you can make confident decisions.

4. **Act As If**

Show up like the CEO you're becoming—even before the results catch up.

5. **Take Inspired Action**

Move forward with purpose, trusting that clarity and momentum will follow.

1. Know What You Want

Define success before you begin. Are you testing proof of concept? Building visibility? Generating cash flow?

Before you start anything new — especially a business, offer, or launch—you need to define what success looks like at this specific stage. This is not about your five-year vision. It's about your next step.

For example:

- If you're testing a new product or service, your goal might be validation and feedback, not sales.
- If you're trying to build your audience, engagement might matter more than profit.
- If you're in need of quick cash flow, your launch strategy will look different than one built for brand awareness.

Set intentional and tangible expectations upfront. You don't need perfect results—you need relevant ones. And the only way to measure relevance is by being crystal clear on your goal.

Think of it like target shooting. I enjoy the challenge of aiming at clay pigeons, sporting clays, and traditional paper targets. Each one demands a different stance, strategy, and level of focus. You wouldn't shoot a moving clay pigeon the same way you'd aim at a stationary bullseye—and you wouldn't judge your accuracy the same way either.

Business is no different. Your "target" determines your entire approach:

- *Are you launching a course to validate the content, or to drive revenue?*
- *Are you pitching yourself to podcasts for brand awareness, or to land a high-ticket client?*
- *Are you offering a low-ticket product to build trust, or a premium service to increase cash flow?*

The clearer your aim, the more aligned your actions.

Once you have clear goals, make sure they align with *your* business model, not the loudest voice on social media or the latest industry trend. A service provider will have different metrics than a speaker. A coach will measure success differently than a product-based business. A nonprofit founder might be aiming for donations and volunteer engagement, while an e-commerce brand is focused on conversion rates and return on ad spend.

And remember—there's a big difference between hitting your target and hitting *a* target. It's easy to let other people's success metrics distract you from your own. *But someone else's bullseye might be completely irrelevant to your growth.*

So ask yourself:

- *What target am I aiming for in this season?*
- *What result would tell me I'm moving in the right direction?*
- *And am I measuring my success by my own terms — or someone else's highlight reel?*

One of the worst things you can do is judge your efforts unfairly because you never defined what success looked like in the first place. A launch with low revenue but high interest might be a total win—*if* your goal was proof of concept. Your short-term goal matters. Let it guide your evaluation and your energy.

When you know what you want, you give your actions focus—and your results context.

2. Know How Much It Costs

Budget before you build. Know the minimum viable version that lets you test without draining your resources.

Moving fast doesn't mean being careless with your money. Every launch has a cost—not just financial, but in time, energy, and opportunity. Having a clear understanding of these costs helps you move with confidence instead of crossing your fingers and hoping for the best.

Start by identifying your minimum viable product or offer. What is the leanest version you can launch that still delivers value and allows you to gather meaningful feedback?

Next, outline the real costs:
- Tech tools
- Design
- Advertising
- Time and labor
- Materials or fulfillment
- Opportunity cost (What are you not doing while pursuing this?)

This isn't about over-analyzing or planning yourself into paralysis. It's about creating smart guardrails that protect your resources while giving your idea the chance to breathe.

The goal isn't perfection—it's sustainable experimentation. Lean doesn't mean cheap. It means wise, focused, and informed.

Just like setting a financial budget for your household, budgeting in business keeps you grounded. It allows you to test and refine without risking everything.

You don't have to be a financial wizard, but you do have to lead with awareness. Because in business, confidence isn't built on how good your idea is—it's built on knowing the cost of bringing it to life.

When you know what it costs, you move with intention—not desperation.

3. Know Your Numbers

One thing my business coach would say is,

"If you don't know your numbers, you don't know your business."

Track everything—clicks, conversions, cost-per-lead, feedback. Don't just guess or "feel your way through." Data tells the story of what's working and what isn't.

This is where a lot of creative business owners tend to drift. They're passionate about their work and excellent at launching, pivoting, and reinventing—*but if you don't track your data, you don't learn from your data.*

Start by tracking what matters:
- Revenue vs. profit
- Conversion rates (from landing page to sale)
- Email open and click-through rates

- Cost per lead or sale
- Where your leads came from
- Engagement data (likes, comments, shares, etc.)

Numbers give shape to the story of your business. They move your decisions from emotional to informed. Without them, you're making wild guesses. With them, you're making strategic adjustments.

Data tells you where to double down, where to refine, and when to pull back. It takes the guesswork out of your next move.

Numbers don't have to be scary. Think of them as your business's pulse. When you track regularly, you can catch patterns early. You can see what's trending up or down and make adjustments long before a crisis hits.

Let's be clear: tracking your numbers isn't about being obsessed with metrics — it's about being a responsible steward of your business.

And remember this mindset tip: Numbers aren't personal. They're information. They don't determine your worth—*they inform your strategy.*

You're not failing if the numbers are low. You're learning. *But only if you look.*

And in case you need it, here's one more critical reason to know your numbers: your tax status. If you're running a business and consistently not showing a profit, the IRS may start to view your venture as a hobby rather than a legitimate business. That means you could lose deductions and be at risk for an audit.

Even if you're making money but reinvesting everything without tracking profit, it sends up red flags. Business owners who don't take this seriously can end up in trouble—even when their intentions are good. So be sure your books are clean, your profit is intentional, and your numbers show that you're building a real, viable business. And that's the difference between staying stuck and scaling up.

4. Act As If

Show up like a confident leader—even if your offer is new. Confidence isn't pretending to know everything—it's trusting that you'll figure it out.

If you've ever suffered from impostor syndrome but *know* you have a purpose, this is your moment. The "Act As If" principle is the bridge between wondering if you're good enough and stepping into the future you're meant to lead. I've lived this. And I can tell you: this step is critical. It's how you shift your thoughts, your posture, and your strategy from questioning to clarity.

When you're in launch mode, the energy you bring to the table matters just as much as the strategy you execute. If you want others to take your offer seriously, you have to take it seriously first.

That doesn't mean faking results. It means:
- Leading with integrity.
- Owning your value.
- Showing up with consistency and belief in your process.

Step into the mindset of the business owner you're becoming—not just the one you were yesterday. Even if you're still refining your offer or figuring things out behind the scenes, act like it's already delivering results. This is what it looks like to lead with intention:
- Speak about your pricing with confidence.
- Follow up with leads promptly and professionally.
- Respond to slow starts with calm clarity, not panic.
- Stick to your value instead of discounting out of fear.

This is less about pretending and more about choosing a new baseline. You're showing up *as if* you are already the kind of person who runs a successful business—and that belief becomes the engine behind your behavior.

This is also a powerful moment to shift your language. Change the way you talk about yourself and your work:
- Instead of *"I'm trying to grow a business,"* say *"I run a business."*
- Instead of *"I hope this works,"* say *"I'm building something meaningful."*
- Instead of *"I don't know if I'm ready,"* say *"I'm learning as I go, and that's enough."*

Remember: Leadership during a launch isn't about having all the answers. It's about:
- Clarity of purpose
- Commitment to the process
- Consistency in how you show up

Your audience can feel your energy. If you carry yourself like a trusted expert, they'll treat you like one. If you hesitate, they'll hesitate too.

The confidence you lead with becomes the permission they need to believe in your offer.

The beauty of this principle is that it creates a feedback loop. When you act as if you're already successful, you start to:

- Make bolder decisions
- Take more aligned risks
- Create more professional experiences
- Attract higher-quality clients

And over time, that posture becomes your new normal.

So ask yourself:

- *How would I act if I already knew this launch would succeed?*
- *What would I do differently if I fully believed in my value?*
- *Where am I downplaying myself out of fear—and what would change if I owned my brilliance?*

The truth is: your future success isn't waiting for perfect timing. It's waiting for you to *act as if* you're already in motion.

Confidence isn't a finish line—it's a decision. And this is the moment you make it.

5. Take Inspired Action

Trust your gut, test fast, and iterate often. What you do teaches you more than what you plan. This is one of the KEY things that differentiates you from an employee. You GET to take inspired action, so take it!

Inspired action doesn't mean being reckless. It means taking action that is aligned with your deeper vision, based not only on instinct but also informed by the data you've gathered so far. You move quickly, but not blindly. You trust your intuition, but you also read the room.

Maybe your first offer didn't perform like you hoped. Inspired action means you pause, ask the hard questions, review your numbers, reflect on what feedback you received, and try again, with smarter tweaks. That's wisdom in motion.

Maybe your low-ticket test product attracted a handful of buyers. That's a win. Ask yourself, what's next? What upsell or next-level offer serves them even better? Inspired action isn't a one-time leap—it's the discipline of brave, continuous movement and realignment.

It also means asking for help when needed. You're not meant to do it all alone.

- If you're unsure how profitable your launch was, hire a bookkeeper.
- If your messaging isn't resonating, bring in a copy coach.
- If you're drowning in backend tasks, delegate them.

Taking inspired action is a mark of maturity. It says: *"I believe in this enough to keep going, even if I don't have all the answers yet."*

And here's a powerful truth: you don't get momentum from thinking. You get it from doing. You don't need 20 more courses—you need more courageous next steps.

Inspired action means:

- You trust yourself to figure it out.
- You move forward *because* of your vision and purpose, even in uncertainty.
- You believe that what's meant for you will reveal itself once you start walking toward it.

So don't wait for the perfect plan. Take inspired action. Refine as you go. And keep showing up.

You've already got everything you need. Stay in motion. That's where the magic happens.

A Story of Missed Action

Let me tell you a quick story. A few years ago, I worked with a brilliant woman named Tina. She had everything—a compelling vision, a unique approach to care, years of experience as a clinician, and a dream of opening her own bilingual clinic that would serve her community in a deeply personal and values-driven way. Tina was passionate, smart, and absolutely qualified. She had everything it takes to succeed.

But she hesitated. She got stuck in the loop of preparing, planning, and second-guessing. She wanted to take another certification course, then another business workshop, then wait for another logo redesign. Her email list? Still sitting in a spreadsheet. Her website? Still unpublished. She kept saying, "I'll launch next quarter," and then, "maybe next year."

Meanwhile, someone else opened a clinic in the same community. It wasn't as unique. It didn't have her personal touch. But it was open — and it was growing.

Tina eventually admitted that it wasn't a lack of knowledge that held her back. It was fear of imperfection. She was waiting to feel 100% ready, 100% certain, and 100% safe. And while she waited, her dream faded.

Her story isn't about failure—it's about missed momentum. Inspired action would have looked like starting small. Testing a pilot program. Renting a room by the hour. She gathered real feedback and learning as she went. She didn't need a polished clinic to prove her concept. She needed movement.

Tina's lesson reminds us: the cost of not acting isn't just money— *it's missed purpose*. It's regret. It's watching someone else serve the people you were meant to help.

So if you've been sitting on a dream, take this as your invitation. Do the small version. Take the next brave step. Momentum doesn't wait for perfection. It waits for courage.

You don't have to get it perfect. But you do have to get it moving.

Here's the truth: The universe (and your business) doesn't respond to what you *intend*—it responds to what you *do*.

Are you ready?

Grab the pen. Move your feet. And keep tracking that inspired action like it's your most powerful business strategy—because it just might be.

The 5 Financial Success Principles are your blueprint for moving from vision to execution, without stalling in perfection. They embody the *Ready, Fire, Aim* approach: prepare enough to move wisely, launch before you feel fully ready, and refine as you go.

Instead of waiting for certainty, you learn by doing. These principles help you course-correct with purpose, turning motion into mastery. You don't need a flawless plan—just the courage to begin, the wisdom to track what matters, and the discipline to aim again, hitting closer to your red bullseye each time.

---

6. Thought Leadership — Wisdom from Jack Canfield, co-creator of *Chicken Soup for the Soul*® and *author of The Success Principles™:How to Get from Where You Are to Where You Want to Be.*

*Excerpted with permission from The Train the Trainer Online manual by Jack Canfield ©2016. All rights reserved by Jack Canfield and Self Esteem Seminars, Inc.

The Financial Success Principles was written by three friends who decided to create something meaningful together: we are the 3 Wise Women. Each of us brings a different background, a different voice, and a unique lens on what success means. One of us is a Jack Canfield Certified Success Coach (you'll find Jack's name on the cover of the book)—and she's the one who took the first step. She acted on a spark of inspiration, shared the idea with the others, and here we are: writing the final chapter of this book. Jack Canfield's name is on the cover of this book for many reasons. Most importantly, because he believes in this message and supports this work.

His writing and wisdom in *The Success Principles™* inspired much of this book and can add one final layer to our work together, offering a mindset shift that pulls everything together.

*In *The Success Principles™*, page 132, Jack Canfield writes:

> *"You can begin right now to act as if you already have achieved any goal you desire, and that outer experience of acting as if will create the inner experience, the millionaire mindset that will take you to the actual manifestation of that experience."*

He continues:

> *"How would you act if you were already a straight A student, top salesperson, highly paid consultant, rich entrepreneur, best-selling author? Once you have a clear picture of that, start being it now."*

This isn't wishful thinking—it's practical psychology. When you act as if, you activate a chain reaction. Your behaviors start to match your desired identity. Your decisions become sharper. Your energy shifts. And most importantly, your outcomes begin to mirror your mindset.

What does this look like in business?

- You price with confidence—even before you feel "ready."
- You share your message—even if your audience is small.
- You pitch the client, apply for the opportunity, submit the proposal — even if your voice shakes.
- You walk into the room—or Zoom—with the energy of someone who belongs there.
- You stop waiting for permission and start owning your vision.

This mindset is not about faking it. It's about aligning your actions with your vision before the external evidence fully arrives. And the more you do this, the faster that evidence tends to show up.

It also means dressing, speaking, and presenting in a way that mirrors your goals. If you want to be a sought-after speaker, how would you show up to your next meeting? If you want to run a high-level coaching business, how would you communicate your value? Each small act of alignment brings you closer to the business you want to build.

Here's a quick self-check to help you integrate Canfield's principle:

Exercise: Act-As-If Alignment Audit

- *What is the role or identity I want to grow into? (Coach, CEO, speaker, author, etc.)*
- *What would that version of me be doing differently today?*
- *Where am I still playing small or waiting for "proof" before I act?*
- *What is one bold move I can take this week to close that gap?*
- Now add this layer:
- *What would I need to believe about myself in order to make that move with confidence?*

Because at its core, "acting as if" is about belief. Believing you belong in the room. Believing you have something valuable to offer. Believing your work is worth seeing.

Pro Tip: Start an "Act-As-If" journal. Document your thoughts, actions, and observations as you begin showing up as your next-level self. Note what changes in how others respond, what new opportunities come your way, and how you feel internally. This small practice becomes proof that mindset does, in fact, move the needle. Success doesn't start with resources. It starts with *resourcefulness*. When you show up with belief and aligned behavior, you'll find that the right people, tools, and opportunities meet you halfway.

So don't wait for someone to knight you with a title. Step into it now. Choose to believe in your work, your message, and your momentum —even if it's still in its infancy.

This isn't just a motivational nudge from us to you—it's a proven mental framework to fast-track your progress. It's your reminder that the business you want to build is already within reach—you just have to act like it.

7. Your Call to Action—Ready, Fire, Aim!

Because the truth is: you're already on the path. You've got the map. Now, it's time to get out there and walk it (or run it!) like the leader you are becoming.

To make this more concrete, go back to section five of this chapter and complete the reflection exercises outlined there. They will set you up for your greatest call to action yet: moving on your very own "ready, fire, aim"—whatever "that looks like for your business.

And remember, success doesn't start with money. It starts with intention. And once you begin acting as if, you'll attract the people and opportunities that help bring your vision to life.

Final Thought from the 3 Wise Women

This project began with one inspired action, and now it's grown into a movement.

What you're holding is just the beginning. A workbook companion is on its way to help you apply everything you've learned, bringing the principles to life in your daily decision-making. But we're not stopping there. We're planning more books in the 3 Wise Women series—each one diving deeper into the real-life challenges and breakthroughs that shape entrepreneurs, leaders, and everyday changemakers.

And there's more. We're launching a podcast where we'll bring these conversations to life. In it, you'll hear the three of us—friends, founders, and fellow journeyers—sharing raw, real conversations about money, mindset, leadership, and the messy middle of building something meaningful. We'll welcome guests and invite contributing authors to share how these principles have shaped their stories, too.

Why? Because we don't just teach these principles—we live them.

Every risk, every pivot, and every brave step has led us here. And if you've made it to this page, you're ready, too.

Throughout this book, we've walked through the 5 Financial Success Principles:

1. **Know What You Want**
2. **Know How Much It Costs**
3. **Know Your Numbers**
4. **Act As If**
5. **Take Inspired Action**

These aren't just theories—they're tools. And now, they're yours.

Know You Are Never Alone

You are not alone. It is never too late.

Entrepreneurship is lonely—and business owners need a team.
No one builds success solo. So ask yourself: *Who's on your team?*
— *Doreen M. Letofsky*

This book is also an invitation to stop doing business alone. Business ownership can be lonely, but it doesn't have to be. What you're reading isn't just advice. It's a hand reaching out. A reminder that building success takes a team, not just tenacity.

Whether you're a seasoned business owner or just starting out, you belong here. We believe in community over competition, and this movement is your invitation to link arms with others who are building something that matters. In fact, read this book again in a year and see how far you've come! I bet you will be surprised.

So if you've been waiting for the "right time" or a sign from the universe—this is it.

Start by picking one principle and applying it this week. Or better yet, share what you've learned with someone who needs to hear it.

Ready. Fire. Aim.

Start small. But start. And start now.

You've got thi$.

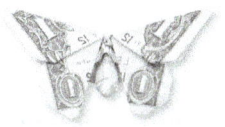

BONUS Chapter:
Financial Roles and Descriptions

Who Should You Get for Help—And What Do They Actually Do?

The truth about credentials, roles, and what needs to change in the financial industry

First of all—**congratulations!!**

If you're reading this bonus chapter, that means you finished the book and made the most important investment of all: in yourself. You're not just learning financial principles. You're choosing to think differently, take control, and build your business with intention.

And if you're like many business owners, one of the first questions you might ask is:

"Should I hire a CPA?"

Most people assume the answer is yes—because CPAs have credentials.

But the truth is, the financial industry is full of alphabet soup:

CPA, EA, MBA, CMA, CFP, CFA, MAcc, CRTP, CTEC, ABA, ATP, CFE, ProAdvisor...the list goes on!

It's no wonder business owners are confused. So let's break it down. But first—let's look at this from **Becca's perspective**.

A Note From Becca: Credentials ≠ Clarity

I didn't become a CPA. I actually have an AAS degree in Agricultural Business, grew up in Iowa, and loved driving tractors. I chose agriculture because it sounded fun and familiar. But after a few years of burnout in corporate jobs, I stumbled upon a receptionist position at a CPA firm—and my world changed.

What started as answering phones quickly turned into bookkeeping, then sales, then business advisory. But here's the thing…

I learned more riding in the passenger seat of a CPA's car—listening to her talk with business owners—than I ever would have sitting in a classroom.

My parents *begged* me to go back to school to become a CPA. I was great with numbers. I loved business. I even attended a college accounting institute for fun during my high school summers .

So why didn't I do it? Simple. I'm a visual learner. I absorb by doing, seeing, and applying—not by memorizing and test-taking.

The CPA exam is a four-part test, taken in a strict order, under tight timeframes. And while I absolutely respect the hard work it takes to pass…I believe CPA training should be an apprenticeship, not a standardized test.

Why? Because the tax laws change every year. Presidents change every four years. So do things like:

- Mileage reimbursement
- Standard deductions
- Medical expense thresholds

CEUs are required to maintain credentials, but even those don't guarantee that every CPA is updated or equipped to communicate with business owners.

A Wake-Up Call: Credentials Don't Equal Connection

In my years working with hundreds of small business owners, I heard it all:

"My CPA yelled at me."

"My CPA files extensions without telling me."

"I don't even know what my CPA is asking for."

"My CPA says I should know this—but I don't."

Let me be clear: **This is not about blaming CPAs.**

It's about understanding that our system is broken.

Most CPAs are trained to file. Not to teach.Not to coach. Not to empower.

What if, instead of passing a test, CPAs had to walk alongside entrepreneurs, learn their fears, their questions, their overwhelm—and develop the communication skills to help them grow?

Because here's the truth:

Out of every business I've ever supported, **no two financial stories have ever been the same.**

Some had Schedule C + rental properties.

Some had W-2s + side gigs.

Some had multiple businesses + investments + family complexity.

No textbook can prepare you for that. But **empathy and experience** can.

Let's Talk About the Reality Behind the Numbers

Eighty-six percent of business owners make less than $100,000 a year.

That's not because they aren't talented, driven, or capable—it's because most of them were never taught how to run a business.

Think back to elementary school. When a teacher asked, "What do you want to be when you grow up?" you probably heard answers like:

- Firefighter
- Teacher
- Astronaut

But how many kids said, "I want to be a business owner"?

And more importantly—how many teachers had any idea how to nurture that path?

Entrepreneurship isn't taught early. Financial literacy is barely covered. And yet, as adults, many people choose to start businesses in search of time freedom, financial independence, or the chance to build a legacy.

What they're not prepared for is the reality: being a business owner means becoming your own sales team, marketing department, operations manager, and bookkeeper—often all at once.

And that gap between vision and reality? That's where burnout begins. That's where business owners feel like they're failing—not because they lack the passion, but because they lack the support and systems that make success sustainable.

That's why education, access, and financial empowerment matter. Not just at tax time, but all year long. Not just in the boardroom, but at the kitchen table.

Because when entrepreneurs are equipped with the tools, language, and team to run their business well—they don't just survive. They thrive.

Let's introduce you to your partners who will help you survive and thrive.

So Who Does What in the Financial World?

Let's break it down in plain English:

Table 13.1 Financial Roles and Descriptions

FINANCIAL ROLES & DESCRIPTIONS
ACCOUNTING ROLES
Accountant Analyzes and prepares financial records to ensure accuracy and compliance with laws. Prepares financial statements, budgeting and forecasting. Assists with tax preparation and advising on accounting principles.
Junior Accountant / Staff Accountant Entry-level accountant who supports senior accountants with financial reporting and data entry. Assists in month-end close. Posts journal entries and supports audits. Assists with managing general ledger.
Senior Accountant Oversees accounting operations and supports financial strategy. Works with complex reconciliations and internal control implementation. Supports audit and period-end closing.
BOOKKEEPING ROLES
Bookkeeper Tracks day-to-day financial transactions, including sales, purchases, receipts, and payments. Creates bank and credit card reconciliations and often manages accounts receivables and payables. Creates basic financial reports. YOU NEED A BOOKKEEPER THAT SENDS YOU MONTHLY REPORTS.
Full-Charge Bookkeeper Handles full accounting cycle, including month-end close and payroll. Can handle invoicing and bill payment as well as payroll processing, preferably through a third-party payroll processor. Creates bank and credit card reconciliations and financial statement preparation.

FINANCIAL ROLES & DESCRIPTIONS

TAX & COMPLIANCE ROLES

Certified Public Accountant (CPA)
Licensed professional qualified to offer accounting and tax services, with state-level certification. Can prepare and file tax returns. Can offer audit and assurance services, as well as financial planning and business consulting.

Tax Enrolled Agent (EA)
Federally licensed tax practitioner who can represent taxpayers before the IRS. Can prepare more complex tax returns. Is able to represent taxpayers with IRS audits and those who need appeals representation. Often provide Tax Planning and Compliance support. Can be more accessible than a CPA.

Tax Preparer
Prepares and files individual or business tax returns. Prepares IRS and state filings while reviewing deductions and credits. Files extensions. Files your taxes. May or may not be credentialed. Not always strategic—often just inputs data.

Tax Advisor / Tax Consultant
Specializes in providing tax planning advice and mitigation strategies. Provides strategic tax planning as well as entity structure consulting. Can assist with estate and gift tax planning and multi-state and international tax consulting.

FINANCIAL PLANNING AND STRATEGY ROLES

Chief Financial Officer (CFO)
Senior executive managing a company's finances and strategy. Manages financial strategy and forecasting. Assists with fundraising and capital planning as well as risk management. Oversees the accounting, tax and audit teams.

Controller / Financial Controller
Oversees internal accounting functions and financial reporting. Manages month-end close. Ensures financial statement accuracy, budgeting, and cost control. Assists with internal controls and compliance.

Financial Analyst
Analyzes financial data to support business decisions. Creates dashboards to display information such as profitability analysis, scenario modeling, trend analysis, and KPI analysis.

Finance Manager
Oversees financial planning and analysis (FP&A) for business units or organizations. Assists with budget management, variance reporting, forecasting, and capital budgeting.

Fractional CFO
Part-time or outsourced CFO offering strategic financial guidance. Assist with Cash Flow optimization, financial modeling, well as investor relations. Ensures there is a growth strategy in place that aligns with the vision and mission.

FINANCIAL ROLES & DESCRIPTIONS

UDIT, ASSURANCE, & ADVISORY ROLES

Auditor (Internal or External)
Reviews financial records and systems to ensure compliance and accuracy. Creates Internal and External financial audits, risk assessments, and Sarbanes-Oxley (SOX) compliance.

Compliance Officer (Financial)
Ensures adherence to laws and internal policies. Prepares regulatory reporting, risk management protocols, compliance audits and policy development.

Forensic Accountant
Investigates financial irregularities and fraud. Assists with litigation support, fraud investigations, asset tracing, and financial crime analysis.

ASPECIALIZED ADVISORY ROLES

Business Owners Advocate (Becca Heissel, co-author of this book)
Helps entrepreneurs understand their numbers, create strategy, set goals, build confidence, and feel financially empowered year-round.

Financial Advisor / Planner
Guides on investments, insurance, and long-term personal wealth. Regulated differently than tax pros.

Financial Coach
Helps individuals build money management skills and behavior. Assists with budget creation, debt repayment plans, habit based financial education and financial goal setting.

Financial Planner / Certified Financial Planner (CFP)
Guides individuals in personal financial planning. Manages retirement planning, investment strategy, estate and tax planning, as well as insurance and risk management.

Investment Advisor / Registered Investment Advisor (RIA)
Manages investment portfolios and gives investment-related advice. Helps with asset allocation, portfolio management, investment strategy and securities analysis.

Profit Strategist (Caroline Passmore, co-author of this book)
Oversees company-wide financial strategy. Specializes in financial analysis, budgeting, and internal strategy. "Bookkeeping is fun."

FINANCIAL ROLES & DESCRIPTIONS

BUSINESS & OPERATIONAL FINANCE ROLES

Business Valuator
Provides formal valuation of businesses for mergers, acquisitions, or litigation. Manages business appraisals, fair market valuation, valuation for divorce or disputes, and Mergers & Acquisition support.

Cost Accountant
Specializes in evaluating the cost structure of operations. Prepares cost analysis and control, manufacturing costing, margin analysis, and inventory valuation.

Treasurer
Manages liquidity, investments, and financial risk in large companies. Creates cash flow management, investment oversight, risk mitigation, and financial policy enforcement.

GOVERNMENT, NONPROFIT, & PUBLIC SECTOR ROLES

Fund Accountant
Focuses on tracking and reporting for investment or nonprofit funds. Manages NAV calculations, fund performance tracking, investor reporting and regulatory compliance.

Grants Accountant
Manages funds and reporting for grant-funded programs. Prepares grant budgeting, compliance reporting, reimbursement tracking and grant audits.

Municipal Accountant
Manages financials for local government entities. Handles public fund management, governmental audits, compliance with GASB standards, and tax levy administration.

ADDITIONAL PROFESSIONAL DESIGNATIONS

Certified Management Accountant (CMA)
A professional designation specializing in financial management and strategic management. CMAs are experts in cost management, performance evaluation, and internal control. Manages budgeting and forecasting as well as performance management. Helps with cost analysis and control, Internal control oversight and strategic financial planning.

Financial Auditor
A specialist who reviews financial statements and processes to ensure accuracy and compliance with accounting standards and regulations. Specializes in conducting audits of financial statements, as well as assessing risk of material misstatement. While also evaluating internal controls, providing audit reports and recommendations, and ensuring compliance with GAAP and IFRS.

FINANCIAL ROLES & DESCRIPTIONS

SOFTWARE & CERTIFICATION PLATFORMS*

This is only to support the software used by the professional. Comprehensive knowledge of Accounting is still required.

FreshBooks Partner, Certified
Specialist in FreshBooks software, supporting freelancers and service-based businesses with cloud accounting.

MBA (Master of Business Administration)
Business strategy-focused. May have knowledge in finance but not always hands-on with small business money.

NetSuite Certified Consultant
Specialist in implementing and managing NetSuite for mid-size to enterprise-level companies.

QuickBooks ProAdvisor Level 1
Certified expert in QuickBooks who assists with setup, training, troubleshooting, and optimization of the software.

QuickBooks ProAdvisor Level 2
Advanced-level QuickBooks Online specialist with deep expertise in QBO features and workflows.

Sage Accounting Advisor
Expert in the Sage family of products, including Sage 50 and Sage Intact.

Wave Pro Network Member
Professional listed in Wave's directory who assists with bookkeeping and tax preparation on the platform.

Xero Certified Advisor
Professional certified in Xero accounting software, helping businesses transition and manage their finances in the cloud.

Zoho Books Advisor
Advisor certified in Zoho Books who helps automate accounting for small businesses.

Build Your Financial Dream Team

You don't have to do it all alone. When it comes to managing your finances, you can either work with a one-stop shop or assemble a team of trusted professionals who each bring their expertise to the table.

Both options can work—it just depends on what fits your business model, values, and goals. The key is this: you need people you can trust who truly understand your business.

Becca's Approach: Strategy + Support Year-Round

Becca partners with EAs (Enrolled Agents) so that when it's tax time, your return is reviewed by a licensed tax expert—but you're never left in the dark during the rest of the year.

She supports clients with ongoing financial clarity, helping you track your numbers, plan for growth, and make empowered decisions all year long—not just in April.

In her earlier work with retail stores, Becca could often spot profit margin errors immediately—just by opening the books. She now focuses on service-based businesses, especially coaches, speakers, and authors, because she loves helping high-impact entrepreneurs understand their numbers and build with confidence.

Caroline's Approach: Bookkeeping with Purpose

Caroline trains bookkeepers to do more than just enter numbers. She believes that bookkeeping should be accurate, insightful, and empowering. When bookkeepers are trained to understand the "why" behind the numbers, they can provide the level of service that business owners truly need.

She specializes in working with nonprofits and mission-driven businesses, as well as skilled construction trades that utilize field service applications such as ServiceTitan, Jobber, and Housecall Pro. Her team provides a full range of services—from bookkeeping to virtual CFO support—helping organizations stay organized, audit-ready, and fully aligned with their financial goals.

Mattie's Approach: Messaging that Aligns with the Math

Not to be left out on this most important page, Mattie is a ghostwriter who supports thought leaders in telling their stories and growing their impact through books. Her emerging understanding of financial principles allows her to help clients write with clarity and purpose. She helps authors define the bigger vision for their book—where it can take them, their business, and the people they want to influence—so every chapter moves them closer to that goal.

Her strength lies in listening deeply, capturing her clients' voices, and helping entrepreneurs communicate their value with confidence.

As her understanding of business finance deepens, Mattie becomes an even more powerful partner in helping clients write books that build both credibility and income.

Choose a Specialist in Your Industry

Just like you wouldn't go to a foot doctor for heart surgery, you shouldn't settle for generic financial help when you can work with someone who knows your industry inside and out.

Find professionals who understand your business model, your challenges, and your growth potential. Whether you build a custom team or work with a firm that provides multiple services, make sure they speak your language—and have your back.

What Needs to Change in This Industry?

Let's be honest:
- Small business owners don't need more jargon.
- They don't need another year-end extension.
- They don't need a CPA who only shows up once a year.

They need:
- Clear guidance
- Ongoing support
- People who listen
- People who explain

We need professionals who aren't afraid to say,

"Let me break that down for you."

"Let's make a plan you understand."

"You're not alone."

Final Thought

This bonus chapter isn't about telling you who to hire. It's about teaching you who does what, what they are each responsible for, and to support you in intentionally choosing the financial professional you need to move from Vision to Impact! We want to encourage you to choose people who help you feel empowered.

Credentials are great. But communication, compassion, and consistency? That's what will actually change your business.

If you don't understand what your financial professional is saying—or worse, if they make you feel small—it's time for a change.

You deserve support that meets you where you are—and helps you grow from there.

Acknowledgments

Becca's Acknowledgement

This book is for every entrepreneur who felt they should have it all figured out but didn't.

To the clients who trusted me when they were overwhelmed, afraid, or stuck—you were my greatest teachers. Your courage to take the first step inspired every word on these pages.

To my husband & children, whose strength and resilience taught me what true success means. You are my "why" and my reminder that anything is possible when led with love.

To Maddie Brown, thank you for showing me what entrepreneurship looks like when it's done with heart, service, and strategy. You gave me a front-row seat to the real stories behind the spreadsheets and sparked my purpose to serve.

To Jack Canfield and *The Success Principles*™—your work rewired my belief system and gave me tools I now pass on to others every day.

To the other three wise women:

To **Caroline**, for holding the highest credentials y

et reminding us all that heart is more important than hierarchy.

To **Mattie**, for turning our rough words into clear magic, showing how language can lift lives.

To **our readers**, for allowing our three voices to carry one shared message—*you are not alone, and success is not a secret.*

To my tribe of collaborators, friends, and fellow dreamers—you gave me accountability when I needed it, belief when I doubted myself, and celebration when I finally said, "I'm doing this."

And finally—to you, the reader. Thank you for investing in yourself. You're not just holding a book. You're holding the blueprint to impact, income, and freedom.

This is only the beginning.

With deep gratitude,

Becca Heissel

Caroline's Acknowledgement

This book is for every hardworking dreamer who dared to step off the beaten path and build something of their own, even when it felt like walking through fog with a flashlight and a toolbox.

To my clients: the builders, the fixers, the founders. You are the backbone of this work. Your determination to bring order to chaos, to understand your numbers, and to chase your vision even when the dollars don't make sense. You are my daily inspiration. It has been my honor to help you turn messes into margins and fear into forecasts.

To my husband, thank you for your unwavering support and endless belief in me. For standing beside me when the days were long, the stress was thick, and our time together was sacrificed for the sake of my mission. You've always told me how proud you are, even when you didn't quite know what I was wrangling behind the scenes. I love you more than spreadsheets love reconciled accounts.

To my son, my eternal cheerleader, thank you for seeing the best in me, even when you didn't understand why I talk to QuickBooks more than people. Your love is my anchor and your pride is my fuel.

To Seth David, thank you for opening the door that changed everything. Your mentorship, generosity, and real-talk approach lit the way when I was figuring it all out. Your impact ripples through every client I serve.

To all the bosses who didn't see my value—thank you. Truly. You lit a fire in me to rise beyond every box you tried to keep me in. I'm soaring with eagles now, and it's far above the ceilings you set.

To the three wise women:

To **Becca**, who brings soul to systems and never lets a message fall flat—thank you for helping me find my voice on the page.

To **Mattie**, the quiet storm of clarity, who polishes every thought until it shines.

And to **our readers**—thank you for investing in yourself. You are not alone, and this book is your permission slip to dream bigger, earn smarter, and lead with impact.

May this be your turning point.

With all my heart, Caroline Passmore

Mattie's Acknowledgement

This book exists because of collaboration, courage, and the belief that sharing what we know can change lives.

To my co-authors and now dear friends, Becca and Caroline—what an honor it has been to create this with you. Becca, your enthusiasm and sheer determination to make meaningful change were the heartbeat of this project from day one. Your fire reminded us all why this work matters. Caroline, your wisdom, experience, and connections to some of the greatest minds in the financial world gave this book both depth and reach. I have come to respect and admire you greatly—not just for what you know, but for how you show up with grace and strength.

To my children – Hope, Ian, Seth, Josh, and Britton – you are not only my heart and soul but also my teachers. Watching you navigate your own financial lives with wisdom and courage humbles me. You are doing better, faster, and braver than I ever did—and that is exactly how it should be. Everything I do, including this book, carries my hope that you will always feel the freedom and power to write your own brave new endings. You lead lives of integrity and I am proud of you all.

To Cathy Juilfs and her incredible team at AIS Planning—including Nathan Goebel, Sarah Noble, and Janet DeZurik—who have become a trusted voice of financial wisdom. You took me from a place of vulnerability, exposure, loss, and shame to a place of strength, confidence, and knowledge. What sets you apart is more than expertise; it's the way you lead with values and genuine care. You don't just manage numbers—you nurture relationships and futures. You are a shining example of how it should be done—and done right. You have my heart and my trust.

To my very dear business group girlfriends at Next Monday and our fearless leader, Becky Estby (and Michelle Pape)—thank you for pushing me, cheering me on, and reminding me to think bigger. You embody what happens when strong women lift each other up.

To all my previous and current authors—you make me a better writer every single day. Every book, every story, and every brave conversation with you has shaped how I approach my own work, and I carry those trusted lessons into everything I write.

And to my family, friends, and even those who underestimated, doubted, or overlooked me—thank you. Those moments forged my courage, strengthened my resilience, and deepened my commitment to living fully and giving generously.

Because in the end, true success isn't just measured by what we gain, but by how much courage we show, how much hope we inspire, and how much better we leave the world than we found it.

Your invisible scribe,

Mattie Murrey

Author Bios

Becca Heissel – Business Mentor | Author Advocate | Success Strategist

Becca Heissel is a business strategist, financial clarity mentor, and certified Jack Canfield Success Principles Trainer who helps authors and speakers turn their words into wealth.

With a background in bookkeeping, marketing, and mindset coaching, Becca created the MAP Framework (Mindset + Action/Accountability + Profit) to guide entrepreneurs from Vison to Impact. She's known for turning overwhelm into organized plans, procrastination into inspired action, and good ideas into lasting income.

As the founder of Business Owners Advocate, Becca is on a mission to flip the statistic that 86% of business owners make under $100,000 a year and to mandate financial literacy education in all 50 states. She helps her clients conquer time freedom, master their message, and grow businesses that work—for their life, their mission, and their bottom line.

Becca's blue butterfly logo symbolizes the transformation she brings to every business she touches. Becca is a Keynote speaker, 4x best-selling author featured on NBC, CBS, ABC, FOX, KTLA, the CW, and more national and international media and she is your advocate and accountability partner.

As a special needs mompreneur, she built a business that allows her to be the mom she needs to be—without sacrificing her life's mission to serve others. Her story is proof that you can build a business that gives you time freedom, serves your clients, supports your family, and makes the world a better place. Becca is the go-to advocate and accountability partner for entrepreneurs ready to grow a business that works—for their life, their mission, and their bottom line.

www.businessownersadvocate.com

Caroline Passmore – Accountant | Financial Advocate | Profit Strategist

Caroline Passmore is a Profit Strategist, accountant, and the founder of CRP Specialists Inc., where financial chaos meets its match. She helps nonprofits and the skilled construction tradespeople who use field service applications such as ServiceTitan, Housecall Pro, etc, business owners build sustainable profitability using powerful systems, financial literacy, and a whole lot of heart.

Known for her sharp eye and even sharper wit, Caroline is fiercely dedicated to helping clients "know their numbers" and take inspired action. Her work transforms businesses from surviving to thriving, empowering founders to make confident decisions and finally pay themselves what they're worth.

Her signature butterfly logo isn't just pretty branding—it symbolizes the transformation her clients go through: from overwhelmed and underpaid to profitable, focused, and flying high.

When she's not untangling balance sheets or building strategic workflows, Caroline is probably training her team of powerhouse women to take over the bookkeeping world.

With a fierce love for her family, her clients, and the big dreams behind every small business, Caroline brings empathy and strategy to everything she touches.

www.crpspecialists.com

Mattie Murrey — Ghostwriter | Author Advocate | Story Strategist

Mattie Murrey Tegels is a globally recognized ghostwriter and copy-writer whose work has caught the attention of an Oscar-qualified director and an Emmy-nominated journalist for its powerful story-telling and emotional resonance. A former assistant professor in a graduate program and a speech-language pathologist who worked in medical settings around the world, Mattie now channels her expertise in human connection into crafting award-worthy books and content that inspire, influence, and leave a lasting impact.

As the founder of My Own Ghostwriter, Mattie is building an award-winning team of writers specializing in non-fiction, fiction, and high-impact copywriting. She and her team provide trusted, concierge-level connections for authors—pairing exceptional writing with the right publishing, media, and speaking opportunities. Her writing services include full ghostwriting, guided authorship, a DIY book-writing course, book coaching, editing, copywriting, and speechwriting for thought leaders, entrepreneurs, and change-makers who want their message heard on the biggest stages and in the quiet of meeting rooms where real decisions are made.

Mattie's authors have earned national awards, keynote speaking engagements, and placement in the Library of Congress. Her own work has been showcased at VIP publishing events in New York City, and her copywriting has been featured in Forbes, Inc., and other major outlets. She's been featured in a forthcoming Amazon documentary about dementia and is known for her thought leadership on writing, storytelling, and building authority through books.

A single mother of five after her husband's death, Mattie built her career on courage, resilience, and an unwavering belief in the power of storytelling—not just as entertainment, but as one of the most profound tools for learning, connection, and change. An avid motorcyclist and in-demand keynote speaker, she delivers standing-ovation talks that inspire authors, entrepreneurs, and change-makers to share their stories with courage and authenticity.

www.myownghostwriter.com